Teaching by Design

Using Your Computer to Create Materials for Students with Learning Differences

Kimberly S. Voss

Woodbine House ■ 2005

© 2005 Kimberly S. Voss
First edition

All rights reserved under International and Pan-American copyright conventions. Published in the United States of America by Woodbine House, Inc., 6510 Bells Mill Rd., Bethesda, MD 20817. 800-843-7323. www.woodbinehouse.com

AppleWorks® screen captures used with permission. Apple®.
> Apple
> 1 Infinite Loop
> Cupertino, CA 95014
> Phone: 408-996-1010
> Web site: www. apple.com

FreeHand® screen captures used with permission. Macromedia®.
> Macromedia, Inc.
> 601 Townsend Street
> San Francisco, CA 94103
> Phone: 415-832-2000
> Fax: 415-832-2020
> Web site: www.macromedia.com

The Picture Communication Symbols™ ©1981–2005 by Mayer-Johnson LLC. All Rights Reserved Worldwide. Used with permission.

Boardmaker™ is a trademark of Mayer-Johnson LLC.
> Mayer-Johnson LLC
> P.O. Box 1579
> Solana Beach, CA 92075-7579
> Phone: 858-550-0084
> Fax: 858-550-0449
> email: mayerj@mayer-johnson.com
> Web site: www.mayer-johnson.com

Official LSU logo used with permission from Louisiana State University, Baton Rouge, Louisiana.

Backcover and interior B&W photographs used with permission. Ervin Photography, Tulsa, Oklahoma and Peevyhouse Photography, Jenks, Oklahoma.

Front cover and interior color photographs taken by Fredde Lieberman, Lieberman Photography.

Chimi's® logo used with permission. Chimi's, Tulsa, Oklahoma.

The following trademarks are owned by the parties noted below and are being used by the author without permission solely for the purpose of illustrating the lesson plans described in this book. This book and the lesson plans described in this book are not associated with and have not been authorized or sponsored by the owners of such trademarks.
> Hellmann's® Mayonnaise of Unilever
> Sara Lee® Bread of Sara Lee Corporation
> StarKist® of Del Monte Foods
> Vlasic® Pickle Relish of Pinnacle Foods Corporation
> Chutes and Ladders of Hasbro®
> Ready to Read Box™ of Lakeshore® Learning Materials
> Rolodex® of Eldon®
> Xyron® of Xyron, Inc.

The following illustrations depict copyrighted materials owned by the parties noted below. Such materials are being used without permission solely for the purposes of illustrating the lesson plans described in this book. This book and the lesson plans described in this book are not associated with and have not been authorized or sponsored by the owners of such materials.
> *Sheila Rae, the Brave* by Kevin Henkes (Greenwillow Books, 1987)

Library of Congress Cataloging-in-Publication Data

Voss, Kimberly S.
  Teaching by design : using your computer to create materials for students with learning differences / by Kimberly S. Voss.—1ˢᵗ ed.
    p. cm.
  Includes index.
  ISBN 1-890627-43-7 (alk. paper)
  1.Learning disabled children—Education—Audio-visual aids. 2. Teaching—Aids and devices—Computer-aided design. 3. Remedial teaching. I. Title.

LC4023.V67 2005
371.9'0285—dc22   2005048293

Manufactured in the United States of America

10 9 8 7 6 5 4 3

To my husband, for believing in me.

To our children, for the important lessons you have taught us.

And especially to Ashley, for redefining love, life, and purpose.

You have enriched our lives.

TABLE OF CONTENTS

ACKNOWLEDGEMENTS

A book is not just a collection of words and images but it is a composite of experiences that have influenced the views and values of the author, impacting what is ultimately put on paper. All of us have crossed paths with persons who have played pivotal roles, good and bad, affecting both the direction of our lives and the ways in which we live them. I have had my collection of people, some of whom I would like to acknowledge for shaping the way I see the world, the way in which I have accepted challenges, and the manner in which I have chosen to affect the lives of others. They have all influenced my life and this book.

K.L. Higgins founded Hummingbird Music Camp in the beautiful Jemez Mountains of New Mexico in 1959. He created a place where I not only went to play music for many summers but a place where I could be creative, taking risks without ever being judged for playing a wrong note. Mr. Higgins once said if you are going to play a note, right or wrong, "play it like you mean it." That has proven to be sage advice for the way I have chosen to live my life.

"Charlie," a young man at Louisiana State University, befriended me in a computer science class in the late 70s and dubbed me one of his "Angels." In a wheelchair and unable to speak, he had to hold his "words" from one class meeting to the next, composing and typing his thoughts on index cards to deliver to me the next time we saw one another. He made me aware of the immeasurable frustration of being unable to verbally communicate and taught me to respect the many less "conventional" ways one can "speak": a touch, a hug, a gesture, a groan, a wail, a laugh. I had no idea how important those lessons would become later in my life.

My former employers, Roger Hebert and Dave Morgan, formerly of Baton Rouge Exploration, conceived what initially seemed a far-out notion: to send me back to college in geology after I graduated with a degree in biochemistry. By doing so, I learned another area of science as they personally taught me to "slip logs" and map subsurface geological features. The entire experience gave me the opportunity to learn to "see" things with a different eye; that is, observing what is on the surface and what it infers is underneath. It taught me the valuable skill of gathering small clues to unravel a puzzle, an enormous gift when unraveling the puzzle of Ashley's many struggles.

Terry Johnson of Mayer-Johnson, L.L.C. essentially gave me my "start" in the field of computer technology as it relates to persons with disabilities by agreeing to publish my first proposal within days of its receipt, as well as the subsequent decision to publish a series of "dashed fonts" I designed. One particular employee of Mayer-Johnson, Sally Long, often gave me the encouragement I needed to persevere.

I have been blessed to have an editor for this book who, like many individuals at Woodbine House, has been profoundly and personally touched by the lives of persons with disabilities, a gift that I believe has greatly affected the editing. I am deeply grateful for the commitment to see this project to its completion. I am very proud of what we have accomplished as I have been challenged to continue to learn and to do my very best.

And I must acknowledge my family, for the enormous sacrifices you have all made, not only as a steadfast father and sisters to Ashley, and as advocates for others with disabilities, but for your commitment to the belief that Ashley's struggles and triumphs should be shared with others.

INTRODUCTION

If you have picked up this book and are reading this introduction, then we may already have something very significant in common: We both need creative and meaningful ways to help our children learn. Maybe you walked out empty-handed from your last trip to the teacher supply store or turned up nothing appropriate after an extensive search of the Internet. Ready-made materials may not be the answer. Luckily, you are only pages away from realizing that you have an extraordinary capacity to create wonderful educational materials to help your child learn.

As a parent of a child with disabilities, and many learning challenges, I have had to readjust my thinking about a lot of things. From the day our daughter Ashley was born, I have had to rethink and reassess my expectations for what our daughter's life might look like and who our daughter might become. Upon her birth, I immediately grappled with the reality that she might never be a mother, a doctor like her father, or a scientist like her mother. I came to terms with that. Within days of her birth, I had to face the fact that I would have to manage her pain and suffering, and that I might even have to face the possibility of her premature death, something no parent should have to face. I had to redefine my quite reasonable expectation that all my children would outlive me. Following a devastating stroke, I had to face the hard reality that Ashley might never talk as others do, see like others see, or dress or feed herself like others who take these basic skills for granted. I dealt with the fact that we, as a family, might have to make some rather extraordinary accomodations and sacrifices for Ashley to participate in life to the best of her ability. I accepted that.

But there were some things I have been unwilling to accept. I have refused to accept that Ashley was not deserving of an education. My expectation was that Ashley deserved to be taught and that she deserved the opportunity to learn, and that access to meaningful educational materials should not stand in the way of her learning. If I could not find exactly what Ashley needed then I would thoughtfully create it myself. And you can, too.

I know that human beings are capable of designing and building magnificent bridges that can span great distances over extreme heights. We attempt such extraordinary feats of engineering because we are convinced it can be done, and we believe that there is good reason to traverse a deep chasm, creating a bridge that will leave no one behind.

This concept of "bridge building" is not only a matter of engineering but also a matter of philosophy, believing in its importance. And educating children, no matter their ability, or disability, should be no different.

I have participated in authoring some rather well written IEPs, and you probably have, too. They look both reasonable, achieveable, and "bullet proof." Yet, with IEP in hand, we walk away to use dated or meaningless materials, worksheets, or nothing at all, to create this "special education." And when the goals cannot be met, we are quick to assume that the goals must have been too difficult rather than looking at the approach to teach the goals and the materials used to teach them.

What seems to be missing is often the strategy. We forget that, like the bridge, we must not only imagine it, we must build it. For every goal in life, we must ask ourselves, "How are we going to achieve it?" We don't build a bridge without first hiring all the necessary people, drawing the detailed plans, and gathering all the required materials long before we ever start construction. We design around obstacles. We find the most solid ground to begin construction and, when we run into problems, we readjust, making the necessary modifications, and then forge ahead.

Our school district acts very much like a team of bridge engineers when it comes to athletics. Recently listed in *Sports Illustrated* as one of the the "top high school athletic programs in America," man, do we know how to play football (and a number of other sports). The coaches don't just tell the players "We are going to win!" The coaches design the best plays; they know their players' strengths and weaknesses and play to their strengths both on and off the field; they build a state-of-the-art weight room facility; and they provide the best equipment, not only to protect them but to allow them to win. One half as much commitment in special education could yield similar results, but that does not happen. Like many school districts, it is often left to the parents to be the bridge builders in their child's education and future.

We can all share in this important responsibility of educating our students with learning differences. Parents, teachers, paraprofessionals, and others can help create the necessary accomodations. We can tap into the skills of more "gifted" students who learn quickly, utilizing their talents to synthesize and create materials to help their classmates who learn more slowly. We can tap into the talents of high school students learning computer graphics to design what might help others. We can create libraries, within our schools and school districts, of materials for students with learning differences for teachers to check out only to be required to return them after adding one new set of materials and one additional novel teaching strategy. We can upload the files of customized materials to school networks for parents and teachers to download, to make minor modifications before printing, laminating, and presenting to other new students.

We can do this!

Granted, even with the greatest effort, not all of our children, disabled or nondisabled, will have the cognitive ability to become a brain surgeon, the grace to become a prima ballerina, or the athleticism to become a world class athlete. But the point of education is not to prove disability but to prove and improve ability, not to prove what we cannot become but to help us to achieve what we can.

We must embrace the philosophy that all children can learn. We must look at assistive aids and services, and accomodations, as a "first line of defense" rather than as a "last resort." And we must not blame the child for their inability to learn but look at the methods and materials we are using to teach them. By writing this book, I hope you will see potential: the learning potential in your child and the creative potential in yourself. I hope that you will not feel bound by what I show you how to create but that you will begin to visualize a greater plan, selecting the most appropriate images and fonts, using the best layout, and choosing the best inkjet media to create your own novel materials.

We can build magnificent bridges that leave no one behind, bridges that acccomodate the learning styles of many different students. Read on and realize that you, too, can begin teaching by design.

ABOUT ASHLEY

On November 16, 1984, our beautiful baby girl was born. With attentive eyes and small ears like her mother, the foundation of a family had begun with the birth of Ashley Lynn Voss. Following an uneventful pregnancy, the prescribed prenatal weight gain, and delivery by natural childbirth, everything seemed just how it should be.

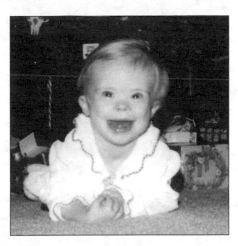

But life seldom goes as planned. Within 45 minutes of Ashley's birth, a pediatrician appeared looking concerned. He told us that he was relatively sure Ashley had Down syndrome. The diagnosis was later confirmed with genetic testing. Like a movie that had gone awry, I desperately wanted to rewind the scene and start over, hoping I would hear a completely different dialogue. But all I could say at the time was "We'll cope."

Because as many as 50% of all children with Down syndrome have some congenital heart defect, a screening for possible cardiac defects was performed on Ashley when she was only three days old. It was determined that Ashley had an atrioventricular septal defect (an AV canal), a large hole common to all four chambers of her heart. The diagnosis was quite serious. It would require close medical attention and future open heart surgery.

From that day forward, Ashley's Down syndrome was never our primary focus. The health and mortality of our child became our principal concern. As expected, within 2 weeks Ashley began showing the early signs of congestive heart failure. I had been warned what to look for and had had little opportunity to take pleasure in the simple joys of motherhood—I had been anticipating the worst. Once the signs appeared, I made the prescribed run to the pediatric cardiologist, the first of many visits. Within days Ashley was back in the same hospital where she was born. There she was continuously monitored and placed on medication to alleviate some of the problems related to her heart failure.

Ashley's weight gain was of paramount concern because her doctors felt that she must reach "an operable weight" before her open heart surgery could be performed. In other parts of the country, surgeons were beginning to operate "sooner rather than later" on infants with Ashley's condition, but her doctors were taking a "wait and see" approach. Visits to the pediatric cardiologist were frequent and disheartening. She remained quite small, having a difficult time eating, keeping food down, and burning fewer calories than she consumed.

> **WHAT IS DOWN SYNDROME?**
>
> Down syndrome (also called "trisomy 21") is a chromosome abnormality, defined by the presence of a third copy of the 21st chromosome, affecting both physical and intellectual development.

Ashley's first surgery occurred when she was only 3½ months old. An incision was made in the left side of her chest and a band was placed around her pulmonary artery to reduce the blood flow to her lungs. This was intended to lower the risk of pulmonary hypertension, a fatal condition that can result from certain heart defects. Additionally, the doctors felt this procedure would allow Ashley to gain the necessary weight. Her open heart surgery was still to come.

With our lives now somewhat stable, Ashley began participating in an early intervention program. Although Ashley's future was uncertain—back in 1986, 1 out of 3 children did not survive her particular surgery—early intervention was my way of staring down her potential mortality. I was determined that she was here to stay. Not a moment was to be wasted.

Another daughter, Megan Katherine, joined us 14½ months after Ashley's birth. Megan gave sweet balance to our lives and served as a wonderful playmate and "role model" for her sister. With no health problems, Megan rapidly surpassed Ashley in size and weight and, before long, "hand-me-downs" became "hand-me-ups."

A move soon followed Megan's birth from New Orleans, Louisiana to Tulsa, Oklahoma as my husband Hal finished his medical residency in anesthesiology at the same hospital where Ashley and Megan were born. We made the decision to have the same surgeon perform Ashley's future open heart surgery as had performed her open chest surgery, so we returned to New Orleans to have Ashley followed medically in the months after our move.

At 2½ years of age, Ashley finally reached her operable weight of 20 pounds, a weight Megan reached long before her first birthday. Her surgery date was set. As the date grew nearer, we no longer openly discussed her mortality, although it was on our minds constantly.

Knowing there were no guarantees she would survive, I quietly set about capturing Ashley's last days before her surgery in pictures and video. I scheduled an appointment for Ashley and Megan to have portraits taken together. And we borrowed a video camera from a friend to videotape our babies playing together, bathing together, using sign language together, and talking together. Early intervention services had done wonders for Ashley. A recent visit to the developmental pediatrician found her with few developmental delays, testing at age appropriate levels in nearly all developmental areas except for those impeded by her heart condition, such as crawling and walking. There was much to be proud of and many wonderful memories to preserve.

Surgery day arrived. On May 19, 1987, Ashley was taken to the operating room. My job as Ashley's mother was to protect her and keep her safe, but now her fate was totally out of my hands. I felt completely helpless as I handed our baby over to doctors and nurses who were strangers to me. After many hours, the surgeon finally appeared in the family waiting room. We were given a brief, matter-of-fact report: "all had gone well." We were told to wait to be called to the pediatric intensive care unit where we could see Ashley shortly. We waited and waited, but we were not called. Unable to stabilize Ashley in intensive care, we were suddenly herded to a doorway to see her pass on a gurney as she was returned to surgery. Looking so small and fragile, I was desperately afraid it would be the last time I would see her alive.

Ashley survived surgery, but it did not take long to realize something was not right. We were told she had bled where the band that had previously been placed around her pulmonary artery was removed during the surgery. We were told that her blood pressure had fallen very low. But that was all we were told. When we saw her in intensive care, I immediately noticed she seemed stiff. Her feet and ankles looked strange, as if she were permanently pointing her toes. Her tongue was stiff as a board. And my beautiful, loving daughter did not even seem aware of who I was.

Ashley's stay in intensive care was "touch and go." She experienced just about every possible complication. For days, questions to staff brought no answers until a pediatric resident offhandedly remarked to my husband that Ashley might have sustained brain damage. Hal ran to find me to break the news. My "mother's intuition" had told me all along that something was horribly wrong and now my worst nightmare had been realized.

Neurological testing followed. Later, the pediatric cardiologist, along with 3 residents I had never seen before, appeared while I was alone with Ashley. In a clinical tone, the cardiologist informed me that Ashley had, in fact, sustained brain damage. There, in front of indifferent outsiders, my world fell apart. I asked where they would all be when I was left to deal with their medical failure. There was no response.

We never saw her surgeon again after that one conversation in the family waiting room when "all went well." His chief resident came to our room and cried with us. Staff continued to provide very little information, although we were told, "If she does not improve significantly within two weeks, we don't know how you will be able to care for her at home." I was overwhelmed with dread. Though their veiled suggestion to institutionalize Ashley was never an option, I wanted to scream at them at the top of my lungs!

The severity of Ashley's complications were not completely revealed until we read her hospital discharge summary. Her blood pressure had fallen even lower than we were originally told. Ashley had experienced a severe ischemic encephalopathy: Not enough oxygen had reached her brain for so long that brain cells had died. Only time would reveal how much she might improve.

Ashley returned home to us a profoundly changed child. Drawn up and tight on the right side of her body, she was fitted with a resting hand splint to try to keep her arm in a more "relaxed" position and prevent her muscles from permanently contracting. In contrast, her left side was completely limp. Her left eye was turned in. She was unable to perform even the most rudimentary physical tasks, such as holding her head up or moving it from side to side.

Ashley was now unable to nurse or drink, having lost her sucking reflex. I fed her a high calorie liquid formula with a needle-less syringe, letting the formula slowly roll down the inside of her mouth and down her throat. Her ability to swallow had also been affected, causing her to gag so easily that feeding her took hours of painstaking work. The touch of anything in her mouth caused her jaw to spastically clench, making it impossible to use a spoon to feed her even the most finely pureed foods. Highly sensitive to sound, Ashley would break into an uncontrollable wail when certain noises "set her off." The cry of a cat or her little sister's laugh would cause her to convulse, her entire body moving uncontrollably, unrecognizable sounds coming from her throat. To alleviate this, we initially kept Ashley in a quiet room where noises and other unpleasant stimuli could be kept to a minimum.

Ashley's thermal regulation had also shut down. She seemed to have "hot spots." While her temperature taken under her arm was normal, her rectal temperature was over 104 degrees. We learned, in that moment of desperation, that if we lowered her into a bath of cool water, her system, oddly enough, would "reset."

Hardest of all to cope with, Ashley was capable of going for days on end without sleep, often dozing only 15 minutes in a 24 hour period. Assuming it was from the pain of her body being so drawn up and tight, I would massage her for hours, trying to alleviate the rigidity. Once her body relaxed, I would carefully place my leg or arm across her limbs, trying to keep them more comfortable, allowing her to drift off to sleep. I even resorted to using the "white noise" on a radio to block out auditory stimuli to try to lull her to sleep.

In struggling day and night to just keep Ashley stable and calm, I began to wonder whether this life would be all Ashley—and I—could expect forever. I daydreamed of driving off with only a tank full of gas and a charge card. Toying with these thoughts at least gave me the sense that maybe I really did still have some control over my life, even if my only choices included abandoning my family or staying to fight for my daughter's life.

On the verge of total exhaustion, I called my sister Tristan and asked her to come. Never being one to ask for help, she realized the seriousness of our situation and came quickly. By the time she arrived, Ashley had improved somewhat although much had remained the same. Her convulsive responses to noise had lessened and there were moments when we felt she was present with us: Ashley might respond with her old laugh to hearing her sister Megan enter the room, only to fall apart and moan uncontrollably again. The rest of the time, she mostly sat rigid and motionless in a special chair that kept her from falling over.

Tristan had not seen Ashley in quite some time and it was clear to me that she did not realize the magnitude of what had happened. One evening, I showed her the videotape of Ashley and Megan just before Ashley's open heart surgery. I could not see Tristan's face until the video ended. She turned to me with tears running down her cheeks and cried out, "Ashley's in there! We've got to get her out!"

That became my mission with Ashley: to get her out. The Ashley I knew died that day in the hospital. Now there was another little girl locked inside her body who wanted out. I dedicated my heart and mind to finding the keys to the doors that imprisoned my daughter, trying each key one at a time, eventually opening one door, sometimes just in time to watch another one shut. This has continued over many years until I solved the puzzle of how the keys must be used. There are no longer so many doors locked tight. And many remain open permanently. What Ashley has taught me is what is shared in this book.

Unfortunately, Ashley's surgery continues to haunt her. The challenges she faces that result from Down syndrome are always eclipsed by these additional acquired disabilities. She is legally blind, a result of a decreased field of vision and loss of depth perception. She has a severe language disorder, including expressive aphasia and apraxia, which greatly limits her ability to speak. And she is agraphic which impairs her ability to write. Other health-related hardships have also followed, including another open heart surgery to repair her mitral valve, major hip surgery to correct a dislocating hip, arthritis, and chronic pain.

This odyssey has been—and remains—one of "getting Ashley out." Trapped inside a body that does not always do what she asks it to do, we have had to invent and create from scratch numerous methods that allow her to emerge. Her medical diagnosis and developmental label have not and cannot measure her human potential. Unwilling to accept "can't" as an option, we have focused on "what if." Ashley's determination, as well as mine, has been our key to unlocking door after door, everyday revealing more of Ashley's abilities and character. While she lives with many challenging and complex disabilities, Ashley has emerged as an assertive, independent, loving, and spirted young woman with a zest

WHAT IS FIELD OF VISION?

Field of vision is the space in which objects can be seen without moving the eyes.

WHAT ARE APHASIA AND APRAXIA?

Aphasia is the partial or total loss of the ability to speak, write, or comprehend spoken or written words resulting from damage to the brain.

Apraxia is the partial or total loss of the ability to make purposeful, coordinated movements, despite having the desire and physical ability to execute the movements.

WHAT IS AGRAPHIA?

Agraphia (also called anorthography) is a form of aphasia defined by the inability to write.

for life and a wonderfully keen sense of humor. She will face adversity throughout her life, but we will face it as we have all the challenges that came before: one day and one creative solution at a time.

I invite you to use this book for your own creative solutions to help address the challenges your child may face. And remember, there is nothing you—and your child—cannot accomplish together.

I grew up when a "bit" meant a small amount of something and a "byte," well, a byte was a typographical error. "Ram" was a male sheep and a "mouse" was a rodent. Those were the years before personal computers or laptops, when a computer typically filled an entire room.

I saw my first computer when I was a junior in high school while visiting a university for a week-long science symposium. A graduate student in the physics department introduced me to my very first computer game. It was a simulation of a lunar landing. I watched in amazement as the capsule was successfully landed and a tiny astronaut emerged to sink a tiny American flag into the surface of the moon. I saw many other amazing scientific instruments during that visit, but it was the primitive, black and white computer program that I talked about with my classmates when I returned to school.

The summer after graduating from high school, I participated in a national science camp. To my shock and dismay, I learned that many of the students from other states already had extensive exposure to computers. At the camp, an engineer from NASA taught us APL (which stood for "A Programming Language"), a sequence of characters used to feed information into a computer. As far as I was concerned, though I never let on, it could have as easily been AFL, "A Foreign Language," because it was "Greek to me."

In college, I finally stuck my toe in the technology water, enrolling in a computer science class only because it was a graduation requirement for my biochemistry degree. I found I had a bit of a knack for this class, not because of my knowledge of computers, but because I was good at problem solving. Feeling inspired, I decided to take one additional computer science class as an elective. That was in 1978.

Things were very different back then. Programming was accomplished by punching holes in a series of cards, each about the size of a legal sized envelope. The pile of cards comprising the program was called a "stack" and the stack of cards was read by a mechanical card reader. The success or failure of your program was revealed by a pile of green and white striped paper spit out by the computer. Typically, the shorter the pile of paper, the better the outcome of your program. Needless to say, I spent many hours in the Computer Center, wrangling with a huge machine that had a fraction of the computing power of today's cell phones.

Then everything changed. Toward the end of my second semester in computer science, someone, somewhere hooked a cathode ray tube (CRT) to a computer. Before long, a room full of these newfangled computer monitors appeared in the Computer Center, networked to the university's "main frame," stored somewhere on campus in one of those enormous buildings. Punch cards instantly became obsolete. Students began entering their programs into the computer by keyboarding their instructions. But the CRTs were too high tech for me; I stuck with my familiar punch cards through the end of the semester. A bit embarrassed of my intimidation by technological advances, I tried not to be seen with my cards, or near the mechanical card reader. Pushing my luck, I signed up for one additional computer science class in "Assembler," another computer language, which consists of a series of ones and zeroes. What was I thinking? Enough was enough. I dropped the class. You could definitely say, "I wanted only so much technology in my life."

But technology's relentless advance, and my growing anxiety about keeping up, did not end there, of course. While traveling through the Atlanta airport, my husband and I encountered voices in the mobile trams, seeming to come from nowhere. Somehow sensing our presence, the voices issued warnings and directions: "Step back from the edge of the car." "You are now approaching Concourse B." I felt like I was part of George Orwell's *Nineteen Eighty Four*, and "Big Brother" was watching. My husband, Hal, found it amusing but I found it disturbing. A talking computer? "No, thank you."

Coerced by Hal, we purchased our first personal computer, an Apple IIGS, a few years later in 1987. He began putting it together early one evening. When I woke the next morning he was still working on it. Determined to finish, he had worked through the night, taking nearly 24 hours to get it up and running.

Now forced to deal with a monitor and keyboard, I made a bold attempt to play the computer game that came with it. Called *Tass Times in Tone Town*, it was entertaining but primitive by today's standards. I also began fooling around with creating images using a simple paint-draw software application that came with all Apple computers. I thought it was rather cool to be able to "draw" using a computer and set about creating Ashley a customized placemat with an image I drew of Big Bird. Sure, it was clever, but nothing really inspired me to spend a lot of time using it. It was only when faced with Ashley's intense needs did I begin to sense the potential for these programs to really help.

I began reading about and slowly purchasing various hardware and software specifically for Ashley's use. I initially felt overwhelmed and intimidated working with a personal computer but the rewards were immediate and I was inspired to forge ahead. The computer proved engaging for Ashley.

It provided immediate feedback and a wonderful multi-sensory approach to learning. Ashley made great strides utilizing computer technology.

Having immersed myself in the literature, I learned that computers were being used to "speak" for individuals with various expressive language disabilities. After extensive research, I purchased Mayer-Johnson's *Speaking Dynamically*® and created my first computer-based augmentative communication system for Ashley. In the beginning, just having two programs open on the desktop at the same time seemed incredibly confusing, copying clipart from one program and pasting it into another. But I worked through my challenges and quickly created a dynamic system for Ashley to express herself.

What power!

Before I knew it I was hooked. I realized that computers not only could run clever programs and perform certain tasks faster than I could, but even more importantly, they could assist Ashley in learning new skills, supplement the skills she had already learned, and even substitute for skills Ashley had not yet learned or might never learn. Computers could assist children like my daughter to overcome many different disabilities.

Although Ashley made wonderful progress in many areas by utilizing assistive technology, she still needed more. Because of her disabilities, readymade educational materials typically did not work for her. Perhaps the text was too small. Or visual clutter was too prevalent. Or the reading level was too high, or too low. Or the images were not engaging, or meaningless, or unfamiliar. To help her learn, I frequently found myself redesigning store-bought educational materials. I initially used scissors and a copier to redesign for Ashley—copying and pasting the old-fashioned way. But as I became more and more proficient with the computer, I found myself learning to create wonderful educational tools using paint-draw software and a color inkjet printer.

I was amazed at what I could create, and at how fast and easy it was. My "homemade" materials were customized to Ashley's individual needs. They were dynamic and motivating. The content, background, presentation, and text type and size could all be carefully chosen and controlled. The images could be selected to be meaningful. "Cutting" and "pasting" was quicker than doing so by hand. The materials could be consistent, and of high quality. They could be designed to be predictable, thereby making learning easier. If Ashley needed it, I found I could create it more easily than I had ever imagined. I was starting to have fun, and my efforts were paying off.

Because so few educational materials meshed with Ashley's learning style, teachers were quick to assume she was simply incapable of learning.

WHAT IS AUGMENTATIVE AND ALTERNATIVE COMMUNICATION?

Augmentative and alternative communication (also known as AAC) describes a collection of methods used to help persons with disabilities to communicate. From high tech (such as voice output devices) to low tech alternatives (such as gestures, sign language, and pictures and photographs), these methods can be used to either supplement (augment) or to replace verbal communication for individuals who cannot speak or have difficulty speaking.

WHAT IS ASSISTIVE TECHNOLOGY?

The Individuals with Disabilities Education Act (IDEA), the federal special education law, legally defines assistive technology as "any item, piece of equipment, or product system... that is used to increase, maintain, or improve functional capabilities of individuals with disabilities."

Surely, Ashley's failure to learn was her fault, right? Wrong. I was convinced that, if blame were to be placed, it should be placed not on Ashley, but rather on our inability to teach her appropriately. I began to explore how changing the teaching strategy could change the outcome.

It was not my lifelong dream to learn to create customized learning materials. It became my passion only when Ashley's education and development were at stake. I was convinced Ashley had an enormous untapped capacity to learn. However, there were a great many challenges to overcome: "Input" and "output" were both issues for Ashley. Her inability to see and decipher visual materials readily made it difficult to get information in. And her inability to speak gave the impression that she could not understand what she was being taught.

Ashley's educational challenges were compounded by the low expectations of her teachers. It was often difficult to convince those working with her that she had something there to tap into. Instead, it seemed all too easy to assume she was just too disabled and throw hands up in defeat.

I found that it is possible to legally gain access to a classroom where an education is purportedly occurring and it is even possible to write well articulated goals, but there is no guarantee an education will occur without the proper strategies and materials in place. To tap Ashley's true potential, it would take a commitment to create the necessary educational materials, not just to settle for what was commercially available. It would take attention to detail, not one-size-fits-all methods. It would take the ability to learn from Ashley's challenges, not just to celebrate easy, superficial successes.

Convinced of the power of assistive technology for persons with disabilities, I began to share the knowledge I had gained in my work with Ashley. I attended my first international conference on technology and disabilities as a speaker, conducting a workshop entitled *Using Speaking Dynamically® to Promote Phonological Development*. This presentation followed the publication of my first computer program, called *See, Hear, and Say*, by Mayer-Johnson in 1996, a computerized approach to addressing Ashley's severe language disorder. Publication of two additional products followed: *School Fonts for Beginning Writing* and *Transitional Fonts for Emerging Writers*.

Through the software I have designed, the workshops I have given, and now this book, I have attempted to put to practical use what has taken me years to learn in solving Ashley's educational challenges. In the end, the real reward has been in discovering the most effective methods to reach and teach my daughter, not the programming skills I had to learn to execute those methods.

As my skills using computers and other assistive technology have grown, I often remember my initial anxious encounters with advanced technology. I feel rather silly when I think back to my discomfort with the idea of a talking computer, and each time I make some technological advance, Hal is the first to remind (and maybe tease) me. Drawing with vectors, designing fonts, creating frame animation, learning web design, devising augmentative communication systems, utilizing digital photography, creating digital panoramas: I have learned by doing, by identifying a problem and creating a solution to address it. There could be no greater inspiration for me than my own child.

Although I have had to learn the hard way, by endless hours of trial and error, I am here to make it easy for you. Using a computer no longer requires mastering arcane programming languages with funny acronyms. Computers no longer require hours to set up, now typically only taking a matter of minutes to remove from the box and plug in. Software makes things simple, and, honestly, the only skills required to create everything in this book are as easy as "pointing and clicking," "copying and pasting," and "dragging and dropping."

So don't just stick your toe in the water. Dare to dive in. The payoff for your child can be enormous. And, I promise, the experience of using a computer for creating personalized educational materials won't byte!

CONTROLLING VARIABLES
Identifying Them

WHY DESIGN VARIABLES ARE SO IMPORTANT

In her great little book *The Non-Designer's Design Book,* Robin Williams (Peachpit Press, 1994) discusses the importance of giving something a name. She shares a story about identifying a particular tree, a Joshua tree, in her parents' yard. Although she had lived in the house for over a decade, she had no name for that type of tree. But when she got a book that identified it, she realized it was not only in her parents' yard but was in just about everyone's yard in the neighborhood.

For me, her story brought to mind shopping for a new car. I am personally not a car afficionado. I see vehicles on the road everyday but have little interest in the make and model. I could drive by the same model dozens of times in the course of a busy afternoon and never note the types of vehicles around me. I don't believe it is because I am unobservant but, more so, because I have little interest in cars. I give little thought to the changes from one model year to the next or, for that matter, what a particular model is called.

That is, until I begin to shop for a new vehicle. All of a sudden, I begin to notice the aesthetics of the various cars on the road: their color, their shape, their size. I observe the components that give a car its overall appearance and appeal.

As I begin to narrow my choices, I become acutely aware of the presence of my top choices on the road. I not only begin to notice the frequency of a particular model but I begin to take note of the frequency of particular colors.

Although I have driven by certain makes and models for weeks, even months, I have paid no attention to their presence. But once the model has a name, and I have a reason to notice, it seems as if I cannot drive down the street without noticing "my car."

This is also true for design elements: once a name is assigned to various design elements, their presence or absence is noticed. Williams suggests, "Once you can name something, you're conscious of it. You have power over it. You own it. You're in control."

When I walk into a well-designed room, I experience a feeling of peacefulness. I'm no expert in design but I do have a sense when something feels right, whether I am conscious of the elements contributing to that feeling or not. But when I walk into a poorly designed room, I not only experience a feeling of agitation but my eyes begin to dart around the room to locate and identify all that is contributing to my sense of agitation.

That is the purpose of the next four sections: I want you to become aware of how choices you make can influence the appearance of what you create. Your design choices can directly affect whether your child can learn from the materials you create. You can either become aware of creating a sense of peace or a sense of agitation. You can begin to recognize elements that may inadvertently increase the cognitive demand on students trying to absorb information, or ways in which you can reduce that load. How information is arranged on a page, the selection of text and images, and the type of media it is printed on can make a difference.

I assume that this is the sort of thing that designers of educational materials are aware of (although, I often see things in readymade materials that amaze me!). For the sake of argument, we will assume they do. So if we are creating curricular adaptations or customized educational materials, we need to be aware, too. We need to recognize what the variables are, how they can change the educational outcome, and how the decisions we make can enhance or detract from their intended use.

WHAT IS A VARIABLE?

A variable is something that is subject to change or variation.

THE APPEARANCE OF TEXT: MAKING TEXT VISUALLY ACCESSIBLE

Almost all educational materials contain words printed on paper—words you hope your child will be able to read. Whether or not she can do that depends largely on the shape and layout of the letters and words on the page. This section of the book is important for you to read because it explains how to make the words on your educational materials easiest for your child to read. After all, what is the point of creating educational materials that you inadvertently render unreadable for your child. If she can't read it, she can't show you she knows it. So, here is my version of "Typesetting 101." Dive in—I guarantee you an "A" in my class!

TEXT AND THE FLUENT READER

Fluent readers probably give little thought to the way text appears in the books and magazines they read. For most people, the way a typeface looks is a mere afterthought because numerous typefaces, called fonts, can be substituted and read with relative ease: Helvetica for Geneva, Courier for Times, or Garamond for Palatino, to name a few. Whether **bold** or *italicized*, single or double spaced, proficient readers read them all interchangeably. From billboards to menus, books to newspapers, fonts may vary but the proficient reader can read them handily.

Fluent readers have become proficient in the visual skills needed to discrimate between the various letters of the alphabet, whether upper or lowercase. They understand what each letter looks like and can instantly and effortlessly identify them. Fluent readers can also apply their sophisticated deciphering skills to the many uniquely designed fonts, as well as cursive and printed letters.

TEXT AND THE "READER IN TRAINING"

Although the appearance of typefaces may go unnoticed by fluent readers, this may not be the case for readers with cognitive or visual impairments and for "readers in training." They may have far more difficulty visually discriminating among fonts depending upon a number of factors, including: type design and type style (plain, bold, or italic), type size, letter and line spacing, competing background, whether the text is handwritten, or whether it is printed in all uppercase or all lowercase letters.

For many early readers, each new typeface may appear as if it were an alien language. He or she might understand that this collection of shapes and symbols stands for something, but their exact meaning is out of reach. Each new typeface—however close in shape to a familiar typeface—may nevertheless be perceived as unique and foreign until, with time and practice, fluency is gained. Fluency opens the door to reading in a variety of typefaces. To the fluent reader, interpreting different typefaces may be much the same as understanding spoken dialects, where typefaces are used interchangeably and their unique appearance is no longer a barrier to reading. The reader may no longer need to read only one specific typeface (and layout presentation) but can read many.

For some children with disabilities, however, the appearance of typeface may continue to influence how well they can gather information from words. For these children, technology and thoughtful design can make all the difference. The purpose of choosing the right typeface is to allow readers to gather information. Its appearance should not get in the way of that process.

The appearance of typeface is a variable, one which is easily controlled, and as you create customized educational materials, you need to be keenly aware of how its appearance may affect its function. It is one of several variables that may affect educational success, and it is one you can learn to control to your child's advantage.

TYPOGRAPHY AND LEGIBILITY

Like most people, I initially had a very cursory understanding of typefaces. I knew how to select one using a pull down menu in a word processing program. I knew how to enlarge it, bold it, and italicize it. And I had a strong opinion about which fonts I preferred. But it wasn't until I learned to use Macromedia's *Fontographer*® software while designing my *School Fonts for Beginning Writing* that I began to understand what was influencing my intuitive choice of typeface, why typeface is important, and how it can affect the use of educational materials I design.

I will try to avoid overwhelming you with too much information about typeface, but what I say in this section can really empower you to design in just the right way for *your* child. So, here goes.

CATEGORIES OF FONTS

Each characteristic of a font is determined by the font designer, including stroke thickness, letter slant, character width and height, and character spacing. It is these characteristics that your eye sees and your brain interprets into letters and words. No two typefaces are created exactly the same. Each and every one is a unique blend of these characteristics.

Typefaces are typically divided into three basic categories: *serif, sans serif,* and *decorative.*

Serif Fonts

Serif fonts are known for having "feet," little horizontal projections at the end of each letter stroke.

Examples of serif fonts include:

Times   Garamond   Palatino

Serif fonts are most often used in books, magazines, and newspapers. They are the most common reading fonts.

Sans Serif Fonts

Sans serif fonts have "no feet." They are much simpler and cleaner in design.

Examples of sans serif fonts include:

Helvetica   Arial   Comic Sans MS

Sans serif fonts are considered "young" in the world of typography, only gaining popularity since the early 20th century. Their clean shapes were a product of the "modern age," often used to contrast with serif fonts and are frequently seen in advertising layouts.

Decorative Fonts

Decorative and ornamental fonts include all other fonts that do not fit into the other two categories. These include script (which resemble handwriting) and other fonts with a fancy appearance. Examples of decorative fonts include:

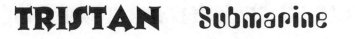

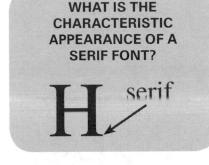

WHAT IS THE CHARACTERISTIC APPEARANCE OF A SERIF FONT?

WHAT IS THE CHARACTERISTIC APPEARANCE OF A SANS SERIF FONT?

Decorative and ornamental fonts are cute and fun but would be tiring to read in large doses. They are typically used in isolation to add style and emotion to documents.

CHOOSING A TYPEFACE

There are differences of opinion over whether serif or sans serif fonts make text more readable. Regardless of which category, some fonts are obviously more readable than others. Interestingly, serif fonts are found in most books, magazines, and newspapers—that is, printed materials with lots of type requiring lots of reading. Even though I personally prefer reading sans serif fonts, most publishing houses must be of the opinion that serif fonts are easier to read. But whether I select a serif, sans serif, or decorative font for designing customized educational materials, my choice is not random. I think about its purpose and the impact it may have on my reader.

VARIATION IN LETTER FORM

"Letter form" is the exact shape each letter is assigned in a typeface. When choosing a font, be aware that there can be significant differences in letter form. For example, the lowercase "a" can vary from an elementary "a" to "Old English." A font with the elementary "a" may be preferable for some readers since this is the character style also taught in early penmanship. There are similar considerations for the lowercase "g."

a	**a**	**g**	**g**
Comic Sans MS	Helvetica	Comic Sans MS	Times
letter style like elementary handwriting	letter style like "Old English" design	letter style like elementary handwriting	letter style like "Old English" design

CONDENSED FONTS

A critical element of font design is how close together or far apart individual letters are placed in a word. In condensed fonts, letters are placed close together with typically little white space in between. This is often done to make text fit into a small space. However, condensing letters makes the typeface more difficult to read and, consequently, is not a good choice for easy reading.

Condensed font letters are crowded together.

SETTING TYPEFACE CHARACTERISTICS

Word processing programs give you the power to control the way text appears by manipulating a number of text characteristics, including letter size, spacing between lines of text, or whether text appears plain, bold, or in italics. Here are some suggestions to picking the characteristics that will make text most easy for your child to read.

PLAIN VERSUS BOLD

Many people assume that changing a typeface from plain to bold makes words easier to read. This is not always true. With most fonts, changing the text characteristic to bold reduces the amount of white space between the letters. Depending upon the font, this can make the text more difficult to read. Bolding text can provide emphasis to a word, but its use must be weighed against its impact on legibility.

Using the plain setting can leave more space between letters.

Using the bold setting can reduce the space between letters.

ITALICS

Italicizing might draw attention to a word, but it is less readable than plain text. Additionally, the italicized version of most serif fonts has a different appearance than its unitalicized counterpart.

Ashley *Ashley*

But the italicized version of most sans serif fonts just looks like the slanted version of the same unitalicized font.

Ashley *Ashley*

My suggestion: Use italics sparingly, especially for serif fonts.

SIZE

The size of a typeface is expressed in the number of "points." Depending upon the software, some standard text size settings include

10, 12, 18, 24, 36, 48, 60, and 72 point. Typeface sizes can also be set to be smaller, larger, and any size in between. The upper and lower limits for text size settings depend upon limitations set by your software.

Enlarging text can improve readability. Text is considered "large print" (an accommodation often used for individuals with visual impairments) from 16 to 18 points.

This type size at 18 points is easy to read.

This type size at 10 points is more difficult to read.

Keep in mind that there is no standard font size. When a font is designed, the font designer chooses the length and width, so size will vary from one font to another.

24 pt. Book Antiqua   24 pt. Birch Std

WHEN ENLARGING TEXT MAY NOT BE A GOOD IDEA

Is larger text always better? Surprisingly, for some individuals with certain visual impairments, the answer is no. Ashley is one of those people. With limited peripheral vision, Ashley sees the world as if she were wearing blinders. Unless something is directly in front of her, she might just miss it.

For people who have lost some peripheral vision, text on a line can begin to run outside their visual field as it is enlarged, making it more difficult to be seen. For these individuals, enlarged text can become too large. When it falls outside their visual field they must be made aware that they must not only track with their eyes from left to right but they may also have to move their head from left to right as well. Otherwise, what is " out of sight" is " out of mind."

The following illustration shows what happens when the text is only slightly enlarged for a person with a limited visual field.

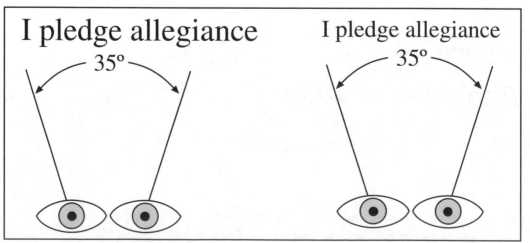

BALANCING TEXT SIZE AND LINE LENGTH

When you enlarge the size of text keep in mind that it can threaten the balance between text size and layout. It is much easier to read short sentences as a single line of text—the eyes only having to track from left to right—than it is to have the sentence wrap around to another line. As the example below shows, it is possible to enlarge the text and still keep an entire sentence on one line in the same available space.

As the length of a line of text increases, there will be no choice sometimes but for the text to wrap around. However, it is still important to limit the length of a line of text. As a rule of thumb, keep the lines of text to no more than 50 to 65 characters. Also, avoid splitting words at the end of lines by turning off your program's automatic hyphenation tool.

SPACING BETWEEN LETTERS

Most word processing applications, like *Word* and *AppleWorks*®, let you "expand" or "condense" the space between characters in a word. This can be a helpful feature because it can improve the readability of certain fonts that may otherwise have characters too far apart or too close together.

Check the space between letters.

Check the space between letters.

> **USING "EXPAND"**
>
> If you use bold typeface, consider using your program's "expand" feature to increase the amount of white space between letters.

SPACING BETWEEN LINES OF TEXT

Most word processing programs and most graphics programs (like *FreeHand*® and *Illustrator*®), enable you to increase the vertical spacing between lines of text. In typesetting, this is called "leading." Most people are familiar with setting their documents just to single or double spacing, but may be unaware that the spacing between lines of text can be set to almost any distance. For example:

Increasing the distances between lines of text can increase its readability by making it easier to visually discriminate between each line of text. Or, it can hinder readability—it depends upon the needs of the reader.

Fourscore and seven years ago our fathers brought forth on this continent a new nation, conceived in liberty and dedicated to the proposition that all men are created equal.

Fourscore and seven years ago our fathers brought

forth on this continent a new nation, conceived in

liberty and dedicated to the proposition that all men

are created equal.

A good rule of thumb is to use 1.5 times spacing.

TEXT ALIGNMENT

Aligning text may seem like a simple formatting issue to make things pretty, but aligning text can also affect the way text is perceived.

Choosing to left align is a good idea because it provides a straight vertical edge.

Row, row, row your boat
Gently down the stream.
Merrily, merrily, merrily, merrily,
Life is but a dream.

On the other hand, right alignment is not wise since this creates an irregular left vertical edge which is very difficult to read.

Row, row, row your boat
Gently down the stream.
Merrily, merrily, merrily, merrily,
Life is but a dream.

Justifying text—creating straight margins on both edges—is also not wise because this aligns text in both the left and right directions. In doing so, it creates uneven spacing between words, making text more difficult to read.

Row,   row,   row   your   boat
Gently   down   the   stream.
Merrily,   merrily,   merrily,   merrily,
Life   is   but   a   dream.

USING ALL UPPERCASE VERSUS ALL LOWERCASE

Did you know that it is faster to read lowercase letters than all uppercase letters? Additionally, the appearance of many words in all uppercase does not bear the slightest resemblance to the same words in all lowercase, and yet they are often used interchangeably. Of the 26 letters in the English alphabet, nearly half of the uppercase letters do not closely resemble their lowercase counterpart. Therefore, words containing these letters look completely different from the same words using all uppercase letters.

dig   bar
DIG   BAR

How do readers decipher all this? Some might distinguish one word from another by a method called "text configuration"—that is, looking at the shape of the entire word. Focusing on a word's ascenders (the upward vertical stroke on letters, such as "b" and "h") and descenders (the tail on letters such as "p" and "g") helps to enable them to identify the word by its shape.

ascender

help

descender

However, when a word is presented in all uppercase, text configuration is no help because all uppercase words have the same shape, a rectangle, providing no clues to the word itself.

Instead, words should appear as they normally do: as a mixture of uppercase and lowercase letters.

CONTRAST

In printing, contrast is the difference between the color of text and the color of background. White text on a black background provides excellent contrast, while black text on a white background is a close second.

Printing a page of white text on a black background is tricky and expensive, especially with an inkjet printer. White text can only be achieved by printing the black background with a large amount of black ink. The white text appears where there is an absence of ink. Not only does this use a large amount of ink but it will make the paper excessively wet, causing it to wrinkle, making it difficult to use.

USE OF COLORED INK

Dark or black ink on light paper makes text easiest to see. But, as a general rule, never use dark ink on dark paper or light ink on light paper since neither provides enough contrast to make text easy to see.

COMPETING BACKGROUND

Although clever, placing text on a competing background can greatly reduce its readability. An easy solution is to box the text with a surrounding white background that then provides necessary contrast to the text.

HANDWRITTEN TEXT

We either don't think it makes a difference or don't plan ahead and, instead, throw together handwritten educational materials, rather than generate consistently appearing text from a computer. Substituting handwritten text for a consistently shaped font can make your materials much more difficult to read. Using cursive text can complicate things even further. Unlike a computer generated font, the appearance of handwritten text varies from one person to another, no two words appearing exactly the same, and no one person able to print the same word the exact same way twice. Writing instruments (pens, pencils, and markers) can also influence the readability of text because of differences in line thickness. The ability to read cursive text is a learned skill. The use of handwritten fonts or cursive text can complicate reading.

| Example of printed handwriting | Example of cursive handwriting | Example of text with consistent font |

My suggestion: Use your computer.

DESIGN AND LEGIBILITY OF NUMERALS

In addition to generating words on your computer, your educational materials will undoubtedly include numbers too. Like letters, there are a few things to keep in mind. There are big differences between fonts in the way numbers are designed. Take the number "4;" you will find two different character shapes for the same number depending upon the font.

4   4

Textile   Helvetica

Also, some numbers are not as easy to discriminate as others for certain fonts. At small text sizes, it can be difficult to see that the letter stroke has stopped depending upon the character design.

6   6

Helvetica   Comic Sans MS

Therefore, pay close attention to your font selection.

SPECIFIC FONT RECOMMENDATIONS

I prefer designing Ashley's educational materials using sans serif fonts. Some good ones are:

Arial, Verdana, and Tahoma.

My all-time favorite font for designing customized educational materials is:

Comic Sans MS

It is a sans serif font, simple and clean in design. The spacing between letters is excellent, enhancing its legibility. Its lowercase "a" and "g" closely mimic elementary school printing (similar to Palmer style handwriting). I used this font almost exclusively until I had a large degree of confidence in Ashley's ability to read.

TEXT DESIGN AMBIGUITY

Be aware that some characters of certain fonts can look ambiguous to the reader. I only became aware of this by watching Ashley quietly manipulating materials I had designed for her.

In some typefaces, such as Helvetica, the uppercase "I" and the lowercase "l" are indistinguishable; one character is only slightly thicker than the other (not even visible to the naked eye) but otherwise they both look like simple vertical lines.

love

Ice

Additionally, the lowercase "t" has a strong resemblance to a lowercase "f" except inverted in both Helvetica and Verdana.

f   t   f   t

These are commonly used fonts. You may find other fonts with similar design ambiguities. By observing errors in your child's performance, you may be able to pinpoint an ambiguity in design.

AVOIDING FONT DEPENDENCY

Although I mostly used Comic Sans MS early on when designing for Ashley, I introduced her to other fonts once I had a high degree of confidence in her ability to read, especially those fonts most commonly used in books, newspapers, and magazines, such as:

Helvetica, Palatino, and Times.

Not wanting Ashley to become dependent upon reading only one typeface, I introduced text to her in other fonts *after* I knew she could successfully read what I initially presented to her.

Text design, however, cannot always be so closely controlled. My intent in introducing variability was for Ashley to learn to generalize her reading skills. You've never heard someone pick up a newspaper and say, "Oh, darn, I can't read this font! I can only read Geneva!" The goal is for reading to be fluid and effortless, as much as possible. The appearance of typeface should not be a contributing negative influence to reading success.

TO SUMMARIZE:

Now that I have given you "Kim's Short Course on Type and Typography," I hope you are more aware of the important choices you make every time you begin to create educational materials.

- do not handwrite your text

- do not use all uppercase letters

- do not use condensed type

- use bold and italicized letters sparingly

- do not place text on a competing background

- provide optimal contrast between text and the background

- consider providing spacing between lines of text

- ultimately, introduce a variety of fonts

ADJUSTING TYPEFACE

If it is possible to ask the person you are designing for their preferred format, then do so. With assistance and examples, they should be able to assist you in determining what is best.

CONTROLLING VARIABLES
Images

GRAPHIC IMAGES: MAKING THEM MEANINGFUL

Graphic images include symbols, icons, and photos. They are especially important for visual learners, but can be an asset to all learners. Almost every educational material included in this book, and almost every one you will invent yourself, will include images.

Images add interest to educational materials, as well as provide meaning to individual words, and contextual clues to books and other reading materials. Just about anyone creating an educational adaptation, educational tool, or communication strategy is probably working with some sort of graphic image to enhance their design.

So, if images are so important, where can you get them? Well, the answer is "almost everywhere." There are many, many commercially available graphic images on the market today, and many companies whose sole purpose is the marketing of graphic images. But there are also many other free sources of images. This section provides some direction on available images and how to choose among icons or stock photos, availability of free images, and when it might be time to create your own.

THE IMAGE CHOICE

For all the different types of graphic images available, there are just as many considerations that go into their selection and use. From symbols (such as icons and clip art) and symbol sets (such as *Picture Communication Symbols*) to "real world" images (such as photographs and digital images), there are usually a number of ways to display an image. Icons and symbols might work best for some learners; "real world" images might work better for others. Some children have difficulty understanding some image types. For them, real world images might be better. For other children, using icons can help them to learn that a symbol or icon can stand for something real.

When it comes to choosing an image type, there is no "better" or "worse" choice and no "right" and "wrong" answer. Symbols and photos both have their place. But there may be a "right" or "wrong" answer for a particular user, or in certain situations. Selecting the "best" image is

---

WHAT IS A STOCK PHOTO?

A stock photo is an existing photo that is available for purchase (or use).

WHAT IS A REAL WORLD IMAGE?

A "real world" image is a photo of an actual object and not an illustration, symbol, or icon of that object. For example, a photograph of your dog, Spot, is a real world image, but a drawing of Spot is not.

an important assignment. So there needs to be some understanding of the criteria driving your selection.

USING SYMBOLS AND ICONS

By definition, a symbol is something that "stands for or represents something else." An icon is "a symbol that is universally recognized to be representative of something." Examples might include the red and white *Coca-Cola* icon to represent a can of pop, "Golden Arches" to represent the McDonald's® fast food restaurant, or a red hexagonally shaped sign to represent "stop."

But that is the critical feature: its ability to be "universally recognized." As much as the icon of "Golden Arches" is generally understood by most to represent McDonald's®, this is not always the case. If a child has never been to a McDonald's® or does not possess an understanding of what the "Golden Arches" stand for, the image would have no meaning. The use of symbols and icons is only as valuable as their association to a child's experiences.

I remember observing Ashley with a speech language pathologist when she was quite young. Presented with a card of an image of a football, Ashley was to select the picture card associated with it. One of the possible choices was a football helmet. Unfortunately, Ashley had had no exposure to the game of football (believe it or not); therefore, she could neither identify a football nor make the association with the helmet. Her failure at this activity had nothing to do with the appearance of the icon, or the presentation of the materials. Instead, it was directly related to her lack of exposure to the images she was presented.

It is the nature of many disabilities that exposure to what most people consider "commonplace" is significantly lacking. Physical access to certain activities, as the result of health related issues alone, can drastically reduce opportunities. Sometimes, a child's intelligence is judged by his or her recognition of specific symbols and icons when, in fact, it may have little to do with cognition and more to do with experience. When we use symbols and icons, we must be careful that we are not exacerbating disabilities rather than enhancing abilities. This often requires using symbols and icons to *teach* what is otherwise thought to be "commonplace."

Likewise, exposure to a particular set of images does not automatically provide an understanding of the image: what it is or what it represents. An image of measuring spoons may not initially be recognized—what they are, where they are found in the kitchen, or what they are used for—until the image is associated with the object and its purpose. However, by attaching meaning to even an obscure symbol or icon through frequent and repetitive use, images can begin to be "universally" understood to stand for certain things.

THEIR PRACTICAL APPLICATION

Ashley has used symbols and icons as a form of communication for years. Unable to speak, she learned to point to symbols to express her wants and needs. It was a method used to augment her communication. She quickly learned she had the power to drive an outcome by pointing to objects representing something concrete. She then learned to directly select from more than one concrete choice, such as two popsicle boxes or two video movie covers. Next, she learned to use an image or icon of something concrete to express her choice. She might not have been able to speak but, by using symbols and icons, she sure could communicate!

Soon, icons of restaurants, such as the "Golden Arches," and other logos and images, gave her the power to express her interest in going to a particular restaurant, or participating in a certain activity. Opportunities were created to provide Ashley the chance to make choices. Symbols and icons were the ticket.

Symbols and icons have also been an important component in Ashley learning to read. She had no reliable way to communicate her understanding of an abstract collection of graphic shapes known to you and me as a "word." But, given the opportunity to match text to a symbol or icon, she was able to prove her ability to understand what text stood for. Expanding upon these same methods, Ashley has been able to make incredible strides in the important skill of reading.

So, you see, symbols and icons can be a powerful tool, but their careful selection and thoughtful use must be closely monitored.

AVOID CONFUSION: USE SYMBOLS AND ICONS WISELY

As I began using symbols and icons with Ashley, it was apparent to me that I was often not only providing her the opportunity to communicate or read, but I was also teaching her *language*. Individual images began to take on a specific meaning to her and I had to be consistent in their use. I also had to be selective of how I used symbols. For example, if I used a symbol of a book to represent the concept "reading," I would avoid using that same symbol to also represent "library."

> **WHAT IS AUGMENTATIVE AND ALTERNATIVE COMMUNICATION?**
>
> Augmentative and alternative communication (also known as AAC) describes a collection of methods used to help persons with disabilities to communicate. From high tech (such as voice output devices) to low tech alternatives (such as gestures, sign language, and pictures and photographs), these methods can be used to either supplement (augment) or to replace verbal communication for individuals who cannot speak or have difficulty speaking.

WHAT ARE *PICTURE COMMUNICATION SYMBOLS*?

Picture Communication Symbols (PCS) are a collection of icons representing objects, acitvities, even feelings. Arranged in a searchable database, a software application called *Boardmaker*™ is the simplest method for accessing these images.

I initially decided to stick with one symbol system; I chose Mayer-Johnson's *Picture Communication Symbols*. Over time, I also created some of my own icons as I needed symbols that were not in the symbol set. I kept a library of these images which I could draw upon from time to time. As more obscure symbols and icons were incorporated into Ashley's educational materials and communication strategies, she learned to associate meaning to them when they were used in context. Later, with access to digital photography, the use of real world images was an easy transition to a much larger bank of images.

BOARDMAKER™ BY MAYER-JOHNSON

Boardmaker™ is a searchable graphic database of over 3,500 bit-mapped (older versions prior to version 5.0) and vector drawn (version 5.0 and above) *Picture Communication Symbols* (*PCS*). These icons are provided in a set of color symbols, as well as in black and white. Each symbol is labeled with an identifiable name used as a method to search the database. The images within the database are listed in multiple languages from English and Spanish to Italian and Dutch.

Initially comprised of the most frequently used words, there are now over 5,000 additional symbols in the *Boardmaker*™ database, including a collection of sign language symbols. These symbols now cover a wide spectrum of categories from cooking and grooming to leisure and school activities. They can also be used to create an array of materials for both educational and communication purposes.

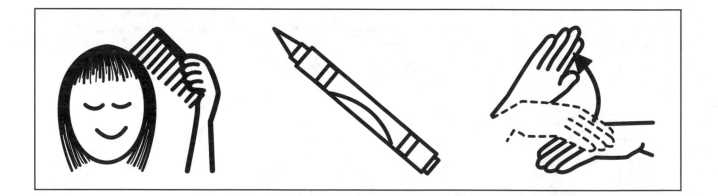

"FULL FIGURE" VERSUS "STICK FIGURES"

Many of the images for words representing verbs, such as "eat," "drink," and "clean" to name a few, are available as both "full figures" and "stick figures." The "stick figures" are more generic, shown without a specific gender, hair length, or hair color. As a general rule, I use the "stick figure" rather than the "full figure" when available since I want the focus to be the action rather than the appearance of the individual.

The *PCS* for "drink" as a "stick figure"

The *PCS* for "drink" as a "full figure"

This has been my practice for years. And, although Ashley cannot articulate her approval of my design decision, other people who create educational materials tell me that their students will ask, "Who's that?" when "full figure" rather than "stick figure" images are used.

MODIFYING "FULL FIGURE" ICONS

Occasionally, I have taken the time to modify a "full figure" icon to look like Ashley using a graphics program. Although somewhat timeconsuming if more than just hair color is altered, I usually reserve this practice only for those icons I intend to use over and over. I do this when I believe the image needs to be more engaging for Ashley and more closely resemble her.

ROYALTY ISSUES WITH *BOARDMAKER*™ AND *PICTURE COMMUNICATION SYMBOLS*

Unlike some commercially available libraries of images, *Picture Communication Symbols (PCS)* allow only for personal use and limited reproduction, and prohibit "commercial use, or for entire school system, hospital system, or institutional system." You are allowed to use *PCS* images as much as you want for creating your own materials, but you should not share the *Boardmaker*™ database with others or create materials using *PCS* images to sell to others without permission. Although this should not typically become a problem, it is something to be aware of.

CREATING YOUR OWN LIBRARY OF IMAGES USING *BOARDMAKER*™

Images of custom clip art, screen captures, scanned images, or digital photographs can be organized in searchable "libraries" making these images as easily located, copied, and pasted as any image found in *Boardmaker*™. By organizing images in this manner, it allows for you to quickly access images to use in other applications.

It is important to create your own *Boardmaker™* library file of new images rather than intermingling your personal images within the libraries of *Boardmaker™* icons. (Version 5.0 and above creates personal libraries automatically, although older versions of Boardmaker™ do not.) Otherwise, your images will be lost if it ever becomes necessary to reinstall the *Boardmaker™* software application, or a future *Boardmaker™* upgrade necessitates reinstalling the software. And it also makes it possible to share your personal library of images with friends who are also *Boardmaker™* users.

If you are a *Boardmaker™* user, or you decide to become one, it is well worth your time to learn how to correctly utilize *Boardmaker™* for this purpose.

BECOMING AN ICON!

There are occasions when I want an icon, rather than a photo, to look like various family members. This gives the image a bit more of a "cartoon character." It is more a generic representation of an individual rather than the person at a particular age, with a particular hair cut, or with a particular set of clothes. I have often adapted available icons, changing hairstyle and color, or adding glasses. I use these icons a great deal for storybooks and communication boards for Ashley.

But this practice of adapting icons to look like people can be a bit tedious and time consuming, and, frankly, I am no artist. So, in an effort to streamline the process and improve the end result, I have used a wonderful service called Iconize me! (http://iconizeme.dv-graphics.com/). For a nominal charge (from $15 per icon for personal use), a digital photo of an individual is e-mailed to their site and an icon is returned to you. This icon can then be used over and over again in various customized educational materials.

Wendy
Ashley's little sister

Wendy
as an icon

DIGITAL IMAGES: REAL WORLD IMAGES

As important as symbols and icons have been to Ashley's development, they have had their limitations. Although invaluable, there are times when icons are ambiguous. For example, an icon of an older bald man with glasses might not be an obvious representation of a child's grandfather. Before digital photography, maybe that had to suffice. But with a digital photo, there is no question: "That's my Grandpa!" Try modifying one icon of a boy to represent more than one blond-haired blue-eyed classmate and you will quickly come to the same conclusion I did: There is an important place for digital images in designing customized educational materials.

I was a very early user of digital photography, purchasing one of the earliest digital cameras on the market (the Apple® *QuickTake 100*) that worked with a home computer. I began experimenting with the use of "real world images" in creating customized educational materials and augmentative communication systems for Ashley when she was quite young. For those personal images of friends, families, pets, or familiar locations, digitized photos are quite often the answer.

STOCK PHOTOS

There are commercially available "stock photos" that can save an enormous amount of time when "real world images" are needed that are not of a personal nature. Using stock photos can save an enormous amount of time from taking a picture, cleaning up, cropping, and sizing the image. Instead, it is a simple matter of copying and pasting the image into a document.

Some stock photos expect a fee to be paid for each time an image is used. But, for others, the purchase price provides for unlimited usage. I look for products that provide the latter.

Products like Hemera *Photo-Objects*® and *The Big Box of Art*™ are a time-saving resource, providing a large collection of high quality, royalty-free images in a searchable database. I am especially fond of *Photo-Objects*® for their "real photo images of people, animals and objects." Their photos are provided with a transparent background (called *pre-masked*), allowing images to be grouped and layered with no additional steps.

See the ***Resources*** section for more information on these stock photos, as well as others.

CREATING YOUR OWN IMAGES

There are also times when it is appropriate to create your own images. Stock images can be expensive and often include images that are

---

WHAT DO THOSE FILE SUFFIXES STAND FOR?

JPEG (JPG): Joint Photographic Experts Group

TIFF (TIF): Tagged Image File Format

GIF: Graphics Interchange Format

PICT (PCT): an Apple graphics format

BMP: a Windows or OS/2 bitmap format

WMF: Windows Metafile Format

EMF: Windows Enhanced Metafile Format

of little to no use. Stock images can be incredible timesavers but when their cost is an issue, it is simple to create your own. Images can also be modified by cropping, combining, and layering to create new ones.

Customized digital images can be easily created using a digital camera (or a single frame of digital video). Digital images can also be created from previously processed photographs by scanning the image using some form of scanning technology. Or, undeveloped film can be processed and the images digitized by many film processing centers. The photographs are then stored in a format that can be recognized by a computer, typically a CD-ROM.

FREE STOCK PHOTOS

The Internet is a wonderful source of web sites with royalty-free and public domain photographs that can be used for personal, educational, and non-commercial use. These images can be screen captured (explained below) or downloaded to your hard drive (also explained below). These images can range from low resolution (72 dpi) to high resolution (300 dpi).

See the *Resources* section for more information on Internet sites for royalty-free and public domain photos.

CAPTURING IMAGES FROM THE INTERNET

For Macintosh® (depending upon your Internet browser):
- Place the pointer over the image you want to copy. Hold down the mouse button and a menu will pop up giving you options to choose from. Choose Save Image As and select a location where you would like to store the image (such as the desktop, hard drive, or designated folder).

- Or, place the pointer over the image you want to copy. Hold down the mouse button and right-click the image. Select Download Image to Disk. Select a location where you would like to store the image (such as the desktop, hard drive, or designated folder).

- Or, place the pointer over the image you want to copy. Hold down the mouse button and begin dragging the image off the web page to the location where you would like to store the image (such as the desktop, hard drive, or designated folder). A copy of the image will appear where you "drop" the image.

For Windows®:
- Place the pointer over the image you want to copy. Right-click the image and choose Save Picture As. Select a location on your hard drive where you would like to store the image and click Save.

Remember that not all images on the Internet are free or public domain. Most of them are copyrighted. (See *Copyright* section.)

SCREEN CAPTURE

A screen capture (also called a screen shot or image capture) is an instantaneous snapshot of the computer screen's contents. The image is saved as a file on the computer's hard drive and can then be opened in a graphics program.

While there are a number of programs commercially available for creating screen shots, such as *SnagIt*® by TechSmith® for Windows® and *SnapzPro*® for Macintosh®, it is easy to screen capture without special programs:

For Macintosh®:
- Press the Command and Shift keys simultaneously, and then press the number 3 key on your keyboard. You will hear a noise that sounds like the shutter of a camera. You have just captured the entire screen. If you press the number 4 key instead, the pointer changes to allow you to select the area of the screen you would like to capture by dragging the pointer over the area.

  The image will be located on your hard drive labeled Picture 1, Picture 2, and so forth. By double-clicking on the appropriate picture, the image will automatically be opened by an appropriate program but can be opened by other graphics programs as well.

For Windows®:
- Press the Print Screen button (usually on the top row of the keyboard) to capture the entire screen. To capture the active window only, press the Alt key and the Print Screen key simultaneously. The screen capture has been copied to the clipboard. The image is now ready to paste into any graphics program.

WHAT IS THE IMAGE QUALITY OF A SCREEN CAPTURE?

The image quality of a screen capture is directly related to the resolution of your computer's monitor (usually 72 ppi/pixels per inch).

CONTROLLING VARIABLES
Layout

IDENTIFYING THE CHARACTERISTICS OF LAYOUT

Over the years, teachers creating curricular adaptations have asked me, "Why do your materials always look so much better than mine? How did you do that?" Initially, I was unable to provide a name for the rules I applied. For me, it was just instinctual. I could show them but I lacked the language to tell them.

For some, this skill of layout and organization is innate; for others it must be taught. Fortunately, it is a skill that can be learned. And it is an important skill to learn since it is in your child's best interest to pay attention to what you may be communicating **through** your layout—by where on a page you place text and images and by how you make your text and images look.

CRAP!

Bet that got your attention! Well, that's exactly what we don't want to happen! In making educational materials, we can inadvertently create visual distraction by not thinking about our actions. But we can avoid producing just that by following some simple rules for this acronym succinctly explained in Robin Williams' book, *The Non-Designer's Design Book* (Peachpit Press, 1994).

CRAP stands for: **C**ontrast
 Repetition
 Alignment, and
 Proximity.

Although her book is not specifically intended for persons creating curricular adaptations and customized educational materials, the information regarding layout can be appropriately applied. When I read this book, I immediately realized that these were the instinctual rules I was using to create materials for Ashley. They are important rules to apply to both text and images.

Read on to learn how layout can affect what you communicate.

CONTRAST

Contrast occurs when two design elements are treated differently, enough so that it is readily apparent. Treating one element differently than another draws attention to the one that is not the same. This can be accomplished in a number of ways, such as (significantly) changing the thickness of a line, or (significantly) changing the color or size of one element.

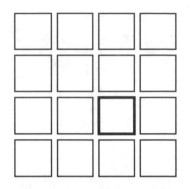

In this example, your eye is first drawn to the square with the different line thickness, before noticing the other 15 like squares.

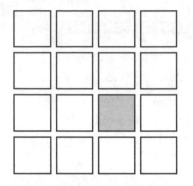

In this example, your eye is first drawn to the square with the different color.

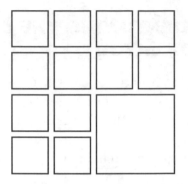

In this example, you notice the square that is different because it is larger than all the rest.

Remember: this is also true for text. If you bold text, change its color, or change its size then you are also providing contrast to surrounding text. But if you want all elements to be visually the same, then you must treat them the same.

REPETITION

The word "repetition" could also be substituted for the word "consistency" (but then the great acronym wouldn't work!). It is the consistency and continuity in the elements of the materials you create, such as type, size, color, background, graphics, and placement of elements.

Repeating design elements, such as using all the same size squares on a lotto board, unifies a document. Repetition also provides visual organizational clues, such as consistently bolding the text of the broad categories in an outline or consistently indenting the text of subcategories.

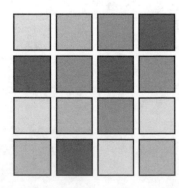

In this example, although difficult to ascertain, there are 4 sets of squares in 4 different colors.

Once the color of the squares are consistently repeated, it is easy to see that there are four distinct colors in four distinct rows.

Although both examples contain the same four sets of colored squares, in which example could you quickly recognize that?

ALIGNMENT

By aligning elements we create order and organization from chaos. And, frankly, most of us perform better with order. When elements on a page are lined up with one another they look organized and connected. Alignment can occur both horizontally and vertically. Providing alignment in text also makes reading easier since the eyes do not have to move all over the page.

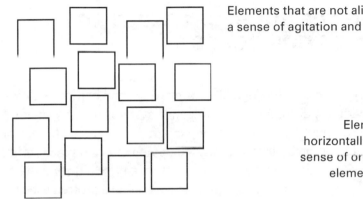

Elements that are not aligned create a sense of agitation and confusion.

Elements that are aligned, horizontally or vertically, create a sense of organization, making the elements appear connected.

Although both examples contain the same number of squares, which example could you count more easily?

PROXIMITY

A visual relationship is established by the proximity between various elements—where they appear on a page in relation to each other. The closer together elements appear the more related they are assumed to be, and the farther apart they appear the less related they are assumed to be.

Shapes, such as rectangles or circles, can also be used to group related elements. Or, lines can be drawn between less related elements.

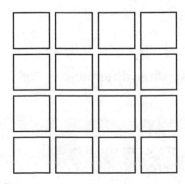

Grouping and aligning similar items make them appear related.

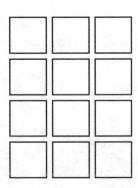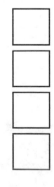

Elements that are farther apart appear less related, although the set of 12 squares appear related and the set of 4 squares appear related since they are in close proximity to one another.

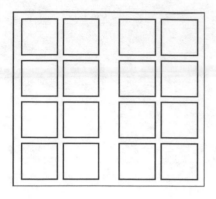

Elements that are grouped together by enclosing them in a shape appear related.

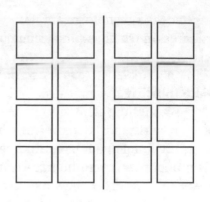

And when a line is drawn between the two sets each set appears related.

APPLYING THE RULES OF LAYOUT TO COMMUNICATION BOARDS

In her book *Early Communication Skills for Children with Down Syndrome* (Woodbine House, 2003), Libby Kumin defines a communication board as "individually designed communication systems that may involve the use of pictures, photographs, rebus or pictographs, alphabet letters, or words." Communication boards are used to supplement or replace verbal communication for individuals who may otherwise have a difficult time communicating. *Picture Communication Symbols* (PCS) are often used for creating communication boards. And *Boardmaker*™, a searchable graphic database of PCS, makes creating communication boards a snap.

There are many available resources that describe the purpose of communication boards and the process of selecting their content, including Kumin's book. Therefore, I have not provided instructions on creating communication boards in this book. But I would like to use the creation of a communication board to show you how the rules of layout—contrast, repetition, alignment, and proximity—can enhance or detract from their design and use.

I always try to create materials for Ashley that need few, if any, directions or explanation, and I can do this successfully through thoughtful layout. While the very simplified communication board in *Illustration 1* gives very few visual clues to indicate that words are to be selected from each category to create a sentence, the communication board in *Illustration 2* is much improved by doing a few simple things:

- keeping all parts of speech in vertical alignment (alignment)
- assigning three distinct colors to the three different parts of speech (repetition and contrast)
- offsetting the alignment of the verbs (contrast)
- drawing a rectangle around the entire set of squares and drawing lines in between each group (proximity)

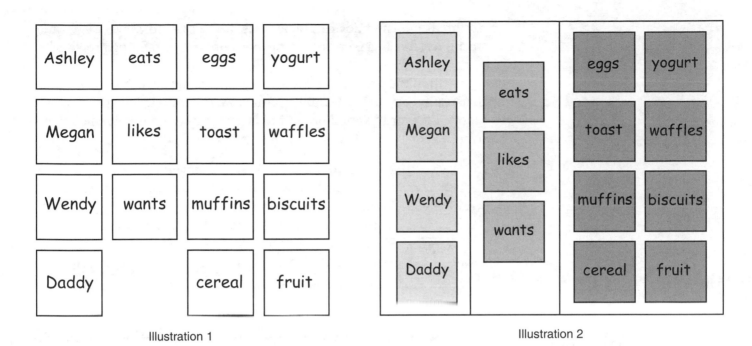

Illustration 1   Illustration 2

The content has not changed but visual clues have been provided to what previously looked like fifteen individual words. Now it looks like a well organized communication board!

A CASE AGAINST AMBIGUITY: DESIGNING FOR SUCCESS

We tend to work very efficiently when there is predictability designed into our routines and habits. For many things, our responses are automatic because the circumstances are predictable and our responses are rote. It is comforting to be able to successfully handle what is thrown our way. And predicatability can be a significant contributor to success.

Take check writing, for example. No matter what bank you use, or in what part of the country you live, checks all essentially look alike. (This is because their layout has been standardized.) They are designed with the date in the upper right hand corner, the signature line in the lower right hand corner, and the memo line in the lower left corner. It is probably not something you have given much thought to because that is, fortunately, just the way it is. Always. Therefore, filling out a check is very automatic. No one must read the text before the line to make sure it says "Date." We perform very efficiently at this task because the presentation is predicatable.

But doctor's office forms are, by contrast, a totally different story. Although generally asking for the same information, they vary from office to office and are completely unpredictable in their layout. Personally, I am always a bit anxious at new doctor visits, not just because of having to "break in" a new doctor, but because of having to fill out those blasted forms as I feel like I am beginning a test of my "form filling prowess."

Often the first line of the form is the beginning of many pages of frustration and unpredictability. Am I to write my name on the line just above the word "Name" or am I to begin writing on the line below it? And if I don't begin correctly then everything is off.

Name
_____

Address
_____

City   State   Zip
_____

Ambiguity could have been easily eliminated by making minor adjustments in the design of the form. For example, if the word for the requested information were simply moved *before* the line, I could have filled out the form with a high degree of confidence that I had placed the information on the correct line starting with the first line.

AVOIDING AMBIGUITY IN YOUR EDUCATIONAL MATERIALS

I share all of this with you because I want you to begin thinking about not only what you place on a page but the way in which you place it, otherwise known as the layout. The manner in which information is organized can communicate a great deal of information (by certain characteristics): whether elements are the same or different, whether elements are related to one another or not, whether elements are of more or less importance.

Remember what applying the rules of layout did for the simple communication board on the previous page? It transformed what was otherwise only a series of squares holding words with an ambigious purpose into something that is easy to use and understand.

IN CONCLUSION

Organizing information well on a page can provide a successful format that can then be modified for new activities. And by doing so, you are providing predictability in your design and reducing the cognitive demand on your child.

AND ONE MORE THING...

Don't include elements on a page just to be cute. Instead, focus on what is necessary and purposeful. Copy text and images to the clipboard, but *think* before pasting them!

CONTROLLING VARIABLES
Media

The variety and quality of media available for use with inkjet printers is amazing. Go to any office supply or computer store, or search the Internet, and you will find dozens and dozens of inkjet compatible products. You are probably most familiar with multipurpose paper but may be unaware of the availability of other inkjet compatible media, including iron-on transfers, magnets, decals, and more. Each has unique qualities that influence whether it is best suited for specific projects. The choices you make about media will control the variables in your teaching and may influence whether your child learns easily or not. I'll describe them and explain how they can be used to create interesting educational materials. I have also included a chart to show which media to use with the "recipes" in the book, so you know how the different media can be used to create useful educational materials.

PAPER MEDIA

(WHITE) MULTIPURPOSE PAPER

You are probably most familiar with white, multipurpose paper. It is typically a lightweight 20 lb. paper that is not as dense as some heavier papers. As a result, images printed on the back side will show

through to the front. For this reason, 20 lb. paper is not a good choice if images will be printed on both sides of the paper.

Multipurpose 20 lb. paper is also less rigid and does not produce as durable a product as heavier, denser paper. But, because multipurpose paper is typically the least expensive, it is best suited for "one time use" materials, such as worksheets, or for materials that do not require high durability. If the paper is going to be laminated, multipurpose paper may be just fine since a great deal of durability will be acquired from the lamination itself. Or, slide the paper into a sheet protector and place it in a three-ring binder. This will also improve the life of the materials. But look for nonglare sheet protectors for those students who are affected by glare.

INKJET PAPER

Inkjet paper is a bit heavier paper (approximately 24 lb.) and a bit more expensive than multipurpose paper, but is specifically designed to be used with inkjet printers. Inkjet paper is smoother so color is applied more evenly, producing a sharper image. Additionally, the paper is designed to absorb just the right amount of ink and is less inclined to smear.

Inkjet paper is also brighter, designated by a number on the packaging: the higher the number, the brighter the paper. The increased brightness changes the paper's reflective quality, producing more vivid colors and better image quality.

WHITE PRINTABLE CARD STOCK

White printable card stock is a heavier, denser paper and, therefore, is more opaque. It is typically a 65 lb. paper. Because it is heavier and denser, it is more rigid and more durable. It is ideal for customized educational materials requiring printing on both sides since the images will not show through from one side to the other. This is especially useful for printing flashcards when information will appear on both sides.

COLORED PAPER

Inkjet papers are available in a wide variety of colors. Colored paper can be used to group similar items printed on the same color paper.

Using gray paper to print colored items can make the colors appear more vivid (similar to how trees appear greener against a stormy sky).

But using colored paper may not always be the best choice visually. Printing text and images on some colors can reduce the contrast between the images or text and the paper itself, making them more difficult to see. When colored paper is used, it is best to choose colors with the greatest difference between the background (paper color) and the foreground (image or text color). One excellent option is black ink on "bright" or "neon" yellow paper. The contrast between the paper color and black ink will be especially high.

Use colored paper with a purpose and not just to be "cute." Pay attention to how the contrast is affected by the color of the paper, and choose colors that provide the highest contrast.

INKJET VELLUM

Inkjet vellum is a translucent paper. It might remind you of "tracing paper." It is a bit slick and not as porous as multipurpose paper or cardstock. Therefore, the ink does not dry as quickly on vellum.

Consequently, you must be careful when handling vellum after printing until the ink is completely dry, otherwise it may smudge.

But, the slow drying quality of vellum makes it ideal for embossing images printed from your inkjet printer. I will show you how to emboss using your inkjet printer to create interesting and useful educational materials.

While inkjet vellum is perfect for embossing, it can also be used for layering a page of images or text on top of another media, or for creating something that will be held up to the light, since the vellum is translucent.

> ### MAINTAINING THE INK PRINTED ON INKJET PAPER
>
> Ink from inkjet printers is sprayed onto the paper in a series of little dots (measured in dpi or "dots per inch") and can come off or run if exposed to water or other liquids. To maintain the integrity of the image on most inkjet media, especially those enduring hard or lengthy use, it is best to use an acrylic spray, such as Krylon® Matte Finish or Crystal Clear (www.krylon. com), to seal the ink on the printed media.

SPECIALTY MEDIA

PHOTO PAPER

Photo paper is specifically used for printing photographs from your inkjet printer. The paper is quite smooth, reflecting light in such a way that the images appear brighter. The papers themselves can be found in different finishes, including gloss (high gloss, gloss, soft gloss, or semi-gloss) and matte. To reduce glare, it is advisable to use paper that has a flat or matte finish rather than a glossy or shiny finish.

One of the problems with using inkjet printers and photo paper is that the images are not archival quality: they fade over time. Improvements are being made to printers, inks, and paper to print digital images but they are currently not of the same quality as traditional photo processing. Instead, digital photos can be taken to many photo processing labs on a floppy disk, CD-ROM, or other digital media (such as CompactFlash (CF) and SmartMedia (SM)). Or, they can be uploaded via the Internet to a number of online digital photo print service sites, such as www. mpix.com. There, they can be printed on photographic paper that will produce a longer lasting image that resists fading.

But it is typically unnecessary to spend the additional dollars for photo paper when creating customized educational materials since their "life" is usually short lived.

TRANSPARENCY FILM

Transparency film is typically used for producing transparencies for presentation on overhead projectors. Transparency film can also be an excellent media for producing customized educational materials for practicing handwriting utilizing a dashed font (*School Fonts for Beginning Writing* or *Transitional Fonts for Emerging Writers*). Printed on the transparency film, write-on/wipe-off pens, such as Vis-a-Vis®, can be used to trace over the dashed text. The transparency film can then be wiped clean and used over and over again.

Transparency film can also be used for creating layered, see-through materials, such as a book of the human body, printing each of the body's systems (circulatory, respiratory, etc.) on a separate transparency film, layering them, one on top of another, and then binding them together.

A disadvantage to using transparency film for creating customized educational materials is that the surface is shiny and can cause reflection and glare, making the images printed on the transparency film more difficult to see.

PLAYING CARD PAPER

PlainCards® are printable playing cards on 8½ x 11 inch cardstock. The cards can be purchased either blank on both sides, or blank on one side and with a red or blue design on the other. Add your own text and graphics on one or both sides. The sheets are comprised of 8 perforated cards per sheet; once the cards are printed, it is easy to pop them out. The card corners are rounded and similar in size to a standard deck of cards. They come with their own card box, or a protective plastic box can be purchased.

PRINTABLE MAGNET SHEETS

Although we have always been told to keep magnets away from computers, printable magnet sheets are safe for inkjet printers. Printable magnets are a versatile product that adhere to most metal surfaces. They are easily cut apart to create magnetic stickers, picture frames, puzzles, and more.

A disadvantage to using the printable magnetic sheets is that they are quite thin (9 mils), making the magnets difficult to pick up and move. If the magnet is going to be handled a lot, a better alternative may be to print the image on a piece of multipurpose paper and then adhere the image to a thicker, more durable magnet.

CLEAR DECALS

Clear decals are one of my favorite inkjet compatible media. Clear decals can be printed and then adhered to clean, smooth, dry surfaces by static-cling, such as glass, mirrors, refrigerators, and write-on/wipe-off boards. Clear decals are also wonderful for creating upright rather than tabletop materials. Placed on a magnetic surface and paired with magnets, clear decals can be used for charts, graphs, fill-in-the-blank sheets, and more.

LABELS AND STICKERS: PERMANENT AND REMOVABLE

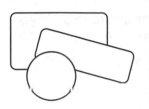

Labels and stickers come in countless sizes, from a single label the size of an 8½ x 11 inch page, to many individual labels per page. They come in various shapes (rectangles, squares, ovals, and circles). Clear, white, foil, and assorted colors (both pastel and fluorescent) are all available. Labels are also available for specific purposes, including CD/DVD labels, videotape labels, and photo stickers.

Permanent labels are just what the name implies: permanent. But the adhesive on repositional labels is similar to the glue found on Post-it® notes, allowing them to be moved or removed. There are obvious advantages to using repositional labels. I often create labels for Ashley to label Valentine cards, envelopes, or to "fill in the blank" on an answer sheet. If they are permanent, then she has only one opportunity to correctly place the label. But if it is removable, then she has more than one opportunity for the label to find its mark.

At first glance, the layout for creating labels might appear to be labor intensive. But templates for formatting the creation of labels are found in word processing programs, such as Microsoft® *Word* and *AppleWorks*®. They can also be downloaded from label manufacturers' websites (such as Avery® at www.avery.com) to be used in *Word* or other software programs that can create labels.

ROTARY CARDS

Rotary cards are created from printing on perforated paper sized to fit standard rotary card files, such as Rolodex®. Sheets are available for creating (standard) 2¼ x 4 inch and 3 x 5 inch rotary cards.

Although the instructions for their use does not mention printing on both sides of the paper, the paper is heavy and dense enough for the image not to show through from one side to the other, making it ideal for creating image and word banks. These can be alphabetized and safely stored in card files. Paired with transparent card protectors, it produces a durable and long lasting product.

Templates can be downloaded from the manufacturers' websites (www.rolodex.com and www.avery.com) for creating these cards in word processing programs, such as Microsoft® *Word*.

INDEX CARDS

Printable index cards come in two sizes: 3 x 5 and 4 x 6 inches. Because the paper is similar to the weight and density of card stock, it is possible to print on both sides of the paper without the image showing through from one side to the other. Although printable index cards may cost a bit more per sheet than plain card stock, they can make quick work out of creating flash cards if one of the available sizes suits your needs since the perforated paper requires no time-consuming cutting.

PRINT & SHRINK

Print & Shrink is a wonderful inkjet compatible media, similar to the *Shrinky Dinks*® product introduced decades ago. An image is printed on this media using an inkjet printer and then shrunk to approximately ⅓ the original size by baking it in a warm standard kitchen oven.

IRON-ON TRANSFER PAPER

Images can be printed onto iron-on transfer paper and then adhered to t-shirts, sweatshirts, special jigsaw media, and placemats by simply using a hot household iron.

FABRIC PAPER

Images can be printed onto fabric paper (available in cotton and silk) and then incorporated into quilts, t-shirts, and the like. Some do not require sewing but can be fused to other fabrics. Many of these products also provide colorfast results. But check the packaging carefully to determine the care instructions.

Another alternative is to use a fabric carrier. This is a sticky piece of paper that a piece of cotton or cotton blend fabric up to 8½ x 11 inches can be adhered to. The fabric can then be fed through an inkjet printer. Once printed, the fabric is removed from the carrier.

WATERSLIDE DECAL PAPER

Waterslide decal paper allows for images to be used for decoupaging and other craft projects. Once the image is printed and dried on the special paper, the image can be cut out, soaked in water for 60 seconds, and then transferred from the backing sheet and applied to another surface, including wood and ceramics. The image for this product becomes waterproof after 30 minutes.

TEMPORARY TATTOO PAPER

Temporary tattoo paper allows you to be able to design and create your own temporary tattoo from an inkjet printer. Consider creating a temporary tattoo of text designating "left" and "right" to put on your child's hands when reinforcing this skill. Or, use temporary tattoo paper for printing something simple like an image of your school's mascot to wear for "Spirit Day."

PUZZLE

Customized jigsaw puzzles can be created using an inkjet printer and your favorite photo or image. There are several commercially available options for creating them.

Precut card stock puzzles can be directly fed through an inkjet print, making them simple to create. These precut puzzles vary in complexity from just a few pieces to many pieces. Some are even designed for creating double-sided puzzles.

Heat transfer puzzles are made of a specially coated surface and precut pieces. The image is printed on an iron-on transfer and adhered to the puzzle surface using a household iron. It is not quite as simple as the precut cardstock puzzles, but the puzzle pieces are thicker, making them a better alternative for students needing a thicker manipulative.

EMBOSSING PAPER

Embossing paper is specifically designed for inkjet embossing. The ink dries slowly on this paper, providing enough time to sprinkle embossing powder onto the image. An embossing heat tool is then used to melt the embossing powder which produces the raised effect.

FUZZY PAPER

Fuzzy paper is just that: fuzzy! It feels a bit like a very low-pile velour. It can be used in your inkjet printer like any other paper and is a bit stiffer than multipurpose paper. Since laminating it is out of the question, consider glueing your printed image to another media, such as poster board, to make it stiffer.

Consider using fuzzy paper for printing images of animals for interactive books; it will provide your student the sensation of fur.

MEDIA AVAILABILITY BY VENDOR

	Multipurpose	Card Stock	Inkjet	Colored	Vellum	Photo	Transparency	Labels/Stickers	Rotary Cards	Magnet Sheets	Playing Cards	Puzzles	Clear Decals	Other Specialty
Epson® www.epson.com	●	●	●			●	●	●						●
Hammermill® www.hammermill.com	●	●	●	●		●								
Hewlett-Packard www.hp.com		●	●			●	●	●						●
Kodak www.kodak.com	●		●			●	●							
Strathmore® www.strathmoreartist.com					●	●		●						●
Great White® www.greatwhitepaper.com	●		●			●	●							
Wausau Paper www.wausaupapers.com	●	●	●	●										
Xerox® www.xerox.com	●	●	●	●			●	●		●				●
PlainCards® www.plaincards.com											●			
Avery® www.avery.com								●	●	●			●	●
Rolodex® www.rolodex.com									●					
www.decalpaper.com										●			●	●
June Tailor® www.junetailor.com														●
Lazertran www.lazertran.com														●
Compoz-A-Puzzle Inc. www.compozapuzzle.com												●		
Joslin Photo Puzzle Co. www.jigsawpuzzle.com												●		
Micro Format, Inc. www.imaginationgallery.net												●		●
McGonigal Paper www.mcgpaper.com					●	●	●			●		●		●
The Crafty PC™ www.thecraftypc.com					●					●	●	●	●	●

MEDIA USAGE BY RECIPE

	Multipurpose	Card Stock	Inkjet	Colored	Vellum	Transparency	Labels/Stickers	Rotary Cards	Index Cards	Magnet Sheets	Playing Cards	Puzzles	Clear Decals	Other Specialty
Lotto Boards	●	●	●											
Gestalts	●	●	●											
Symmetry Game	●	●	●											
Jigsaw Puzzle												●		●
Counting Hands	●												●	
Magnetic Model	●		●							●				
Flash Cards		●												
Flip Book	●	●	●											
Simple Slider	●	●	●											
Pocket Slider	●	●	●	●										
Double Slider	●	●	●											
Basic Wheel	●	●	●	●										
Complex Wheel	●	●	●	●										
Clock Faces	●		●											
Visual Schedule							●		●					
Telling Time	●		●											
Rotary Cards								●						
Recipe Cards									●					
Menu	●	●	●											

(continued on next page)

	Multipurpose	Card Stock	Inkjet	Colored	Vellum	Transparency	Labels/Stickers	Rotary Cards	Index Cards	Magnet Sheets	Playing Cards	Puzzles	Clear Decals	Other Specialty
Sight Words	●	●	●											
Spelling Your Name	●	●	●											
Interactive Spelling Cards	●	●	●											
Decoding Text with Word Families	●	●	●											
Reading Inventory: Word Magnets & Decal	●		●							●			●	
Fill In the Blank: Word Magnets & Decal	●		●							●			●	
Interactive Books	●	●	●											
Sentence Building: Parts of Speech	●	●	●											
Journal Writing	●		●											
Handwriting Transparency						●								
Name Labels							●							
Color Within the Lines					●									●
Game Spinner	●		●											
Card Games											●			
Custom Game Piece														●
Cards for Audio Card Reader	●		●											

COPYRIGHT

All you really want to do is create interesting and useful educational materials for your child. That sounds like challenge enough. I am sure that you are not thrilled that copyright law can affect your work, but it can. Although all of the different facets of copyright law are complex, its general principle is quite simple: it protects the way a person *expresses* his or her idea. Copyright laws do not protect the *idea* itself. For example, if a photographer takes a picture of a fruit basket, copyright law protects that picture, not the idea of taking a picture of a fruit basket. If a woman were standing next to the photographer when he takes his picture, and she takes her own picture of the same fruit basket that would be allowed. The woman could not, however, copy the photographer's actual picture. Copyright law protects his picture, and she would need his permission to copy and use it.

This means that you can freely use any work that *you create from scratch* (whether it be a photograph, painting, drawing, story, etc.). If you take a photograph of your child, create a diagram, or draw an illustration, it is yours to do with as you wish without limitation. Copyright law is important for the materials in this book only when you want to use a work (photo, text, drawing, painting, etc.) that *has been created by someone else*. As a general rule, you cannot use another person's works without that person's permission. If, for example, you see a picture on the Internet that you like and want to use it, you need to be aware that the picture is likely protected by copyright laws and generally cannot be copied without the photographer's permission. Without copyright protections, people who create art, books, and music could not control the use and enjoyment of their works. With no control over their works, artists, authors, and musicians could not profit, which means that we'd all probably have a lot less art, books, and music to enjoy.

I can already hear you saying, "but I'm not looking to steal anything… I just want to create something that I can use to educate my child. Do I really need to get permission to do that?" Fortunately, there is some latitude and flexibility within the copyright laws that will allow you to create educational lessons for your children. In general, you can use another person's work so long as (1) your use is for purposes of teaching a lesson (like a teacher would), (2) your use is not commercial, and (3) you use only that portion of the work that is needed to teach the lesson (for example, if you need only one photo from a calendar, you should not copy the entire calendar). This type of use is often referred to as "fair use." *Please remember, not all personal use is "fair use."* For example, it is illegal to copy a song for your own personal enjoyment without the musician's permission. Similarly, it is illegal to copy a painting and hang it on your wall without the painter's permission. You could, however, copy portions of the same song or painting to develop teaching materials (similar to what a music or art professor might do when creating his or her lesson plans).

At the end of the day, your best bet is to use your own photos, drawings, text, etc., but so long as you meet the requirements of "fair use," you can also use other people's works.

GRAPHIC SKILLS

What graphic artists used to accomplish by hand with paper and pen, pencil, chalk, or paint can now be done with a computer graphics program and a few clicks of a computer's mouse. Graphics programs are powerful time saving applications that convert a labor intensive activity, like cutting with scissors or pasting with glue, into something that can be accomplished in a matter of seconds. You may have already acquired some of these basic skills using a word processing program on your computer when you have cut, copied, or pasted text.

Graphics programs all start with a blank document (like a blank canvas) into which you place basic shapes (lines, rectangles, circles, and polygons), images (photographs, illustrations, clip art, and icons), and text. You can then manipulate (arrange, move, flip, rotate, enlarge, and reduce) everything in your document to create just what you want. Color can be applied to the text and the lines that create shapes and images, or as "fill" to the interior of shapes. And all of this can be done with minimal computer knowledge or even artistic ability.

NECESSARY COMMANDS

Many graphics programs are available that can handle creating the educational materials included in this book. Most of them have the same tools and commands, and can accomplish the same tasks. The programs may call some tools and commands by different names, and they may locate them in different menus, but they all basically function the same.

For a graphics program to complete the projects in this book, it must at a minimum include the following simple commands or functions. Almost all—even the most basic (cheap) programs—have the ability to do all these things. They include:

- Document Settings
- Cut
- Copy
- Paste
- Duplicate (optional)
- Grid and Rulers
- Select Tool
- Text Tool
- Line Tool
- Ellipse Tool
- Rectangle Tool
- Polygon Tool
- Color Palette
- Arrange
- Flip Horizontally, Flip Vertically
- Rotate
- Scale
- Pen Width and Line Width
- Arrows
- Dashed Lines

TYPES OF GRAPHICS PROGRAMS

Graphics programs are the primary tool you will use to create wonderful educational materials for your child. But the choice of the program you will rely on is an important one, and I'd like to tell you a little about them to help you choose.

BITMAP VERSUS VECTOR GRAPHICS

There are two types of graphics programs: bitmap and vector. Bitmap programs use pixels (tiny squares) and vector programs use smooth mathematically defined lines to create an image.

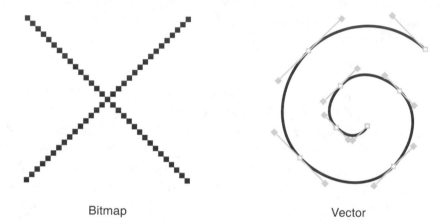

Bitmap   Vector

Both types of programs are similar in many ways, including the appearance of much of their toolbars, but what they are best used for, and the quality of the images they produce, are quite different. Many graphics programs, such as Adobe® *Illustrator*®, *CorelDRAW*®, and Macromedia® *FreeHand*® create and manage both bitmap and vector images. For most of the materials in this book, graphics programs that generate only bitmap images will suffice, although vector programs are preferable.

Bitmap Images

Bitmap programs are called "image editing programs." Bitmap images (also called *raster images*) are created by a series of tiny squares, called *pixels*,

BITMAP FILE TYPES

You can tell a file type by its file name. Bitmap file formats include the following suffixes:

- TIFF (TIF)
- JPEG (JPG)
- GIF
- BMP
- PNG

A photograph of a cow

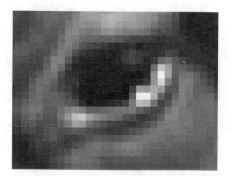

The cow's eye magnified showing the individual pixels

placed on a grid (known as a *bitmap* or *raster*). Each square has a particular location and color that defines it, similar to a mosaic. The appearance of the image is modified by changing the location and/or color of each pixel. When the image is magnified, the lines (particularly curved lines) appear jagged and the individual squares that make up the image become apparent.

Bitmap images require more memory because the computer must keep track of the location and color of each individual pixel. But they are especially effective for photographs because they can provide subleties in color and shading.

Vector Images

Vector programs are called "illustration programs." Images in vector graphics programs are created by straight lines and curved lines defined by mathematical formulas. They are composed of objects rather than pixels.

They produce superior images since lines appear smooth and not jagged. Unlike a bitmap image, scaling (changing the size of) a vector image maintains the same detail and clarity as the original and, therefore, produces a superior image.

The appearance of the image can be modified by dragging the handles (the small boxes on selected lines; each little box is called a handle).

Vector images require less memory than if bitmapped, and are great for images requiring sharp lines and greater detail.

VECTOR OR BITMAP: WHICH IS BETTER?

Changing the size of a bitmapped image makes lines appear distorted and jagged. Graphics programs that create and manage vector images produce a superior printed product. The lines are smooth. And the image is easily scaled while maintaining its clarity at any size.

Vector 100%

Vector 200%

Bitmap 100%   Bitmap 200%

Vector images are also easier to color because color is applied by clicking inside an object or dragging color to it, rather than worrying about the location of individual pixels.

Relatively inexpensive bitmap graphics programs were common in the past. But the companies that published them were gobbled up by the "big boys," like Adobe® and Macromedia®, so that vector graphics programs are now the "industry standard" for creating illustrations while bitmap programs are more commonly used for editing photographs. With the reasonable prices of some vector graphics programs, it makes sense to invest in a vector graphics program to achieve the superior output if you are in the market to purchase this kind of software. Otherwise, use a bitmap program at your disposal until you are inclined to purchase a graphics program that manages vectors.

CHOOSING A GRAPHICS PROGRAM

The many graphics programs available today range in price and complexity. As expected, the complexity is usually commensurate with the price: Programs that cost more typically do more. And, typically, with more capacity and power comes a steeper learning curve. But the simplest commands can be easily utilized in even the most complex programs, ignoring the more complicated "bells and whistles" until you have the inclination to tackle them.

Programs such as Adobe® *Illustrator®* and Macromedia® *FreeHand®* (available for both Mac® and Windows®) are not inexpensive (around $400), but provide a large selection of commands and design shortcuts. *CorelDRAW®* (now Windows® only) and Jasc® *Paint Shop™ Pro™* (Windows® only) are less expensive good alternatives (less than $100) that also provide both image editing (bitmap) and illustration (vector) capabilities.

Graphics programs, such as the paint-draw section of *AppleWorks®* (Mac® only), have adequate sophistication for many projects and carry a lesser price tag (less than $80). *AppleWorks*® has more than enough capacity to complete the projects in this book, although its graphic capabilities are not in the same league as other programs.

All of the programs listed above can, without a doubt, be used to complete all the projects in this book. But if you have a different program in mind, that's just fine, as long as it can execute the necessary commands.

Consider searching the Internet for freeware, shareware, or public-domain software for a graphics program with the necessary commands.

THERE MIGHT BE A SATISFACTORY PROGRAM ALREADY LOADED ON YOUR HARD DRIVE!

If you do not own any of the graphics programs mentioned, and none of the programs I've mentioned even sound familiar, you may still have a hidden treasure already on your hard drive: Microsoft® *PowerPoint*® (part of Microsoft® *Office*)! Although not really intended for creating the same types of graphics as programs like *Illustrator*® and *FreeHand*®, the graphic capacity of this program is pretty amazing. With an understanding of its design format and a few minor mental adjustments on your part, you can use *PowerPoint*® to create everything in this book and more.

Another option is Microsoft® *Publisher* which might also be included in your *Office* suite.

There may be other programs lurking on your hard drive that have come with another software application that can do the job, too. In short, if you already have a graphics program, learn how to use it. If you don't own one, buy one! And when you are shopping for one, consider looking for the following:

- *A graphics program that is manufactured by the same company as another product you already own:* Programs by the same manufacturer often have similar toolbars and a similar "feel," reducing the learning curve for you (such as Adobe® and Macromedia® products).

- *A graphics program that is bundled with other software applications:* Software companies offer "suites" or "bundles" of programs as a way to get you to buy a lot of software at once. Consequently, you can save money buying software bundled together compared to buying programs separately. For example, Microsoft® *Office* is a "bundle" where the cost of purchasing any two of the most popular applications separately (*Word*, *PowerPoint*®, or *Excel*®) is comparable to the cost of the entire suite comprised of 6 or more different programs (depending upon the version). There may be a graphics program included—look for it.

WHAT IS FREEWARE AND SHAREWARE AND PUBLIC-DOMAIN SOFTWARE?

Freeware is a program that is authored by computer enthusiasts and distributed electronically free of charge through users' groups, websites, bulletin boards, etc. It is copyrighted.

Shareware is also authored by computer enthusiasts but is distributed electronically on the honor system. The author might request a nominal fee if you like and use their program. It is copyrighted.

Public-domain software can be used without restrictions and is not copyrighted.

- *A graphics program that is bundled with a selection of graphic images, photo images, or fonts:* If they are giving images and fonts away, hand them over! You will always find a use for them.

- *A scanner that is bundled with software:* Scanners typically come with simple image editing programs used to edit photos.

- *Academic/educational versions of graphics programs:* If you qualify, you can benefit from significant savings.

TOOLBARS IN GRAPHICS PROGRAMS

Whether you are using *Illustrator®*, *CorelDRAW®*, or *FreeHand®*, graphics programs have a similar look and feel to them. Once you are familiar with one toolbar, it is not difficult to move from using one graphics program to another. Users of graphics programs may have their favorite,

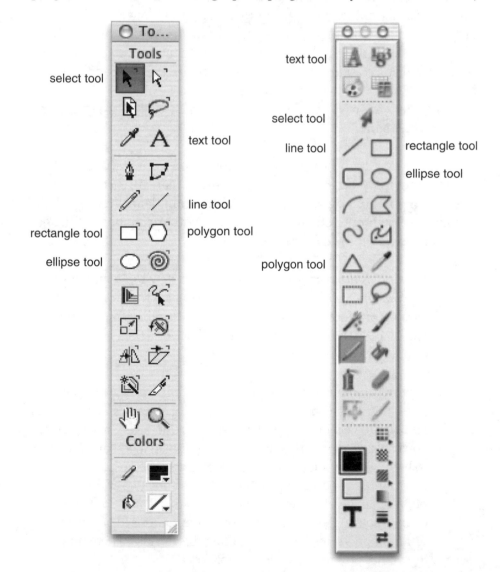

but it is probably due more to familiarity with a particular program than to any significant difference.

Although no two toolbars from different graphics programs look identical, they all essentially do the same thing and are, therefore, very similar. For example, a line segment represents the *Line Tool*, a rectangle the *Rectangle Tool*, and an ellipse the *Ellipse Tool*. Take a moment to compare the two toolbars on the previous page. You will easily recognize the tools by their icons and will quickly identify the similarities between both toolbars.

"USING GRAPHICS PROGRAMS 101"

The instructions that follow will be your introductory class to the world of graphic design. These instructions are not intended to replace the instruction manuals that accompany all graphics programs, nor are they intended to be extensive instructions in graphic art. Instead, they provide an overview and an understanding of only those (simple) skills necessary to complete the projects included in this book.

You will quickly realize that the most difficult skill to master is choosing the proper tool from the toolbar or the proper command from the menu. Unlike a word processing program that only deals with text, you must tell the graphics program what you want to do—create a basic shape, type text, etc.—by selecting a tool or command. And you must first select something by clicking on it before you can move it. The rest is essentially a matter of clicking, holding, and dragging the mouse. Moving anything within the document requires these same mouse skills. It's all that simple!

Read on and begin to understand the capacity you possess with a graphics program to create wonderful materials that will help your child learn.

DOCUMENT SETTINGS

Each time you begin a program, you will be given the option of opening an old document or creating a new one. If you begin with a new blank document, one of the first things you will do is establish the document settings. For word processing projects, document settings can include size of margins (top and bottom, left and right), headers, footers, and the presence of page numbers. More typically for graphics programs, you will be choosing the overall size of the document (usually letter or legal) and the orientation (landscape or portrait). The typical default settings are letter size and portrait orientation, but you always have the opportunity to select settings for each new document. The instructions in this book tell you what document settings to choose.

LETTER OR LEGAL? PORTRAIT OR LANDSCAPE?

Letter sized paper is 8½" x 11."
Legal sized paper is 8½" x 14."

The image is printed vertically for portrait and horizontally for landscape.

The method for defining document settings varies from one program to another. Depending upon the program, it can initially be a bit confusing. Nevertheless, there is always a way to define document specifications in every graphics program so that you generate the document output of your choosing.

Portrait orientation

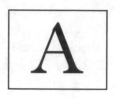

Landscape orientation

BASIC COMMANDS

Cut, Copy, Paste, and Duplicate

Cut, *Copy*, and *Paste* are the commands you will use most frequently. *Cut* completely removes an image or text from a document, while *Copy* leaves the image or text in its original place but makes a copy of it.

When *Cut* or *Copy* is executed, the Clipboard holds the bit of information (text or image) from the document. The Clipboard is a temporary storage location within your computer, much like short term memory. Once information is located on the Clipboard, it is then available to *Paste* within the same document, between documents, or between software programs. Multiple copies of the same image can be pasted as long as it is currently located on the Clipboard. But the content of the Clipboard is replaced each time new information is copied to it.

Duplicate, a related command, makes an exact copy of a selected image with one simple command without the use of the Clipboard. The copy appears slightly offset from the original image. The images can then be selected and moved independently to their permanent locations. *Duplicate* cannot to be used between documents, or between software programs, but is great for creating multiple copies of the same image within the same document.

Duplicate makes an exact copy of the selected image in one simple step.

Grid and Rulers

Grid provides nonprinting horizontal and vertical lines or dots that serve as a guide for the exact placement and alignment of images and text.

Rulers provide a guide for sizing shapes and images to a particular dimension. The *Rulers* typically appear along the top and left side of the document page.

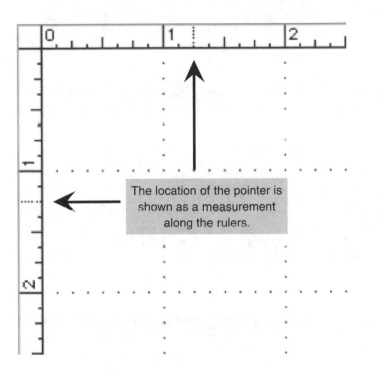

The location of the pointer is shown as a measurement along the rulers.

When using *Rulers*, a thin dashed line appears on each ruler that shows the position of the pointer. This assists in creating shapes to a specific size, and in an exact location.

The ability to appropriately size and place shapes and images is important since many of the included projects require shapes and images with specific dimensions and locations.

Select Tool

The *Select Tool* (also called the *Pointer Tool*) lets you select images by clicking on them. It is necessary to select images before modifying them (such as rotating, scaling, or moving).

 **Text Tool**

The *Text Tool* (also called a *Type Tool*) is used for what you would expect: creating text. It appears in the Toolbar as a capital letter, usually an "A" or a "T."

Different *Text Tool* appearances

Once selected from the Toolbar, the *Text Tool* creates a text frame (also called a text block). A flashing cursor (a vertical line) appears in the text frame at the position where text will be located once keyboarding begins, just like in a word processing program.

This is a text frame.

This is a text frame. → handles

The text frame serves as a mini word processing document, allowing for the adjustment of the text characteristics within its boundaries as in any word processing program. The text within the text frame can be changed by font (such as Helvetica, Geneva, or Times, to name a few), size (such as 12 pt, 36 pt, or 72 pt), and design (plain, **bold**, *italic*, etc.). Text within the text frame can also typically be aligned right, left, centered, and justified.

The text frame itself can also be resized by dragging its handles when the frame is too small to hold all the required text. The text frame can also be selected and repositioned within the document. Text frames may look slightly different in various programs but they all perform essentially the same way.

DRAWING BASIC SHAPES: LINES, ELLIPSES, RECTANGLES, AND POLYGONS

Drawing shapes is a fundamental part of creating the materials in this book. In most graphics programs, the process of drawing a basic shape is rather simple: select the correct tool from the Toolbar (*Line Tool*, *Ellipse Tool*, *Rectangle Tool*, or *Polygon Tool*), hold down the mouse button, drag the pointer, and then release the mouse button when the appropriate size of the basic shape has been reached. This is the method used for making lines, ellipses, rectangles, and polygons.

By utilizing *Grid and Rulers*, it is easy to see the size of the shape being created so that the dimensions of the end product are easily achieved. Additionally, by holding down the Shift key while creating a basic shape, the appearance of the shape is constrained proportionally, making it easy to create perfect squares, circles, and straight lines (horizontal, vertical, and diagonal).

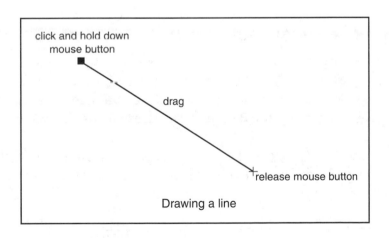 **Line Tool**

After selecting the *Line Tool* from the Toolbar, straight lines can be created by holding down the mouse button, dragging the pointer until the appropriate line length is achieved, and then releasing the mouse button to end the path.

click and hold down
mouse button

drag

release mouse button

Drawing a line

Holding down the Shift key while dragging the *Line Tool* will simplify drawing lines at constrained angles, such as horizontal, vertical, or diagonal.

More involved graphics programs also provide tools for creating curved or calligraphic lines. Although the instructions for customized educational materials in this book do not utilize these tools, play around with them and learn how to use them if they are included in your graphics program.

Ellipse Tool

The *Ellipse Tool* (also called the *Oval Tool*) is used for creating ovals and circles.

After selecting the *Ellipse Tool* from the Toolbar, ovals and circles can be created by holding down the mouse button, dragging the pointer until the appropriate dimension is achieved, and then releasing the mouse button. *(See figure below left.)*

Perfect circles are created by holding down the Shift key while using the *Ellipse Tool. (See figure below right.)*

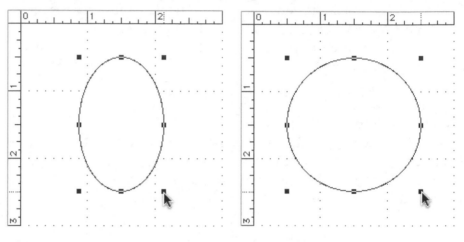

Rectangle Tool

The *Rectangle Tool* is the quickest method for drawing squares and rectangles. Rather than drawing each of the four sides of a square or rectangle individually, the *Rectangle Tool* does it in one easy step.

By holding down the Shift key while using the *Rectangle Tool*, the dimensions of the image are constrained to create a perfect square. *(See figure below right.)*

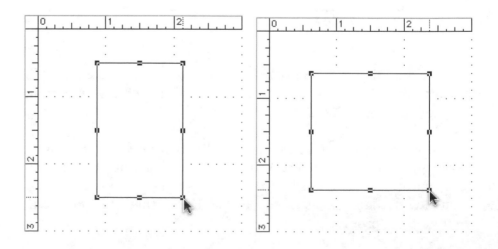

Polygon Tool

The *Polygon tool* produces multi-sided objects, such as triangles, diamonds, and hexagons, in one step.

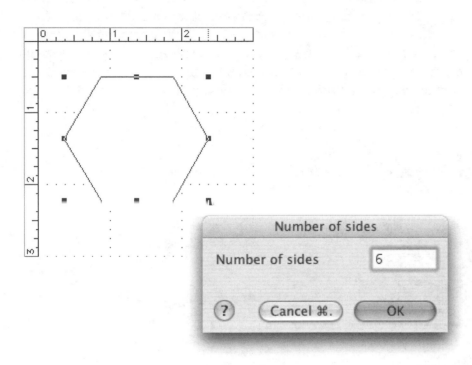

More sophisticated graphics programs, such as Macromedia *FreeHand®* and Adobe® *Illustrator®*, also provide simple command tools to draw stars with various characteristics.

COLOR PALETTE

All graphics programs have a *Color Palette* but, depending upon the complexity of the program, some have more involved *Color Palettes* than others. The more simplistic programs typically provide *Color Palettes* with a limited number of color selections. *(See Illustration 1.)* The more sophisticated programs often provide multiple methods to select colors, including the use of slide bars to "mix" colors with varying amounts of cyan, magenta, yellow, and black (CMYK). *(See Illustration 2.)* No matter, the purpose of a *Color Palette* is the same: to allow the selection of color to apply to lines and fills for images and text.

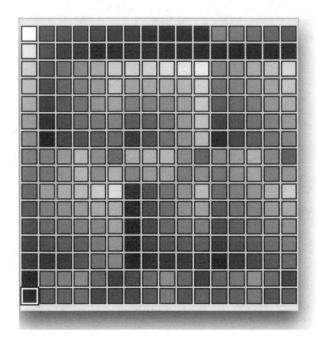

Illustration 1

Illustration 2

The methods to apply color include pens, paint buckets, paint brushes, spray cans, and eyedroppers. Basic shapes, as well as text, can be created with a chosen color. And the lines of basic shapes can be selected to match their fill color. (See **Matching the Line and the Fill Color** in **Graphic Skills: Extras**.)

If you look in the manual of a more sophisticated graphics program, the chapter on color will probably be quite extensive. Managing color for the graphic artist is a complex process, but that level of knowledge is far greater than what is required for generating the materials in this book.

Don't be overwhelmed by the process of applying color. Play with it. Apply it. Print it. You will get the hang of it in no time.

MORE COMMANDS

Arrange

Graphics programs let you create lots and lots of shapes and images on the same page–sometimes one on top of another. *Arrange* lets you order the placement of placed shapes or images within a document. When multiple images are placed, the one placed first will end up behind all the images placed after. If this is not where you want an image to appear, then this command will help. It can assist you in bringing images forward that have been placed on top of one another. There are typically four different options to choose from for the *Arrange* command:

- *Bring Forward* moves an image up one level in the pile.
- *Send Backward* moves an image down one level in the pile.
- *Bring to Front* moves an image to the front of the pile.
- *Send to Back* moves an image to the back of the pile.

Images drawn or pasted in
the following order:
hexagon, square, triangle

Send to Back command
applied to triangle

Send to Back command
applied to square

<aside>
THE DEFAULT FILL FOR BASIC SHAPES

The default fill for basic shapes in some graphics programs, such as *FreeHand*® and *CorelDRAW*®, is transparent: You can see what is underneath the shape until a Fill Color is applied from the Color Palette. In other graphics programs, such as *Illustrator*®, *AppleWorks*®, and *PowerPoint*®, a basic shape is automatically created with its own Fill Color (that is, white or some other default color). For these programs, the *Arrange* command is quite useful to *Send to Back* the basic shape so that you can see what is beneath it.
</aside>

The *Arrange* command is especially nice when drawing a basic shape (such as a square, ellipse, or hexagon) around an already pasted image. By drawing the basic shape *after* the image has been pasted, the shape can be sized appropriately without any measuring. To do so, follow these simple steps: Paste the image, draw the basic shape around the image, and then use the *Send to Back* command while the basic shape is selected. This will move the shape *behind* the image and place the image inside the shape, making it easy to cut out for things like lotto cards and flash cards.

Basic shape is drawn

Square is drawn over the star

Square is *Sent to Back*; star is in front

Flip Horizontally, Flip Vertically

Flip Horizontally, Flip Vertically command moves images along a horizontal or vertical axis. If pasted images are not properly oriented, it is easy to fix them using this simple command.

horizontal axis

Flipped vertically

vertical axis

Flipped horizontally

In more sophisticated programs, the command may be found as a Transform function and is executed as a mirror reflection of an image along a designated axis. In that case, the designated axis is 90 degrees to flip horizontally or 180 degrees to flip vertically.

Rotate

Rotate moves images in a circular fashion, typically either by selecting and dragging it (free rotate), or by choosing the number of degrees to move the selected image around a particular point, either in a clockwise or counterclockwise fashion.

Image in its original orientation

Image rotated 45 degrees counterclockwise

Image rotated 90 degrees counterclockwise

Scale

Scale lets you change the size of an image.

Original Image Size
(100%)

Scaled Size
(50%)

There are a number of ways to resize, or scale, an image. Often an image can be selected, its handles grabbed and then dragged. By holding down the Shift key while dragging the handles, the image is resized proportionally.

Scale by Percent is accomplished by choosing a percent value of the image's original size. A percent value greater than 100 will resize the image larger than its original appearance; a value less than 100 will resize the image smaller than its original appearance. But, although there are sometimes upper limits for scaling, any percentage can be selected from 0 to 100.

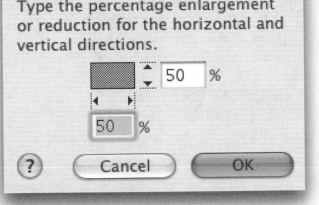
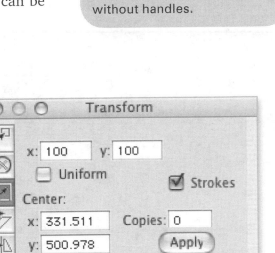

When the same percentage is used for x and y coordinates, the image is scaled proportionally. *(See figure above right.)*

CREATING "DASHED IMAGES"

It is easy to take any image that is comprised of simple lines and turn it into something your child can trace. Just Select All, change the line type to dashed, and then print!

Dashed Lines

Unfortunately, not all graphics programs provide *Dashed Lines*. But for the ones that do, bless them. It is a great feature.

With this feature, it is simple to create a dashed line: select the line and then change it to dashed, or select dashed before the line is created.

Line Width

Like other features of a graphics program, you can control the thickness of any line you draw. The thickness of a pen or line is determined by the *Line Width*.

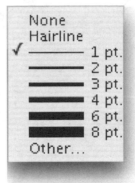

Arrows

Many graphics programs include the feature of adding an arrow at the ends of lines. This often comes in handy. About the only confusing thing when adding arrows is knowing what end of a line the arrow will appear. If all else fails, use trial and error. If it's not on one end, then it's going to be on the other!

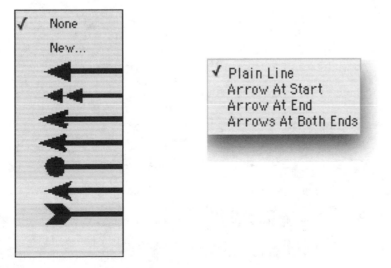

EXTRAS

ADJUSTING LINE THICKNESS WHEN SCALING VECTOR IMAGES

There will be times when you will want to scale a vector image. Whenever a vector image is scaled (made smaller or larger), the thickness of any lines in the image is also automatically scaled. Therefore, an image that is scaled to 50% of its original size will also have a line thickness that is half the width of the original image. This can change the way an image appears, not only by its size but by the prominence of the lines comprising the image.

The thickness of the line is under your control. Although an image has been scaled, you can always use the Select Tool to select individual lines and then change them back to their original thickness.

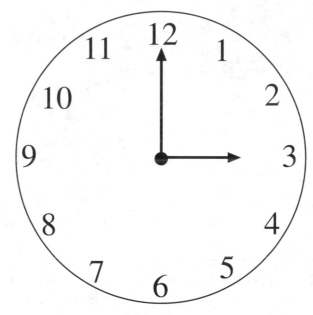

Original Image

Image scaled by 50%
Line thickness
automatically scaled
by 50%

Image scaled by 50%
Line thickness
changed back to
the thickness of the
original image

MATCHING THE LINE AND THE FILL COLOR

Setting the line and fill color in the *Color Palette* to the same color will create a shape without a black line as its outside edge.

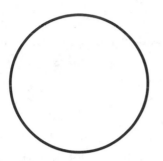

Line color is black and
the fill color is white
or transparent

Line color is black and the
fill color in red;
the line color does not
match the fill color

Line color is red and the
fill color is red;
the line color matches
the fill color

This can also be accomplished by setting the line color to white (if the background color is white) after filling the shape with color.

Or, setting the line width to "None" after filling the shape with color will produce a shape without an outer line.

APPLYING PAINT TO A CLOSED SHAPE

Shapes (like polygons and rectangles) created using individual lines can appear closed (i.e., lines appear to join at the corners), yet they cannot be filled with color or texture. When color or texture is applied to these "open" shapes, it will either "spill over" to the background of your document or the fill color of your shape will not change to the color or texture you are trying to apply. It is analogous to a box with four sides; the corners may be touching but not glued. Therefore, the box will not hold anything.

Instead, lines in vector graphics programs must not only be touching but must be "joined" (according to the computer) to create one continuous line and, therefore, a closed shape. In bitmap graphics programs, lines comprising a shape must at least touch one another or cross over one another for the shape to hold color or texture.

There are a few solutions, but the simplest is to use the tools for creating rectangles, ellipses, and polygons whenever possible since these tools automatically create closed shapes.

WHAT ARE OPEN AND CLOSED SHAPES?

An open shape is one in which the end points are not connected. A closed shape is one where the start and end points meet.

MAKING AN EXACT COPY: USING THE GROUP COMMAND

When text is placed inside a rectangle, the overall image is comprised of two separate components: the rectangle and the text frame. By selecting the rectangle with the pointer, the rectangle can be moved. By selecting the text frame, the text can be moved. Each one can move independently from the other.

But to make an *exact copy* of an entire image that is comprised of two or more items, you want the relative placement of objects to stay the same. To accomplish this, you have two choices:

1. Simultaneously select the rectangle and text by dragging the pointer over both components at the same time. Then use the Copy and Paste, or Duplicate, command, and an exact copy is achieved.

   Or,

2. Simultaneously select the rectangle and text, and then use the Group command found in the pull down menu under Modify in *FreeHand*®, under Object in *Illustrator*®, or under Arrange in *CorelDRAW*®. Grouping objects maintains their relative placement. Once the individual images are grouped, they can then be treated as a single object, copied to the clipboard, and then pasted.

The Group command is useful in lots of situations: when two or more objects need to be moved relative to one another, copied, pasted, or scaled. The Ungroup command will reverse the process, allowing you to independently manipulate objects.

USING REFERENCE LINES

Reference lines are used to correctly place text, images, or basic shapes.

For example, if you need to locate the center of a circle, you can do so by using the Line Tool to draw a horizontal reference line and a vertical reference line through the middle of a circle. The point where the two lines intersect is the center of the circle. Once the center of the circle is located and marked, the reference lines have served their purpose and can be deleted.

MOVING OBJECTS...A LITTLE

Typically, there are a number of ways to move an object in a graphics program. You are probably familiar with using the Select Tool to select an object and then moving it by dragging it with the mouse. But did you know you can use the arrow keys (up, down, left, and right), rather than dragging it with the mouse, to nudge objects into place? If you need to only slightly adjust an object to its correct location, the arrow keys are a great way to go.

DRAWING IN *POWERPOINT*®

If you have Microsoft® *Office* loaded on your computer, you may not realize you also have a rather sophisticated drawing program loaded as well. The toolbar looks a bit different than most graphics programs, but everything is there to create all the materials in this book.

You will notice when you begin using *PowerPoint*® that you must make a selection from the Project Gallery. Choose *PowerPoint*® Presentation and then select Blank for New Slide. You will immediately notice that the default orientation for the document is landscape rather than portrait, but this is easily changed in the Page Setup found under the File menu.

The next thing you will notice is that the page is divided into four quadrants and that, although there is a ruler, it is labeled for the four quadrants and their x and y axes. The appearance of the ruler changes depending upon what you are doing: The ruler's origin is the center for creating shapes, and its origin is the left when creating text. This will require you to make minor adjustments when creating objects of a specific size or a specific location.

The grid is also invisible, but when the grid is on, objects will automatically align to the nearest intersection of the grid.

SAVE YOUR WORK!

Time is something that cannot be bought. It is a valuable commodity. The time it takes to create customized educational materials is well worth it, but it is "expensive" if you must recreate them just because the document was not saved properly. I have had materials lost, stepped on, and drenched with chocolate milk. When files are saved, it takes no time at all to open and reprint them. When they are not saved, you have no other choice but to recreate them from scratch and that takes time!

Here are some basic tips on saving files:

- Give files distinct names that relate to the materials you are creating. For example, use file names like "Fruits and Vegetables Lotto" that describe the type of activity and the design of the materials created.
- Save things with "parts" using the same file name but with an added descriptor, such as Word Wheel Cover and Word Wheel Base, or Word Wheel #1 and Word Wheel #2. Since you can

SAVING TO AN EXTERNAL STORAGE DEVICE

It is not only important to save your work but it is also smart to save your work to an external storage device as well. These include external hard drives, ZIPs, and CD-Rs or CD-RWs.

Although it may seem redundant to save to your computer's hard drive and to an external device, this protects your work from the possible failure of your computer's internal hard drive.

instruct your computer to list files in alphabetical order, files named in this manner will come up next to one another.
- Save projects in folders, especially for those materials that have "parts."

But most importantly, *save your work!*

CREATE WITH TEMPLATES

Templates are patterns or models that can be modified or added to. A template file is the "skeleton" document without the final text and images. Templates can be used again and again. By using templates, it is easy to add new graphics and text, and create an entirely new project in a fraction of the time. And by creating with templates, you are building predictability into your materials, making learning a whole lot more efficient, and designing for success for your student.

LOTTO BOARDS

Types of Lotto Boards

Described in full detail in the next sections.

- Color Lotto, *see page 97*.
- Shape Lotto, *see page 99*.
- Color & Shape Lotto, *see page 103*.
- Size Lotto, *see page 107*.
- Color, Shape, & Size Lotto, *see page 109*.
- Miscellaneous Lotto, *see page 113*.

The picture above might look like Ashley playing Bingo, using what looks like a Bingo game board and placing cards on it. But it's a matching game and it's called Lotto! Lotto has been one of the most important educational tools Ashley has ever used. Without it, she could not have been able to show what she knows. With it, she has been able to demonstrate a remarkable range of knowledge and skills.

Lotto consists of a board of 2 or more images and a set of cards with corresponding images. It is most often used to teach visual discrimination skills. Matching images on the lotto board to identical images on a set of "choice cards" requires understanding the concept of "same" and "different" for countless academic concepts such as colors, objects, and names. Lotto boards and cards can also be used for matching related items, such as an image of a cat to the word "cat." It is an activity often associated with younger children but does not have to be used exclusively for that age group. Lotto is not considered a complex educational strategy. But it is sometimes an important place to begin teaching a new skill, or to test a skill that has already been taught by other methods.

At a very young age, I nicknamed Ashley the "Lotto Queen." She could have probably completed a lotto board in her sleep. I capitalized on that, exploiting her matching prowess to teach her many things. Using lotto, I was able to answer important questions: "Can she see these are the same?" Yes! "Does she understand the correspondence between these two images?" Yes!

Kim's Crash Course to Lotto Design

Detailed explanation of these rules follows on the next pages!

1. Choose the right number of windows.

2. Make all windows the same size and shape.

3. Balance the image with the window size.

4. Make all text the same size.

5. Label with a purpose.

6. Choose the best design orientation.

7. Select the right paper size and printer orientation.

8. Choose the right paper weight and color.

9. Take advantage of your computer's power.

Using lotto, Ashley's visual discrimination skills developed rapidly. She relied upon this skill heavily because it enabled her to compensate for barriers in other areas. She could use lotto effectively to represent her understanding without speaking. This became a powerful tool.

Ashley has used lotto to demonstrate her understanding of scores of facts and concepts, including colors and shapes. But once she exhausted the commercially available lotto boards—which happened very quickly—I was left to design my own. Ultimately, this was a blessing in disguise because it forced me to stretch beyond pre-formatted commercially available products, enabling me to learn to create what would best suit Ashley's needs.

With access to graphic images (including digitized photos and clip art), it is nearly effortless to create lotto boards on your computer. Graphics programs provide a great deal of design flexibility. Designing one is a matter of following a few simple steps (honest!):

1. Decide upon the overall size of the lotto board.

2. Decide upon the complexity of the lotto board; that is, the number of "windows."

3. Draw a square or rectangle.

4. Add horizontal and vertical lines to create a grid.

5. Save the blank lotto board on your computer as a template to be used again and again.

6. Decide upon the content of the lotto board and begin copying and pasting the necessary images.

7. Save each unique lotto board with its own descriptive file name.

8. Print.

9. Laminate.

10. Cut.

It's that easy!

THE POWER OF DESIGNING YOUR OWN LOTTO BOARDS

You know your child's learning style best. Designing your own lotto boards lets you put that knowledge to work! But, it is important to be aware of the decisions and choices you are making when designing your own lotto board and the impact those decision have on its effectiveness. I have spent countless hours over many years designing lotto activities—it's second nature to me now. I have distilled it into 9 simple steps that I call:

Kim's Crash Course to Lotto Design

1. CHOOSE THE RIGHT NUMBER OF WINDOWS

The beauty of designing your own lotto board is that the number of "windows" can be chosen to meet the needs of your child or student. Two choices may be too few while nine choices may be too many. It is easy to create a lotto board with just the right amount of difficulty.

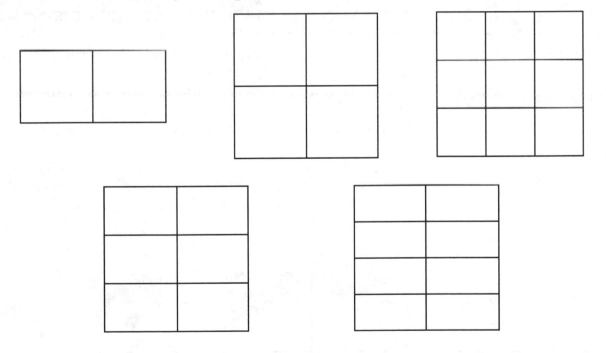

2. MAKE ALL WINDOWS THE SAME SIZE AND SHAPE

The "windows" of a lotto board can be designed in many different shapes. Each "window" does not have to be a square, but all "windows" must be the same dimension. By doing so, each "window" has the same "value" as all the rest on the board. Otherwise, too much or too little attention is drawn to certain windows because of their relative size.

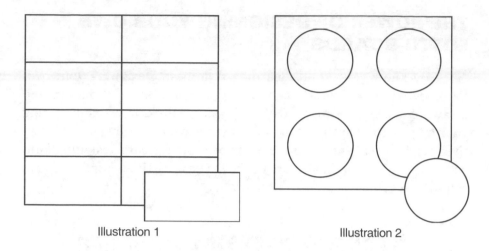

Illustration 1   Illustration 2

Some window shapes are more suited to a particular purpose than others. For example, lengthy words require more space which rectangular shaped "windows" accommodate. *(See Illustration 1.)* Changing the window shape to look like *Illustration 2* is great for simple images and family photos, and can also provide variety and interest.

3. BALANCE THE IMAGE SIZE WITH THE WINDOW SIZE

When designing your lotto board, strike a balance between maximizing the size of the image (which makes it easier to see) and preserving the "white space" surrounding it (which makes each image visually separate from the other images around it). Balancing the size of the window, the scale of the image, and the amount of white space will determine the windows' shape and size.

As you increase the complexity of a lotto board by adding more "windows" (such as going from 4 to 8 choices), your design will need to change. The size of the images may need to be decreased because

Images are rather small; predominance of "white space" around images

Balance between "white space" and size of the images

Image size is maximized but may make visual discrimination more difficult

the overall size of the paper is fixed; placing more divisions on it will require that the size of each individual window decreases. If the size of the image is key to your child using the lotto board, then limit the complexity and the number of "windows" so that the size of each image can remain right for your child.

4. MAKE ALL TEXT THE SAME SIZE

Altering the text size on a lotto board to accommodate words of varying lengths is not a good idea. Doing this makes shorter words look larger, bolder, and more important than longer words that appear in smaller text size. Instead, to make things fit, change the text size or increase the window size to accommodate all the words, long and short, on one lotto board. (Refer to *Scale* in the *Graphic Skills* section.)

cantaloupe	peach	grapes
pear	pineapple	apple
grapefruit	banana	kiwi

Poor design; text size varies depending on length of word

banana	grapefruit
cantaloupe	peach
pineapple	grapes
kiwi	apple

Good design; window size is changed so that text size is consistent for words of varying lengths

5. LABEL WITH A PURPOSE

It is easy to add a label to either an individual image or lotto board, and just as easy to remove it. But remember, labels on lotto boards can enhance their use or detract from their intended purpose. Here are some guidelines:

Labeling Images

Any icon or image on a lotto board can be labeled by pairing it with text. But before adding text, think about your objective for the activity and decide whether labeling the image will add to or detract from the objective. If the objective of the activity is strictly visually discriminating among the various images on the lotto board, then adding text may be a distraction. If your child has mastered visual discrimination and has moved onto introduction of sight words, then by all means consider including text labels of the images.

Labeling Above or Below the Image?

Once you decide to include text labels, you must decide whether to place the label above or below the image. Some say that early readers might use their fingers to run over the text, thereby covering up an image placed above the word. By placing the text label below the word, this problem would be eliminated. Others say that the focus should be the familiar image before the less familiar text and that this is better achieved by placing the text above the image.

The jury is still out on what is considered "best." As is true for many design elements, it is best to look at the objective that text serves and what works best for your child when creating customized educational materials.

Labeling Lotto Boards with Titles

If you are considering labeling an entire lotto board with a title, first ask yourself: "Is the title for the student or for me?" Unless the title is part of the teaching plan, I recommend leaving titles off. The addition of a title could be visually confusing, distracting your child's focus from the images on the lotto board.

If the title is to be used as an educational objective—for example, teaching about categories like "Baby Animals," "Fruits," "Vegetables," "My Family"—where naming the lotto board is part of the lesson, then adding a label might enhance the use of the lotto board.

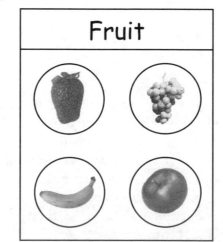

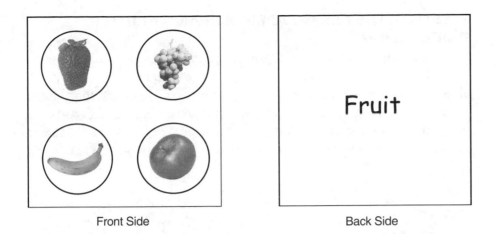

Front Side   Back Side

Some people like to label lotto boards to help to keep them organized. To avoid causing distraction, consider placing the label on the back of the lotto board by printing on the back side of the paper. This can be accomplished by creating a document with the lotto board name only, turning the printer paper over, and then running the paper through the printer a second time. By using card stock, the paper is heavy enough so that the image will not show through from the back side to the front of the lotto board, and you now have a useful label.

6. CHOOSE THE BEST DESIGN ORIENTATION

For some children, the orientation of the lotto board can contribute to success or failure. Some students attend more readily to one orientation than another. By orienting the lotto board vertically, the choices may be more visually accessible, or vice versa.

The lotto board itself can be designed in a horizontal or vertical orientation and then printed accordingly.

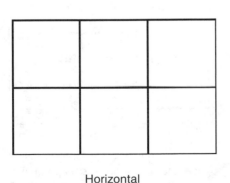

Horizontal

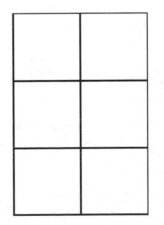

Vertical

7. SELECT THE RIGHT PAPER SIZE AND PRINTER ORIENTATION

The biggest limitation to designing a larger lotto board is the size of the paper used to print it. Although "tiling" can be used when available—printing larger images on multiple pieces of paper and then gluing or taping them together—it is impractical and unnecessary. Boards can be printed on either letter-sized (8½ x 11 inches) or legal-sized (8½ x 14 inches) paper which can accommodate any size lotto board.

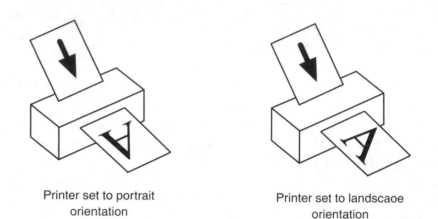

Printer set to portrait
orientation

Printer set to landscaoe
orientation

Larger lotto boards can be oriented to utilize the length of the paper, rather than the width. Print it in either portrait (top to bottom) or landscape (side to side), typically found in the page setup menu of a graphics program. Orienting the design width-wise and printing in landscape utilizes the paper length.

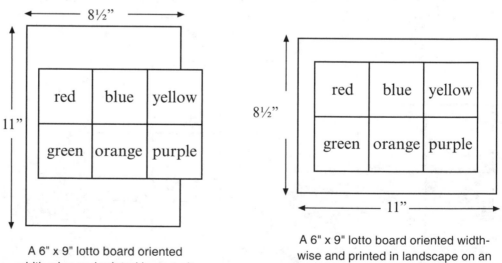

A 6" x 9" lotto board oriented
width-wise and printed in portrait
on an 8½" x 11" piece of paper. As
you can see, it does not fit.

A 6" x 9" lotto board oriented width-
wise and printed in landscape on an
8½" x 11" piece of paper.

8. CHOOSE THE RIGHT PAPER WEIGHT AND COLOR

Printing lotto boards and choice cards on white printable card stock of approximately 65 lbs. produces the best product. Paper thickness and density are measured in "pounds" (lbs.); the higher the number, the thicker and denser the paper. Once laminated, the lotto board and choice cards will be quite durable.

Lotto boards can also be printed on standard 20 lb. white printer paper or colored paper. Printing on colored paper can simplify matching lotto boards to their corresponding choice cards. But, although cute and efficient, printing on some colors of paper can reduce the contrast between the images or text and the paper itself, making the images more difficult to see. Pay attention to how the contrast is affected by the color of paper that you choose, and choose colors that provide the highest contrast. (Refer to *Controlling Variables: Media* on *Colored Paper.*)

9. TAKE ADVANTAGE OF YOUR COMPUTER'S POWER

Because it is so quick and easy to manipulate and change computer files, you can keep your lotto board fresh, and correct problems in your design. Presenting variations of a lotto board—by moving images around—guarantees that you can use a board and its images more than once. It also ensures that success is determined by visual discrimination rather than by memorizing a static layout. Changing the location of images also reduces boredom and provides variety while presenting the same information. It is easy to modify an existing lotto board once the images have been copied and pasted into the drawing document: just select each image and drag it to its new location.

Computers also let you easily fix lotto boards that are not working well for your child. Failure with a lotto board can sometimes be a matter of over attending to one of the images. Rather than looking at all the images on the board, your child may prefer one or more images over all the rest.

This was often the case with Ashley. Presented with a lotto board with images of people's faces, she was fascinated with an image of a crying baby. She did not want to attend to the other images on the lotto board, but instead used sign language to communicate her concern for "baby crying." With the activity going nowhere, I went back to the computer, removed the image of the baby, replaced it with one that was less engaging, and printed the new board. Because I had created my own lotto board, it was easy to modify its presentation. Ashley could then successfully complete the lotto exercise.

OTHER LOTTO TIPS

CONSIDER USING . . .
...cork or felt pads to make it easier to pick up choice cards. Typically used on the bottom of items to avoid scratching wood tabletops or other surfaces, they can be found in most hardware stores. Each comes with a self-adhesive so that it can be quickly placed on the back corner of individual choice cards. This slightly elevates one side of the card above the table surface, making it easier to pick up.

COLOR LOTTO

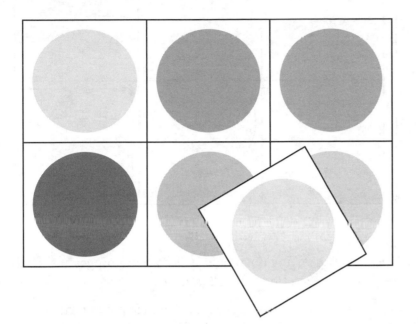

What You'll Need

Materials
- White printer paper or printable card stock, 8½" x 11"
- Laminating pouches, 8¾" x 11¼"

Tools
- Scissors
- Heat laminator

Art
- None

Software
- Graphics program

Hardware
- Color printer

Level of Difficulty
- Simple

Color is one of those wonderful early skills that is always taught by parents and teachers to young children, and one which children tend to learn with ease. "What color is an apple?" "Red!" kids shout. "What color is a banana?" "Yellow!"

But Ashley was unable to call out the names. Although she had learned to sign many color words, she would typically shut down and not respond if asked to name a color or sign the color of a particular object. The expectation to produce a response on demand was challenging for her, a product of her neurological damage. To prove that Ashley could visually discriminate between colors, it was necessary to find some way for Ashley to respond. Lotto was the solution.

The first color lotto board I ever created was not generated from a computer but used numerous pieces of construction paper of various colors. After tracing circles onto the construction paper, I cut them out and glued them onto poster board. To make the choice cards, I repeated the entire process over again, cutting and gluing colored circles onto poster board and then cutting the cards apart. This took hours.

By contrast, completing the process on the computer takes a fraction of the time and produces a superior product. And it is easy to swap out colors and move the colors around to create new lotto boards.

By following these simple instructions, you can create a lotto board for color discrimination in no time at all.

Skills to Teach

- ● Visual perception
- Math
- Language
- Communication
- Reading
- Handwriting
- Self-help

Illustration 1

select
and center

9"

6"

3"

3"

DIRECTIONS

1. Open a new drawing document in a graphics program such as *AppleWorks®*, *FreeHand®*, or *Illustrator®*.

2. In the File Menu, select Page Setup. Change paper Orientation to Landscape. (Refer to the previous section on **Document Settings** in **Graphic Skills**.)

3. Turn on Grid and Rulers. (Refer to the previous section on **Grid and Rulers** in **Graphic Skills**.)

4. Using the Rectangle Tool, draw a 6 x 9 inch rectangle.

5. Using the Line Tool, divide the rectangle into 6 equal parts. To do this, draw a horizontal line to divide the rectangle in half. Then draw 2 vertical lines at 3 inch intervals to divide the rectangle into 6 squares, each 3 x 3 inches. *(See Illustration 1.)*

6. Using the Ellipse Tool, draw one circle that is sized to fit inside one of the 3 x 3 inch squares.

7. Copy the circle to the clipboard and paste 5 identical copies into the document. Using the Select Tool, select and center each circle within the 6 squares.

8. Using the Select Tool, individually select each circle by pointing to and then clicking on it. Using the Fill color in the Color Palette of the Tools window, fill each circle with a unique color from the Color Palette (such as red, orange, yellow, green, blue, and purple).

9. Print two copies (preferably on printable card stock).

10. Heat laminate both copies.

11. Cut one laminated into six individual lotto choice cards. Use the other copy as your lotto board.

QUICK TIPS

DESIGN TIPS
■ **Adjusting the Number of Choices**
If a selection of 6 choices is too great or too few, reduce it to 4 or increase it to 8. That's the beauty of designing it yourself on a computer!

■ **Make the Circle Lines Disappear**
To make the line around each circle disappear, see **Matching the Line and the Fill Color** in **Graphic Skills**.

DRAWING TIPS
■ **Drawing Lines**
To simplify drawing lines horizontally, vertically, or at constrained angles, hold down the Shift key while dragging the Line Tool.

■ **Drawing Circles**
To simplify drawing circles, hold down the Shift key while dragging the Ellipse Tool.

CUTTING TIP
■ **Cutting Lotto Cards**
By cutting just inside the printed line, the black line is removed and the lotto card better fits the lotto board. This is because the card is then just slightly smaller than the corresponding squares of the lotto board.

SHAPE LOTTO

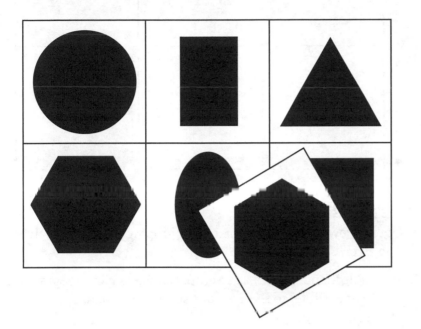

Once Ashley had exhibited her understanding of discriminating by color using the color lotto board, it was time to see if she could discriminate by shape. So, I made a lotto board with different shapes, all of the same color. In the absence of six unique colors, shape would be the only indicator to her of difference among the choices. When selections all appear as one color, color cannot be used as a clue to indicate "sameness."

The illustration above shows you how the board appears when a lotto is created to discriminate solely by shape. Drawing shapes of various types is made simple with a graphics program. Circles and ovals are created using the same drawing tool (the Ellipse Tool), while rectangles and squares are created using a separate drawing tool (the Rectangle Tool).

Although the instructions provided are for shapes appearing all black, the lotto board will function the same when all shapes appear all red, all yellow, or any other single color.

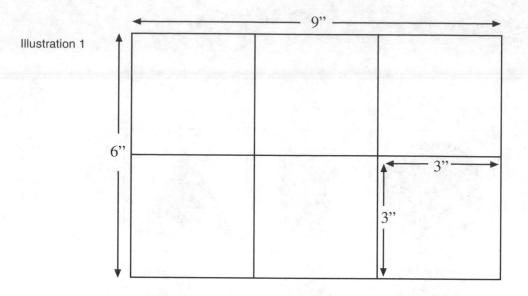

Illustration 1

DIRECTIONS

1. Open a new drawing document in a graphics program such as *AppleWorks®*, *FreeHand®*, or *Illustrator®*.

2. In the File Menu, select Page Setup. Change paper Orientation to Landscape. (Refer to the previous section on **Document Settings** in **Graphic Skills**.)

3. Turn on Grid and Rulers. (Refer to the previous section on **Grid and Rulers** in **Graphic Skills**.)

4. Using the Rectangle Tool, draw a 6 x 9 inch rectangle.

5. Using the Line Tool, divide the rectangle into 6 equal parts. To do this, draw a horizontal line to divide the rectangle in half. Then draw 2 vertical lines at 3 inch intervals to divide the rectangle into 6 squares, each 3 x 3 inches. *(See Illustration 1.)*

6. Using the Ellipse Tool, draw one circle that is sized to fit inside one of the 3 x 3 inch squares. Using the Select Tool, select and center the circle within one of the 6 squares.

7. Using the Ellipse Tool, draw one oval that is sized to fit inside one of the 3 x 3 inch squares. Using the Select Tool, select and center the oval within one of the 6 squares.

8. Using the Rectangle Tool, draw one square that is sized to fit inside one of the 3 x 3 inch squares. Using the Select Tool, select and center the square within one of the 6 squares.

9. Using the Rectangle Tool, draw one rectangle that is sized to fit inside one of the 3 x 3 inch squares. Using the Select Tool, select and center the rectangle within one of the 6 squares.

10. Using the Polygon Tool, draw a triangle (3 sides). Using the Select Tool, select and center the triangle within one of the 6 squares.

11. Using the Polygon Tool, draw a hexagon (6 sides). Using the Select Tool, select and center the hexagon within one of the 6 squares.

12. Using the Select Tool, individually select each shape by pointing to and then clicking on it. Using the Fill color in the Color Palette, fill each shape with black (or any other single color).

13. Print two copies (preferably on printable card stock).

14. Heat laminate both copies.

15. Cut one laminated copy into six individual lotto cards. Use the other copy as your lotto board.

QUICK TIPS

CUTTING TIP
- **Cutting Lotto Cards**
  By cutting just inside the printed line, the black line is removed and the lotto card better fits the lotto board. This is because the card is then just slightly smaller than the corresponding squares of the lotto board.

COLOR & SHAPE LOTTO

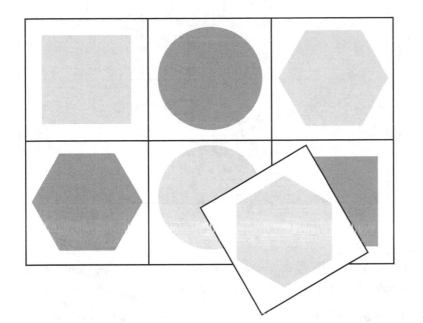

Once Ashley had mastered single variables—specifically color or shape, each individually—it was time to introduce the concept of visually discriminating among two variables simultaneously: color and shape. This was accomplished by creating a lotto board consisting of two of the same shapes but with two distinct colors. Ashley could no longer rely on her ability to visually discriminate only among different shapes, nor could she use color as the sole indicator of two items being the same. Instead, she had to juggle two unique characteristics for each image.

In designing a lotto board with two variables, only three shapes and three colors should be used. Whether the shapes are circles, squares, and hexagons, or any other three distinct shapes, it does not matter, so long as each shape appears in one of only two colors. Create a variation of these same lotto boards by changing the location or color of each shape.

You can take this activity in all sorts of directions. Other distinct shapes can be used in two distinct colors. Or other variables can be combined with color or shape, such as number, position, or size of objects.

Additionally, two completely unique boards can be created consisting of the same set of shapes but each set of shapes appearing in only one color. Then your child could learn to complete two lotto boards simultaneously.

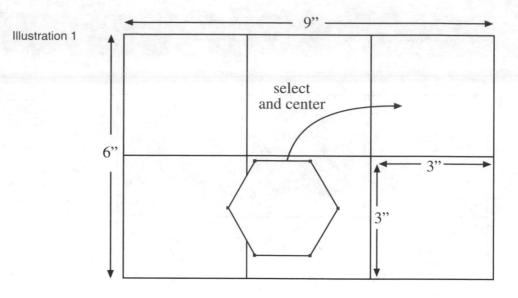

Illustration 1

DIRECTIONS

1. Open a new drawing document in a graphics program such as *AppleWorks*®, *FreeHand*®, or *Illustrator*®.

2. In the File Menu, select Page Setup. Change paper Orientation to Landscape. (Refer to the previous section on **Document Settings** in **Graphic Skills**.)

3. Turn on Grid and Rulers. (Refer to the previous section on **Grid and Rulers** in **Graphic Skills**.)

4. Using the Rectangle Tool, draw a 6 x 9 inch rectangle.

5. Using the Line Tool, divide the rectangle into 6 equal parts. To do this, draw a horizontal line to divide the rectangle in half. Then draw 2 vertical lines at 3 inch intervals to divide the rectangle into 6 squares, each 3 x 3 inches. *(See Illustration 1.)*

6. Using the Polygon Tool, draw a hexagon (6 sides). Using the Select Tool, select and center the hexagon within one of the 6 squares.

7. Copy the hexagon to the clipboard and paste 1 identical copy into the document. Using the Select Tool, select and center the hexagon within one of the 6 squares.

8. Using the Rectangle Tool, draw a square that is sized to fit inside one of the 3 x 3 inch squares. Using the Select Tool, select and center the square within one of the 6 squares.

9. Copy the square to the clipboard and paste 1 identical copy into the document. Using the Select Tool, select and center the square within one of the 6 squares.

10. Using the Ellipse Tool, draw a circle that is sized to fit inside one of the 3 x 3 inch squares. Using the Select Tool, select and center the circle within one of the 6 squares.

QUICK TIPS

DRAWING TIPS

■ **Drawing Circles**
To simplify drawing circles, hold down the Shift key while dragging the Ellipse Tool.

■ **Drawing Squares**
To simplify drawing squares, hold down the Shift key while dragging the Rectangle Tool.

11. Copy the circle to the clipboard and paste 1 identical copy into the document. Using the Select Tool, select and center the circle within one of the 6 squares.

12. Using the Select Tool, individually select each shape by pointing to and then clicking on it. Using the Fill color, fill one circle red and the other circle yellow. Fill one square red and the other square yellow. Fill one hexagon red and the other hexagon yellow (or use two other colors from the Color Palette).

13. Print two copies (preferably on printable card stock).

14. Heat laminate both copies.

15. Cut one laminated copy into six individual lotto cards. Use the other copy as your lotto board.

SIZE LOTTO

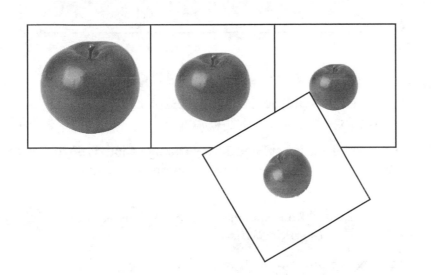

What You'll Need

Materials
- White printer paper or printable card stock, 8½" x 11"
- Laminating pouches, 8¾" x 11¼"

Tools
- Scissors
- Heat laminator

Art
- Scanned image, computer graphic, or clip art

Software
- Graphics program

Hardware
- Color printer

Level of Difficulty
- Simple

In an effort to determine if Ashley could visually discriminate among objects varying in size or dimension, I created a series of lotto boards, each with the same image but in gradations of size: small, medium, and large.

Resizing an image to create such a lotto board can be easily accomplished by one of two methods: Scale by Percent (a command which resizes by a percentage of the original size), or select the image, grab one of its handles, and then drag the handle to create the object's new dimension.

I prefer to design the lotto board in a horizontal orientation. This can encourage left to right progression (a necessary skill for reading). But vertical orientation (top to bottom) is also acceptable and may better suit the user.

Skills to Teach

- ● Visual perception
- Math
- Language
- Communication
- Reading
- Handwriting
- Self-help

Illustration 1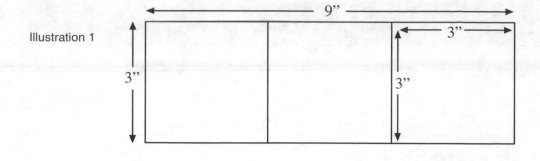

DIRECTIONS

1. Open a new drawing document in a graphics program such as *AppleWorks®*, *FreeHand®*, or *Illustrator®*.

2. In the File Menu, select Page Setup. Change paper Orientation to Landscape. (Refer to the previous section on **Document Settings** in **Graphic Skills**.)

3. Turn on Grid and Rulers. (Refer to the previous section on **Grid and Rulers** in **Graphic Skills**.)

4. Using the Rectangle Tool, draw a 3 x 9 inch rectangle. *(See Illustration 1.)*

5. Using the Line Tool, divide the rectangle into 3 equal parts. To do this, draw 2 vertical lines at 3 inch intervals to divide the rectangle into 3 squares, each 3 x 3 inches. *(See Illustration 1.)*

6. Copy a 2 x 2 inch image to the clipboard. (Or, be prepared to resize a smaller or larger image once it has been pasted. Refer to the previous section on **Scale** in **Graphic Skills**.)

7. Paste three copies of the image into the drawing document. Using the Select Tool, select and move each image into one of the three squares.

8. Resize the image in the middle square to 75% of its original size. (Refer to the previous section on **Scale** in **Graphic Skills**.)

9. Resize the image in the far right square to 50% of its original size.

10. Print two copies (preferably on printable card stock).

11. Heat laminate both copies.

12. Cut one laminated copy into three individual lotto cards. Do so by cutting just inside all printed lines. This will remove the black lines on each card and make them slightly smaller than the squares of the lotto board that they will be placed in.

QUICK TIPS

RESIZING TIP
■ **Maintaining Proportions**
To maintain the original proportions of an object when resizing using Scale by Percent, type the same number to scale in both the horizontal and vertical directions.

To maintain the original proportions of an object when resizing it by dragging the handles, hold down the Shift key as you drag one of the handles diagonally.

COLOR & SHAPE & SIZE LOTTO

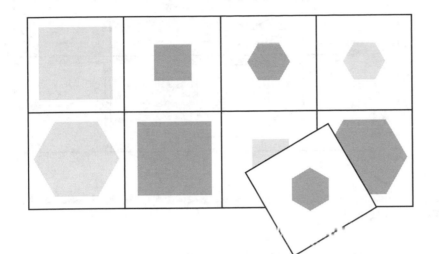

In designing lotto games for Ashley, I was very methodical; I did not add new variables—new colors, shapes, or sizes—until I knew she had mastered the old ones. I wanted to avoid piling too many variables, one on top of the other, making it impossible to pinpoint the variable that might have caused failure. In your work with your child, you should be sure he or she has mastered a skill before you build upon it.

Once Ashley had mastered one and two variables, why not try three! I already knew she could discriminate among various colors, various shapes, and various sizes. But discriminating among three variables simultaneously presented a much greater challenge.

This particular lotto board provides two different possibilities for three different variables (color, size, and shape). I have specifically chosen squares and hexagons in either red or yellow, and small or large. Your child will be challenged to visually discriminate between the "big yellow hexagon" and the "small yellow square," and so on.

Play with the various combinations and come up with other unique lotto boards using three variables. Or four.

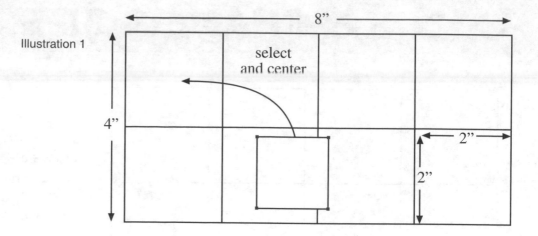

Illustration 1

DIRECTIONS

1. Open a new drawing document in a graphics program such as *AppleWorks®*, *FreeHand®*, or *Illustrator®*.

2. In the File Menu, select Page Setup. Change paper Orientation to Landscape. (Refer to the previous section on **Document Settings** in **Graphic Skills**.)

3. Turn on Grid and Rulers. (Refer to the previous section on **Grid and Rulers** in **Graphic Skills**.)

4. Using the Rectangle Tool, draw a 4 x 8 inch rectangle.

5. Using the Line Tool, divide the rectangle into 8 equal parts. To do this, draw a horizontal line to divide the rectangle in half. Then draw 3 vertical lines at 2 inch intervals to divide the rectangle into 8 squares, each 2 x 2 inches. *(See Illustration 1.)*

6. Using the Rectangle Tool, draw one square that is sized to fit inside one of the 2 x 2 inch squares. Using the Select Tool, select and center it within one of the 8 squares.

7. Copy the square to the clipboard and paste 3 identical copies into the document. Using the Select Tool, select and center the squares within three of the 8 squares.

8. Using the Polygon Tool, draw one hexagon (6 sides) that is sized to fit inside one of the 2 x 2 inch squares. Using the Select Tool, select and center the hexagon within one of the 8 squares.

9. Copy the hexagon to the clipboard and paste 3 identical copies into the document. Using the Select Tool, select and center the hexagons within three of the 8 squares.

10. Using the Select Tool, individually select each shape by pointing to and then clicking on it. Using the Fill color, fill two squares red and two squares yellow. Fill two hexagons red and two hexagons yellow (or use two other colors from the Color Palette).

11. Using the Select Tool, individually select the shapes by pointing to and then clicking on them. Resize one red square and one yellow square to 50% of its original size. Resize one red hexagon and one yellow hexagon to 50% of its original size. (Refer to the *Resizing Tip* on **Maintaining Proportions** in the previous section.)

12. Print two copies (preferably on printable card stock).

13. Heat laminate both copies.

14. Cut one laminated copy into eight individual lotto cards. Use the other copy as your lotto board.

QUICK TIPS

CUTTING TIP
- **Cutting Lotto Cards**
  By cutting just inside the printed line, the black line is removed and the lotto card better fits the lotto board. This is because the card is then just slightly smaller than the corresponding squares of the lotto board.

MISCELLANEOUS LOTTO

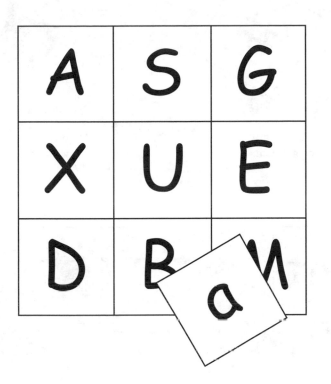

What You'll Need

Materials
- White printer paper or printable card stock, 8½" x 11"
- Laminating pouches, 8¾" x 11¼"

Tools
- Scissors
- Heat laminator

Art
- Scanned image, computer graphic, or clip art

Software
- Graphics program

Hardware
- Color printer

Level of Difficulty
- Simple

The previous instructions have shown you how to create specific kinds of lotto boards. You should now be capable of creating many other lotto boards for many other purposes. The good news is that the possibilities for learning with lotto are endless. Lotto boards can be used for visual discrimination, prereading skills, reading, categorization, and math readiness, to name just a few. They can be used in virtually any way you can imagine or invent.

By saving the layouts for lotto boards as computer files before images have been copied and pasted into them, many unique boards can be quickly created with a new set of icons, photos, or text. Save each lotto board with a unique and descriptive name. Print, laminate, and cut out the cards. It's that easy!

Skills to Teach

- Visual perception
- Math
- Language
  Communication
  Reading
  Handwriting
  Self-help

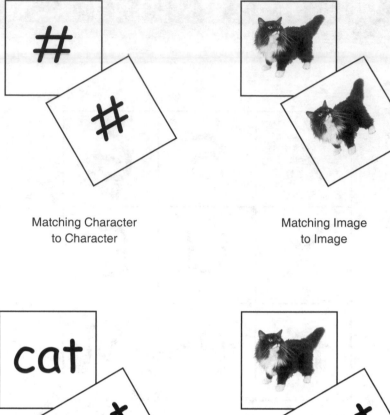

Matching Character
to Character

Matching Image
to Image

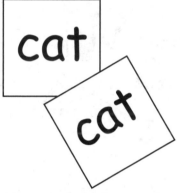

Matching Word
to Word

Matching Word
to Image

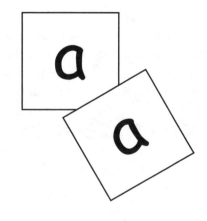

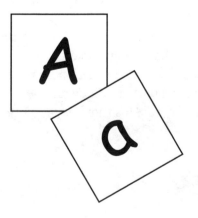

Matching Letter
to Letter

Matching Lowercase
to Uppercase

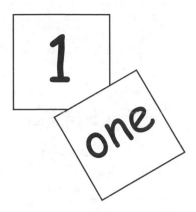

Matching Text to
Numerical Character

Matching Number of Objects
to Number of Same Objects

Matching Number of Objects
to Number of Different
Objects

Matching Numeral
to Number of Objects

Matching Sign to Word

Matching Sign to Numeral

SIGN LANGUAGE SYMBOLS

Mayer-Johnson produces a set of *Boardmaker*™ sign language symbols which I use for various purposes, including creating lotto boards. This is often an extension activity— a method to interact with the same information but in a different way. When the sign I need is not included in this library, I scan the image out of a sign language dictionary, and then copy and paste it into the lotto board.

WHAT IS A PHONEME?

A phoneme is the smallest unit of sound in speech that distinguishes one word from another.

Phonemes are represented in print by the letter sound placed between slashes (/d/). If this is visually confusing to your child, consider leaving them out.

Matching Beginning
Phoneme to Image

Matching Opposites

GESTALTS

What You'll Need

Materials
- White printer paper or printable card stock, 8½" x 11"
- Laminating pouches, 8¾" x 11¼"

Tools
- Scissors
- Heat laminator

Art
- Scanned image, computer graphic, or clip art

Software
- Graphics program

Hardware
- Color printer

Level of Difficulty
- Simple

A number of years ago, Ashley visited her neuropsychologist for developmental and educational testing. The results of these examinations were very valuable, providing more than just test scores. Typically I would leave with information about developmental milestones and ideas for new skills to teach Ashley.

On one particular visit, Ashley was given a test to assess her visual perceptual skills. It was a Gestalt test, comprised of a picture of a cat cut in half along the diagonal. A Gestalt is a shape or structure that comprises a whole which cannot be expressed simply by its parts. Presented with the two pieces, Ashley had to put them together to construct the cat. Ashley had a difficult time. At first, she made no attempt to bring the pieces together; instead she spun the pieces around and around. It seemed as though Ashley could not see the whole, and therefore could not construct it from its parts. Could I design something on the computer to teach her to do this?

When we returned a few days later for additional testing I pulled out the materials I had created. With them, I had been able to teach Ashley to complete a Gestalt. The neuropsychologist was amazed and suggested I ramp up the difficulty of the exercise, first dividing the pictures into more and more pieces and later configuring the pieces into a variety of shapes (triangles, rectangles, and squares). With each new image, I began by dividing it from the simple (2 pieces) to the complex (many pieces in different shapes). This allowed Ashley to process each new "whole" before she had to construct it from its "parts." But as Ashley became more and more proficient, even this became unnecessary. Ashley soon had little difficulty constructing anything I gave her.

The point of this entire exercise was not to "teach to the test" but to determine the necessary skills to complete the task. As much as information can be taught, so too can academic learning strategies.

Skills to Teach

- ● Visual perception
  Math
  Language
  Communication
  Reading
  Handwriting
  Self-help

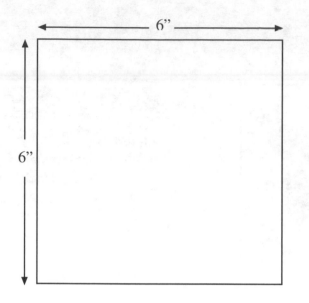

Illustration 1   Illustration 2

DIRECTIONS

1. Open a new drawing document in a graphics program such as *AppleWorks®*, *FreeHand®*, or *Illustrator®*.

2. Turn on Grid and Rulers. (Refer to the previous section on **Grid and Rulers** in **Graphic Skills**.)

3. Using the Rectangle Tool, draw a 6 x 6 inch square. *(See Illustration 1.)*

4. Copy an image approximately 5 x 5 inch (or slightly smaller), or other clip art, to the clipboard. (Or, be prepared to resize a smaller or larger image once it has been pasted. Refer to the previous section on **Scale** in **Graphic Skills**.)

5. Paste the image into the drawing document. Using the Select Tool, select and move the image into the middle of the square.

6. Set the Pen Width or Line Width to Hairline and then, using the Line Tool, draw a diagonal line from the upper left to the lower right hand corner. *(See Illustration 2.)*

7. Print (preferably on printable card stock).

8. Heat laminate.

9. Carefully cut along the outside of the square and along the diagonal line.

QUICK TIPS

DRAWING TIPS

▪ **Choosing Simple Images**
Be sure to use simple images against a white or transparent background when creating Gestalts. That way, the background will not give extra clues to the correct orientation.

▪ **Determining Pen Width**
Setting the Pen Width or Line Width to Hairline will draw guide lines for cutting that will be imperceptible once they have been cut.

DESIGN VARIATIONS

Use the following configurations to divide the "whole" into few to many "parts."

SYMMETRY GAME

Ashley loves using educational materials like the one shown above. Each game board consists of windows showing only the left half of the image. The corresponding choice cards show the right half of the image. Given the set of cards, Ashley must find the other half of each image and then place it on the board.

This activity may resemble lotto, but teaches different skills. It requires your child to understand the concept of symmetry by splitting an image through a central dividing line. Completing the game board requires identifying two corresponding halves of a single image. This skill helps your child develop the ability to see combinations and discern the whole of an object from its parts.

Ashley enjoys this activity and plays it all the time. This raised a problem: With only a limited number of boards and cards available in the commercial symmetry product, she completes it in short order. So I thought, "Why not make her some more?"

It is remarkably easy to create boards and cards for this activity using your computer.

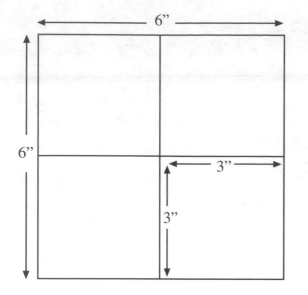

Illustration 1

Illustration 2

DIRECTIONS

1. Open a new drawing document in a graphics program such as *AppleWorks®*, *FreeHand®*, or *Illustrator®*.

2. Turn on Grid and Rulers. (Refer to the previous section on **Grid and Rulers** in **Graphic Skills**.)

3. Using the Rectangle Tool, draw a 6 x 6 inch square. *(See Illustration 1.)*

4. Using the Line Tool, divide the square into 4 equal parts. To do this, draw a vertical line to split the square into 2 equal parts and then draw a horizontal line to divide the square into 4 squares, each 3 x 3 inches. *(See Illustration 1.)*

5. Copy a 2½ x 2½ inch image to the clipboard. (Or, be prepared to resize a smaller or larger image once it has been pasted. Refer to the previous section on **Scale** in **Graphic Skills**.)

6. Paste the image into the drawing document. While the image is selected, drag and center it within one of the 4 squares.

7. Continue this same process of copying, pasting, and centering 3 additional 2½ x 2½ inch images into the last 3 empty squares.

8. Using the Rectangle Tool, draw a 1½ x 3 inch rectangle over the right half of the first image. *(See Illustration 2.)* If the rectangle is transparent (that is, the image shows through from underneath), fill it with the color white selected from the Color Palette. (Also check out the *Drawing Tip* for **Drawing Rectangles with No Lines**.)

QUICK TIPS

BOARDMAKER™ TIP
▪ **IMAGE SIZE**
When using *Boardmaker™* prior to version 5.0, and copying a symbol to another program, setting the Picture Size to 125% automatically sets the image size to approximately 2½ x 2½ inches.

When using *Boardmaker™* version 5.0 and higher, and copying a symbol to another program, the image is automatically set to approximately 2 x 2 inches. Be prepared to resize the image to the desired size.

Illustration 3: The Board

select and drag

Illustration 4: The Cards

9. Continue covering the same half of the last 3 images. *(See Illustration 3.)*

10. Save the game board with a distinct file name, such as "Symmetry Game Board." Once printed, this will be the game board.

11. To create the cards, cover the other half of each image. Using the Select Tool, select and drag each of the four 1½ x 3 inch rectangles to cover the left half of all four images. *(See Illustration 4.)*

12. Save the game board with a distinct file name, such as "Symmetry Game Cards."

13. Print one copy of each of the two distinct game boards (preferably on printable card stock).

14. Heat laminate both copies.

15. Keep one board intact, cutting along the outside black line of the 6 x 6 inch square.

16. Cut the other board apart into 4 choice cards that expose one half of each image. Do so by cutting just inside all printed lines. This will remove the black lines on each card and make them slightly smaller than the squares of the game board that they will be placed in.

QUICK TIPS

DESIGN TIP
■ **Create a Game**
Create a custom game spinner to determine which image must be completed first, second, and so on. (See *Game Spinner*.)

DRAWING TIP
■ **Choosing Simple Images**
Be sure to use simple images against a white or transparent background when creating Symmetry Game boards and cards. That way, the background will not give extra clues to the correct selection.

Illustration 5

DRAWING TIPS

▪ **Drawing Rectangles with No Lines**
When drawing basic shapes, it is possible to do so without the lines showing. This can be done by either changing the line width to "None" or changing the line color to the background color in the Color Palette.

The examples to the right show two different images of the same cow. *(See Illustration 5.)* Although it may not appear that both cows are pasted into boxes, they are! While the one on the left shows the box, the one on the right does not. The "handles" at each corner of the rectangle show on screen (but not when printed), but the perimeter lines do not because they have been changed to either "None" or white.

It may be preferable to use this technique when creating the Symmetry Game board. The presence of the vertical line of the rectangle that divides the image in half may be distracting to the user. *(See Illustration 6 and 7.)*

▪ **Finding Basic Shapes with No Lines in Your Document**
If you misplace something in your document because it has no exterior lines or interior shading, click Select All. The handles of anything that has been pasted or drawn on the page will appear (including basic shapes and text frames), allowing you to locate them.

Illustration 6

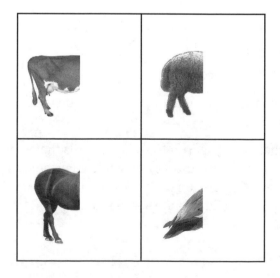

Illustration 7

JIGSAW PUZZLE

What You'll Need

Materials
- Puzzle media
- Iron-on transfer
- Optional: Acrylic spray

Tools
- Scissors
- Pen or pencil
- Household iron

Art
- Scanned image, computer graphic, or clip art

Software
- Graphics program

Hardware
- Color printer

Level of Difficulty
- Simple

How would you like to create a jigsaw puzzle from a picture of your dog, a family vacation, or some other engaging image, just by running a specialty paper through your printer? Creating a custom jigsaw puzzle is just about that easy.

Jigsaw puzzles are great for working on visual perceptual and spacial reasoning skills. These are important skills for reading and mathematics. Jigsaw puzzles can become a dynamic teaching tool when the images are meaningful and when the complexity of the puzzle (that is, the number and shapes of pieces) is controlled by you. By generating the puzzles yourself, you can do just that: creating a puzzle comprised of more and more pieces while using the same image!

You can create puzzles using paper media that has 3, 15, or 40 pieces (www.compozapuzzle.com). Or you can create a two-sided, 16 piece puzzle (Flip Puzzle™ at www.imaginationgallery.net). These papers work on most inkjet printers. But be forewarned: These papers are not thick; they're about the thickness of a business card. (They obviously can't be too thick to run through your printer.)

If your child has fine motor difficulties, or you just prefer a thicker media, there is another alternative that uses inkjet iron-on transfers, a household iron, and a specially coated puzzle media that the iron-on transfer adheres to (www.jigsawpuzzle.com). This media is the thickness of a conventional puzzle and comes in many shapes (rectangles, hearts, circles), sizes (from about 2 x 4 to 8 x 10 inches), and complexities (from a few pieces to over 100).

Read on to find out how to create your very own custom jigsaw. And I promise that you will not find the directions the least bit puzzling!

Skills to Teach

- ● Visual perception
- ● Math
- ● Language
  Communication
- ● Reading
  Handwriting
  Self-help

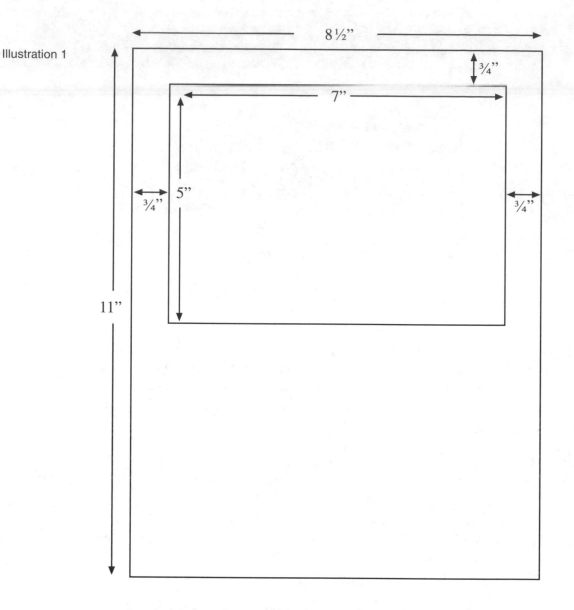

Illustration 1

DIRECTIONS FOR ONE-SIDED 15 PIECE JIGSAW PUZZLE

1. Open a new drawing document in a graphics program such as *AppleWorks®, FreeHand®,* or *Illustrator®.*

2. Turn on Grid and Rulers. (Refer to the previous section on **Grid and Rulers** in **Graphic Skills**.)

3. Using the Rectangle Tool, draw a 5 x 7 inch rectangle. *(See Illustration 1.)*

4. While the rectangle is selected, move it ¾ inch below the top edge of the page and ¾ inch from the right side of the page.

5. Save the document with a distinct file name, such as "15 Piece Jigsaw Template."

6. Open a photo image in a photo editing program such as Adobe® *Photoshop®,* or a graphics progam such as *FreeHand®* or *Illustrator®.*

7. Crop and resize the image to approximately 5¼ x 7¼ inches. (Or, be prepared to resize the image once it has been pasted. Refer to the previous section on *Scale* in *Graphic Skills*.)

8. Using the Select Tool, select the cropped image. Copy it to the clipboard.

9. Paste the image from the clipboard into the new document. Using the Select Tool, select, move, and center the image within the 5 x 7 inch rectangle.

10. Delete the rectangle (but only the rectangle, not the image).

11. Print a test copy on standard inkjet paper. (See *Printing Tip* for **Printing a Test Copy**.)

12. Print the image on the 15 piece puzzle media using the "high quality" setting of your printer.

13. Optional: Spray with acrylic spray to protect the ink.

14. Pop out and separate the puzzle pieces.

DIRECTIONS FOR TWO-SIDED JIGSAW PUZZLE

1. Open a new drawing document in a graphics program such as *AppleWorks*®, *FreeHand*®, or *Illustrator*®.

2. Turn on Grid and Rulers. (Refer to the previous section on *Grid and Rulers* in *Graphic Skills*.)

3. Using the Line Tool, split the page in half by drawing a horizontal reference line the width of the page located 5½ inches from the top edge of the page.

4. Using the Rectangle Tool, draw two 4 x 6 inch rectangles.

5. Using the Select Tool, select and move the first rectangle 1 inch below the top edge of the page and 1¼ inches from the right side of the page. *(See Illustration 2 on the next page.)*

6. Using the Select Tool, select and move the second rectangle 1 inch above the bottom edge of the page and 1¼ inches from the right side of the page. *(See Illustration 2 on the next page.)*

7. Save the document with a distinct file name, such as "Two-Sided Jigsaw Template."

8. Open two photo images in a photo editing software application such as Adobe® *Photoshop*®, or a graphics progam such as *Free-Hand*® or *Illustrator*®.

9. Crop and resize both images to approximately 4⅛ x 6⅛ inches. (Or, be prepared to resize the image once it has been pasted. Refer to

---

QUICK TIPS

PRINTING TIP
▪ **Printing a test copy**
  When using specialty papers, it is always best to run a test copy on standard printer paper first. Place the test copy on top of the specialty paper, hold both up to the light, and determine whether all images and text are properly aligned. This is a good habit when printing such things as labels, decals, and pre-perforated papers. Specialty papers are significantly more expensive than standard printer paper; therefore, it is worth the effort to take the time to run a test before printing your final copy.

A NOTE ABOUT TWO-SIDED JIGSAW PUZZLES

For some students, using a two-sided puzzle with an image on both sides can cause confusion when pieces are mixed up from two separate images. Images on both sides may provide just the level of difficulty you are seeking. Or, it may be too much. Don't feel you must print images on the front and back side of the puzzle. Use only one image placed on one side and still take advantage of the double-thickness of the puzzle media when the two sides are stuck together.

Illustration 2

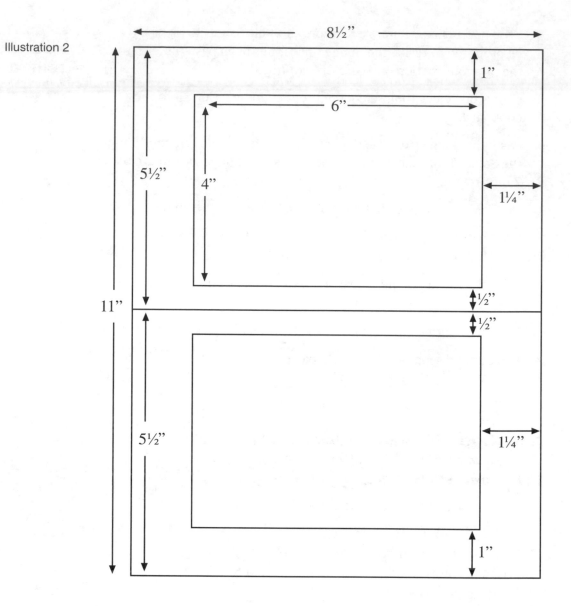

the previous section on **Scale** in **Graphic Skills**.) (Also check out the *Sizing Tip* for **Printing to the Edges of the Puzzle.**)

10. Using the Select Tool, individually select each cropped image. Copy to the clipboard.

11. Paste the images from the clipboard into the new document. Select, move, and center each image within the two 4 x 6 inch rectangles. (NOTE: If you would like your images oriented the same way on both sides of the puzzle, rotate one image 180 degrees.) *(See Illustration 3.)*

12. Delete both 4 x 6 inch rectangles (but only the lines, not the images). (See *Design Tip* for **Where Did That Line Go?**)

13. Print a test copy on standard inkjet paper. (See *Printing Tip* for **Printing a Test Copy.**)

QUICK TIPS

SIZING TIP
■ **Printing to the Edges of the Puzzle**
By sizing a photograph (4⅛ x 6⅛ inches) slightly larger than the size of the puzzle (4 x 6 inches), the photograph is guaranteed to print on the puzzle media all the way to the edge. Otherwise, an unsightly white edge could appear along the perimeter of the puzzle.

Illustration 3

8½"

11"

14. Print the images on Flip Puzzle™ media using the "high quality" setting of your printer.

15. Allow the ink to dry before folding along the preperforated line on the puzzle media.

16. While holding the media on a flat, clean, and dry surface, carefully remove the liner paper to expose the adhesive.

17. Secure the two images together with the adhesive by folding along the preperforated line.

18. Optional: Spray with acrylic spray to protect the ink.

19. Pop out and separate the puzzle pieces.

QUICK TIPS

DESIGN TIP
▪ **Where did that line go?**
Whenever you place one image on top of another object (such as a photograph on top of a line or shape), you may not be able to see the object underneath but your computer knows that it is still there. If you need to see the object to serve as a guide, or would like to delete it, arrange the order of objects by using the "Send to Back" or "Bring to Front" command. This will move one object in front of or behind the other. (See *Arrange* in *Graphic Skills*.)

But if you are only printing to an inkjet printer and do not need the hidden object to show, don't worry about it; just print with the object hidden underneath. Only the image on top will appear when printed.

PRINTING TIP
▪ **The size of objects and the "printable area"**
When drawing and printing larger objects that are close to the edge of the paper, "clipping" can occur if the object exceeds the "printable area." The "printable area" is a characteristic of each printer. To determine whether the size of an object exceeds the printable area of your printer, print a test copy once the object has been drawn.

Illustration 4

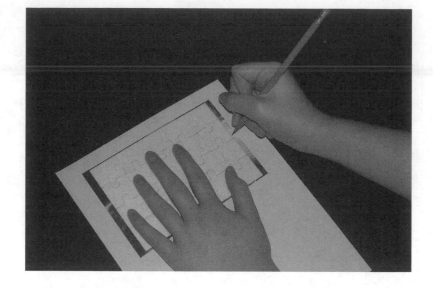

Illustration 5

DIRECTIONS FOR IRON-ON JIGSAW PUZZLE

1. Open a new drawing document in a graphics program such as *AppleWorks®, FreeHand®,* or *Illustrator®.*

2. Turn on Grid and Rulers. (Refer to the previous section on **Grid and Rulers** in **Graphic Skills**.)

3. Using the Rectangle Tool, draw a rectangle slightly larger than the dimensions of the iron-on jigsaw puzzle (i.e., if your puzzle is 4 x 6 inches, make your rectangle 4⅛ x 6⅛ inches). Using the Select Tool, select and move the rectangle on the page, placing it 1 inch or more from any edge of the document to avoid "clipping" from your printer.

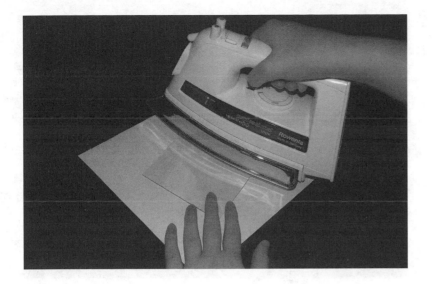

Illustration 6

4. Open a photo image in a photo editing program such as Adobe® *Photoshop*®, or a graphics program such as *FreeHand*®, or *Illustrator*®.

5. Crop and resize the image to the approximate size of the rectangle and the iron-on jigsaw puzzle. (Or, be prepared to resize the image once it has been pasted. Refer to the previous section on **Scale** in **Graphic Skills**.)

6. Using the Select Tool, select the cropped image. Copy it to the clipboard.

7. Paste the image from the clipboard into the new document. While the image is selected, drag and center it within the rectangle.

8. Delete the rectangle (but only the rectangle, not the image). (See *Design Tip* for **Where Did That Line Go?**)

9. If there is text within your image, it is absolutely necessary to flip the image horizontally before printing or your text will be backwards. Or, choose Mirror, Reverse, Flip, or Back Print in the printer options to print your image with the correct orientation.

10. Print a test copy on standard inkjet paper. (See *Printing Tip* for **Printing a Test Copy**)

11. Print the image on the iron-on transfer paper. Be sure to print on the proper side of the iron-on transfer paper.

12. Allow the image to dry completely.

13. Place the iron-on jigsaw puzzle over the image printed on the iron-on transfer paper and mark the dimensions of the puzzle. *(See Illustration 4.)*

14. Cut away the excess transfer paper, making the transfer paper the same size as the puzzle. *(See Illustration 5.)*

Illustration 7

15. Preheat the iron on the highest setting for 8 minutes. Do not use steam.

16. On a flat, solid, and hard surface (not an ironing board), place the transfer paper face down on the fuzzy side of the jigsaw puzzle. Press the pre-heated iron firmly on the iron-on transfer, moving the iron in a constant circular motion to the edges of the puzzle. Continue for approximately 30 seconds for small puzzles (4 x 6 inch) to 2 minutes for larger puzzles (8 x 10 inch). *(See Illustration 6.)*

17. Allow the puzzle to cool for 15 to 20 minutes.

18. Pull away the backing from the jigsaw puzzle, starting at one corner and pulling slowly across the puzzle. *(See Illustration 7.)*

19. Separate the puzzle pieces. Take your time, carefully loosening and separating the pieces one row at a time, and then one piece at a time.

QUICK TIPS

PRINTING TIP

■ **Conserving Your Iron-On Transfer**
If printing more than one image on an iron-on transfer paper, remember to copy and paste all images before printing. Or, print one image at the top of the page, cut off the ragged edges, turn the paper around, and then print the next image on the other end of the paper.

COUNTING HANDS

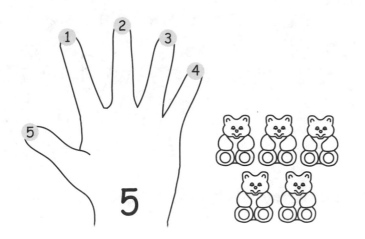

What You'll Need

Materials
- White printer paper, 8½" x 11"
- Laminating pouches, 8¾" x 11¾"
- Bear counters
- Magnets
- Optional: Inkjet clear decal, 8½" x 11"

Tools
- Heat laminator
- Hot glue gun
- Magnetic board
- Stand

Art
- Scanned image, computer graphic, or clip art

Software
- Graphics program

Hardware
- Color printer

Level of Difficulty
- Simple

In an effort to create a strategy that might assist Ashley with counting, I decided to capitalize on using the images of hands to design some of her educational materials for math. Her hands are always with her and, because Ashley uses sign language to represent numbers, I thought it would be natural for her to associate a representation of numbers with an image showing the fingers of the hand.

Interestingly, the word "digit" (used to define numbers 0 thru 9) is also a word for "fingers." In fact, it is believed that our decimal system (based on 10) came about because we have 10 fingers. Fingers were often used for counting and computing. People still use their fingers to count and represent numbers. So using images of a hand to represent the numbers to ten seemed a reasonable accommodation for Ashley.

To create the images of the hands, I scanned my hand and then traced around the image in a graphics program. I added yellow circles (for high contrast) to the tips of each finger and then placed the corresponding numeral within each circle. I added a larger numeral for the total number of fingers represented by the entire hand. I then printed the materials and attached them to a magnetic board.

Using a hot glue gun, I attached magnets to the backs of yellow bear counters. Ashley then placed these bears on each finger, in the proper numerical order, with one to one correspondence as we counted out loud.

I'm giving you the images of the hands (on the CD-ROM in the back of the book), so you just have to open the files in a graphics program, add circles and text, and then print them out.

Surely you were counting on me to make this easy for you! It sure made learning to count to ten easy for Ashley!

Skills to Teach

- Visual perception
- ● Math
- Language
- Communication
- Reading
- Handwriting
- Self-help

Illustration 1

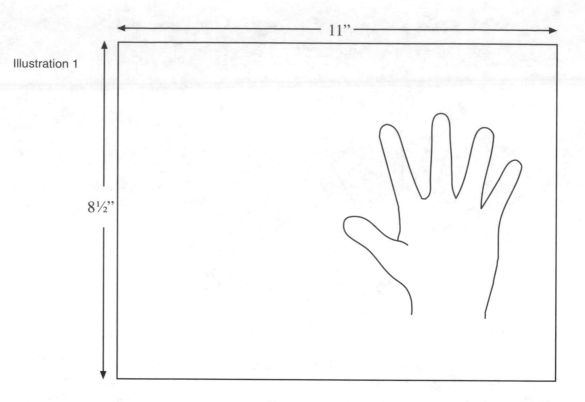

11"

8½"

DIRECTIONS

1. Open a new drawing document in a graphics program such as *AppleWorks®, FreeHand®,* or *Illustrator®.*

2. In the File Menu, select Page Setup. Change paper Orientation to Landscape. (Refer to the previous section on *Document Settings* in *Graphic Skills*.)

3. Turn on Grid and Rulers. (Refer to the previous section on *Grid and Rulers* in *Graphic Skills*.)

4. On the CD-ROM in the back of the book, open the file for the graphic image of the hand you desire.

5. Using the Select Tool, select and then copy the image to the clipboard.

6. Paste the image into the new drawing document and then move it to the right half of the page.

7. Using the Ellipse Tool, draw a circle that is approximately ½ x ½ inch in diameter.

8. Using the color yellow from the Color Palette, change the fill color and the line color of the circle to yellow.

9. Using the Select Tool, select the circle and copy it to the clipboard. Paste enough copies of the circle so that there is one circle for each finger of the hand.

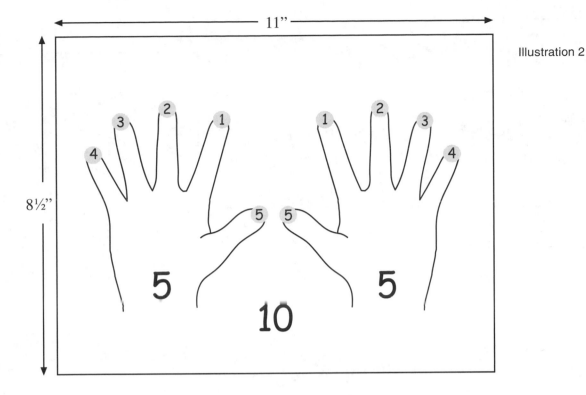

Illustration 2

10. Using the Select Tool, select each circle and move it to the tip of each finger of the hand.

11. Set the text size to 24 pts.

12. Using the Text Tool, type the numbers for each finger so that each number appears in a separate text frame.

13. Using the Select Tool, select and move each number inside the circle on the appropriate finger.

14. Set the text size to 72 pts.

15. Using the Text Tool, type the numeral for the total number of fingers represented for one or more hands.

16. Using the Select Tool, select and move the number at the base of the hand. *(See Illustration 2.)*

17. Optional: Using the Text Tool, type the number that represents all the fingers (that is, when the number is greater than 5 and represented by more than one hand). Using the Select Tool, move the number between the images of the two hands. *(See Illustration 2.)*

18. Print. (Optional: Print on clear inkjet decal and use with magnet board and stand.)

19. Laminate.

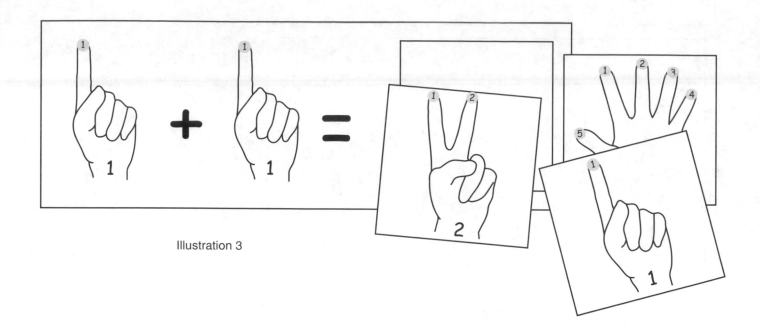

Illustration 3

DESIGN VARIATIONS

Math Problems Using Counting Hands

Consider creating math problems using counting hands as a bridge to more traditional math problems representing numbers with objects or numerals. *(See Illustration 3.)*

Illustration 4

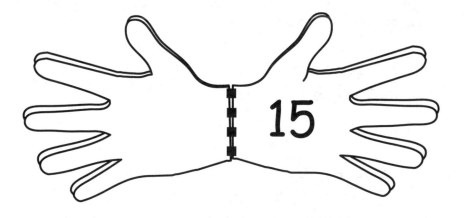

Counting by Fives

Consider creating a math book using hands to show counting by fives. Add numerals to each hand in increments of five on the graphic image of the hand showing five fingers. Comb bind the pages at the "wrist," and then count by fives out loud with your child while turning the pages. *(See Illustration 4.)*

MAGNETIC MODEL

Following a hard fought legal battle on her behalf, Ashley was routinely included in regular education classes through her middle school years. As she advanced in grades, however, the gap between the general education curriculum and Ashley's ability to participate became greater. Never one to easily give up on the tremendous benefit for Ashley to be with her nondisabled peers, there were occasions when I had to become rather creative to design a parallel adaptation for her.

This was very much the case when Ashley was given a 6th grade science assignment to create a model of a cell. Each student was expected to present their model to their classmates. "Edible cells" was the order of the day as many students created models from food: hard candies for Golgi bodies, licorice for mitochondria, and so on. Others created more conventional models from styrofoam or clay.

I headed to the computer once again to create a way for Ashley to construct her own model. Using a graphics program, I designed a magnetic model of a simple image of a cell. I created images of each of the cell's parts, printed them, adhered them to an adhesive magnetic sheet, and then cut them out. I then created a completed cell image. Using this image as a model, Ashley placed the magnetic cell parts onto a magnetic image of an empty cell. She then successfully presented the model to her class by using her augmentative communication (voice output) device. Programmed with descriptions of the cell's parts, Ashley pushed the buttons of her device designated by the various images: a vacuole, nucleus, etc. The communication device did the talking for her.

Did she learn the function of a mitochondria? No. But she learned to create a model by looking at a finished example. She learned to stand in front of her classmates. She learned to accept rousing applause. And she experienced what it felt like to be a contributing member of her class.

I learned that the idea of building a magnetic model can be used for many purposes. The following instructions will show you how to create a magnetic model to construct a pepperoni pizza for a math activity. I hope you find this magnetic idea as attractive as I did!

Illustration 1

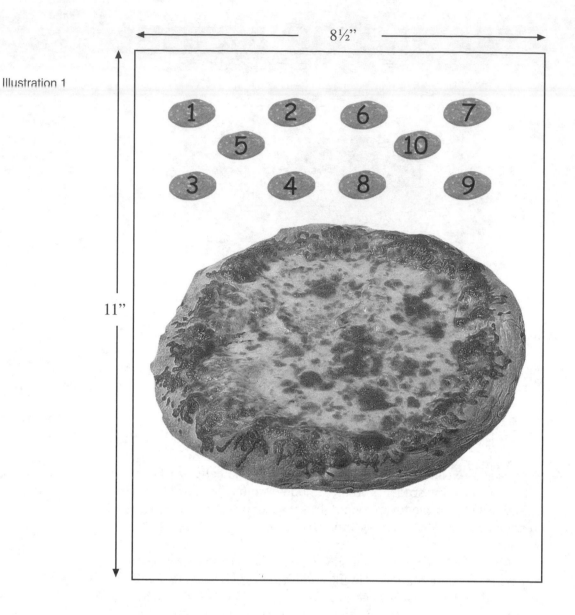

DIRECTIONS

1. Open a new drawing document in a graphics program such as *AppleWorks®, FreeHand®,* or *Illustrator®.*

2. Turn on Grid and Rulers. (Refer to the previous section on *Grid and Rulers* in *Graphic Skills*.)

3. Retrieve an image of a cheese pizza. (One is available in Hemera *Photo-Objects®.*)

4. Copy the image to the clipboard.

5. Paste the image into the new drawing document.

6. Using the Select Tool, select and then resize the image of the cheese pizza to approximately 7½ inches. (Refer to the previous section on *Scale* in *Graphic Skills*.)

7. Retrieve an image of a pepperoni. (One is available in Hemera *Photo-Objects®*.)

8. Copy the image to the clipboard.

9. Paste the image into the new drawing document.

10. Using the Select Tool, select and then resize the image of the pepperoni to approximately 1 inch. (Refer to the previous section on *Scale* in *Graphic Skills*.)

11. While the pepperoni is selected, copy it to the clipboard and paste 9 additional copies (or use the Duplicate command).

12. Using the Select Tool, select and move the images of the pepperonis. *(See Illustration 1.)*

13. Set the text size to 36 pts.

14. Using the Text Tool, number each of the pepperonis with the numerals 1-10. If necessary, change the text color to a color other than black to improve the contrast between the pepperoni and the text.

15. Print.

16. Adhere to a magnetic media. (See *Types of Magnetic Media: Choosing the Right One.*)

17. Cut out the images.

DESIGN VARIATION

Magnetic Model for Teaching Fractions

Food is a hard thing to beat for teaching fractions: halves of a sandwich or banana *(see Illustration 2)*, fourths or eighths of a pie or pizza. *(see Illustration 3 on the next page)*. In the absence of using real food, and as a way to avoid messy manipulatives, photographs of meaning-

Illustration 2

Illustration 3

ful food items can be used to make some awesome magnetic models to represent fractions.

Nothing says the text for the fractions must be black; change the text color to white, or another color, if this improves the contrast between the photograph and the text. (See ***Controlling Variables: Text*** on ***Contrast, Use of Colored Ink,*** and ***Competing Background***.)

FLASH CARDS

Flash cards have lots of uses and are easy to create using a computer and an inkjet printer. They can be used as a communication tool with single words or simple phrases on one side and the corresponding image on the back. And, whether you use a simple image or pair the image with text, it can be a powerful and efficient communication strategy.

Flash cards can also be used for practicing math facts when laid out with a math problem on one side and the solution on the other. Or they can also be hole punched, placed on a ring, and attached to a backpack or purse like the example above.

I'm going to teach you how to create flash cards with information printed on both sides of printable card stock. And, most importantly, you will learn how to match up the information on the front with the information on the back.

These instructions show how to create flash cards for learning new words in sign language. But don't feel limited by this example; flash cards have a myriad of uses and are easy to create once you learn a few simple steps. Use your new skill for many different activities, including:
- ordering food at a restaurant
- learning or reviewing sight word vocabulary
- keeping track of a daily schedule
- learning to associate names and faces, or
- reviewing words and their definitions.

Look at the examples at the end of this section to see many kinds of flash cards you can create!

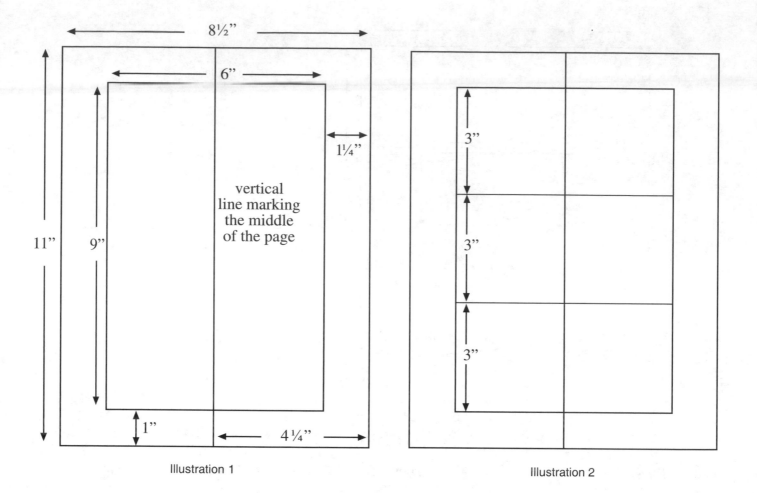

Illustration 1   Illustration 2

DIRECTIONS

1. Open a new drawing document in a graphics program such as *AppleWorks®, FreeHand®,* or *Illustrator®.*

2. Turn on Grid and Rulers. (Refer to the previous section on **Grid and Rulers** in **Graphic Skills**.)

Front

3. Draw a vertical line as a guide, splitting the page into two equal parts. (The line will be placed along the horizontal axis at 4¼ inches.)

4. Using the Rectangle Tool, draw a 6 x 9 inch rectangle centered on the vertical line that marks the middle of the page (1¼ inches from the right edge of the page and 1 inch above the bottom of the page). *(See Illustration 1.)*

5. Using the Line Tool, divide the rectangle into 6 equal parts by drawing two horizontal lines at 3 inch intervals. *(See Illustration 2.)*

6. Save the document with a distinct file name, such as "Flash Card Template" for later use.

7. Copy and paste 6 images (each approximately 2 x 2 inches) into the drawing document. (Or, be prepared to resize a smaller or

Illustration 3: Front Side

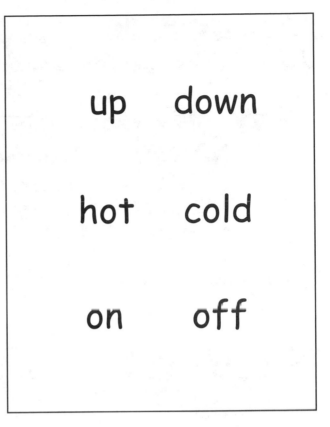

Illustration 4: Back Side

larger image once it has been pasted. Refer to the previous section on *Scale* in *Graphic Skills*.)

8. Using the Select Tool, select, move, and center each image within one of the 6 squares. *(See Illustration 3.)*

9. Save the document with a distinct file name, such as "Flash Card Front."

10. Print a copy of the front side of the flash cards on printable card stock.

Back

11. Open the Flash Card Front file you just created.

12. Set the text size to 72 points.

13. Using the Text Tool, type the names of each of the six images so that each line of text is in a separate text frame.

14. Using the Select Tool, select and move the name of each image in the opposite column that the image appears on the Front. For example, if the image for the sign for "up" appears at the top of the page in the left column, place the word "up" at the top of the page in the right column. *(See Illustration 3 and 4.)*

QUICK TIPS

DESIGN TIP
- **Keeping Two Files Open At One Time**
When creating an educational tool with information printed on both sides of the paper, it is helpful to keep both files for the "front" and "back" open on your desktop at the same time.

DRAWING TIP
- **Making Lines Disappear Without Deleting Them**
You can make lines not appear when printed yet have them remain in a document. This can be accomplished by changing the line width to "None" or the line color to "white." Why bother? If you ever want to use an old file as a template, the lines will guide you as to where to properly place new images or text.

15. Delete all lines (or read the *Drawing Tip* for **Making Lines Disappear Without Deleting Them**) leaving only the text.

16. Save the document with a distinct file name, such as "Flash Card Back."

17. Print a copy of the back side by turning the previously printed card stock over and then running it through the printer a second time.

18. Heat laminate the card stock.

19. Using the printed lines on the front of the card stock, cut the laminated copy into six individual flash cards.

20. Hole punch each flash card and place on a loose-leaf ring.

Flash cards for learning sign language vocabulary

Flash cards for ordering food at a restaurant

Flash cards for learning sight word vocabulary

Flash cards for daily schedule

Flash cards for communication

Flash cards for math facts

Flash cards for learning names and faces

Flash cards for definitions of words

FLIP BOOK

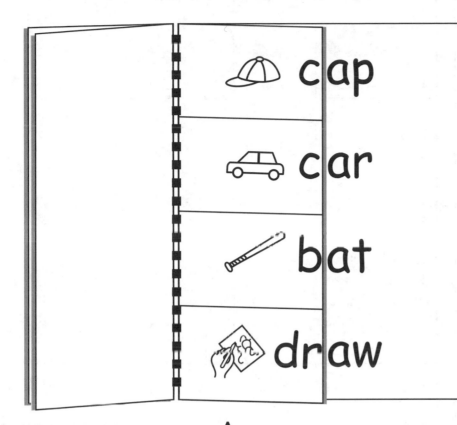

What You'll Need

Materials
- White printer paper or printable card stock, 8½" x 11"
- Laminating pouches, 8¾" x 11¼"
- Plastic binding comb

Tools
- Scissors
- Heat laminator
- Comb binder

Art
- Scanned image, computer graphic, or clip art

Software
- Graphics program

Hardware
- Color printer

Level of Difficulty
- Moderate

Ashley always needs many visual presentations to review previously learned information, or to introduce new concepts. Flip books are just one more idea I have "up my sleeve." And you should, too!

Flip books are comprised of a base page and a series of flip cards layered on top. By changing ("flipping") the flip cards, new words, letter patterns, or images are created. It is a great visual tool, and interactive as well.

With flip books, you can combine pieces of text to create new words:
- onsets and rimes for word families (see p. 151 for definitions)
- -ed endings to create past tense words,
- -s to create plurals.

Or, add different prepositional phrases to a simple phrase to create brand new sentences.

And, flip books are easy to modify and customize, so you make them as easy or challenging as you need. Use photos or icons; alter the shape and layout; and even create double or triple flip books (see the Design Variations). Once you master the simple flip book, you will see lots of uses and design modifications to suit your child's needs, and you'll wonder why you hadn't thought of doing them before!

Skills to Teach

Visual perception
Math
● Language
Communication
● Reading
Handwriting
Self-help

Illustration 1

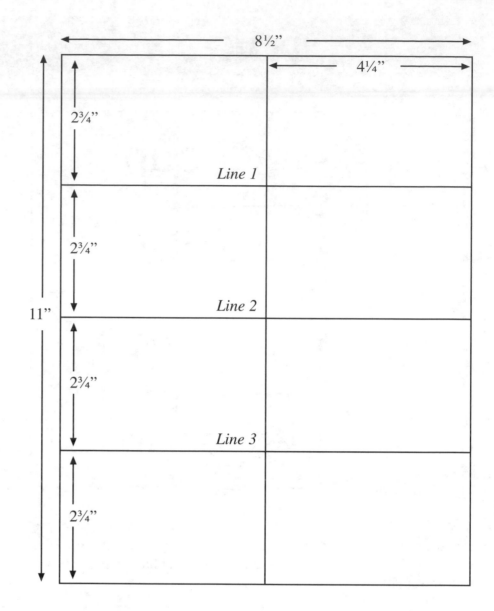

The following directions create a flip book comprised of one base and 4 flip cards.

DIRECTIONS

1. Open a new drawing document in a graphics program such as *AppleWorks®, FreeHand®,* or *Illustrator®.*

2. Turn on Grid and Rulers. (Refer to the previous section on ***Grid and Rulers*** in ***Graphic Skills***.)

3. Using the Line Tool, split the page in half by drawing a vertical line the length of the page located 4¼ inches from the right edge of the page. (This is your cutting line.)

4. Using the Line Tool, draw the following lines:

   ■ **Line 1:** a horizontal line the width of the page located 2¾ inches below the top edge of the page

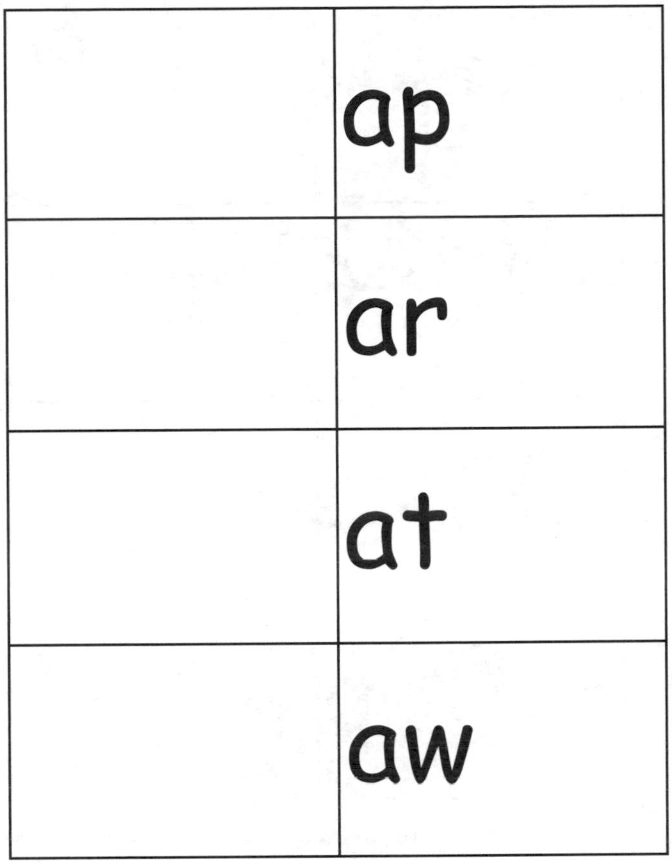

	ap
	ar
	at
	aw

Illustration 2

🧢	cap
🚗	car
🏏	bat
✏️	draw

Illustration 3

- **Line 2:** a horizontal line the width of the page located 2¾ inches below Line 1

- **Line 3:** a horizontal line the width of the page located 2¾ inches below Line 2. *(See Illustration 1.)*

5. Set the text size to 100 pts.

6. Using the Text Tool, type the rimes for 4 word families (in 4 separate text frames).

7. Using the Select Tool, select, move, center, and place each rime inside one of the four rectangles just to the right of the center dividing line. Place the text close to the center dividing line. *(See Illustration 2.)*

8. Using the Text Tool, type the onsets for the 4 word families (in 4 separate text frames).

9. Using the Select Tool, select, move, center, and place each onset inside one of the four rectangles just to the left of the center dividing line. Place the text close to the center dividing line. *(See Illustration 3.)* Note: Be sure that the text lines up horizontally across the center dividing line.

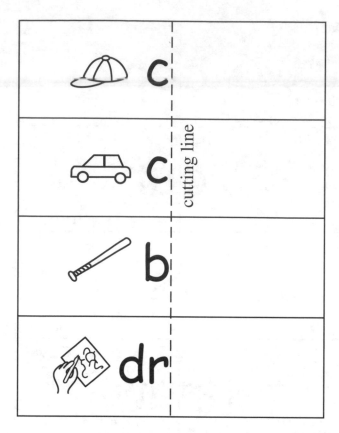

Illustration 4: Flip Card 1

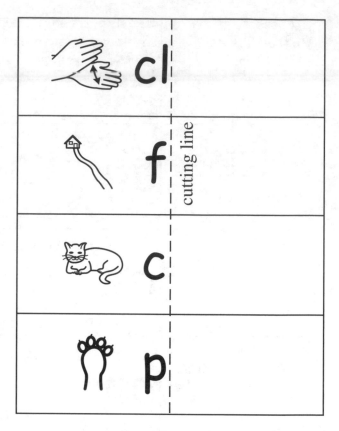

Illustration 5: Flip Card 2

10. Copy a 2 x 2 inch image to the clipboard for the particular word represented by the first onset and rime. (Or, be prepared to resize a smaller or larger image once it has been pasted. Refer to the previous section on *Scale* in *Graphic Skills*.)

11. Paste the image into the document. Using the Select Tool, select and move the image to the left of the initial letter for the word it matches.

12. Copy and paste additional 2 x 2 inch images for each onset and rime. Using the Select Tool, select and move each image to the left side of its corresponding intial letter. *(See Illustration 3.)*

13. At this point, this image needs to be saved. Save it with a distinct file name, such as "Flip Book Base" (you'll work on the Flip Book Base a bit later). Now you will continue to work with the image you've created so far.

Flip Card 1

14. Delete the rimes on the right side of the center dividing line.

15. Save the image with a distinct file name, such as "Flip Book Card 1." *(See Illustration 4.)*

Flip Card 2

16. Using the Text Tool, change the onsets (initial letter) to the next set of words to be created.

17. Replace each 2 x 2 inch image by copying and pasting new images for the particular word represented by the onset and rime.

18. Save the image with a distinct file name, such as "Flip Book Card 2." *(See Illustration 5.)*

Flip Card 3 and 4

19. Repeat steps 16-18.

Flip Base

20. Open the previously saved document called "Flip Book Base."

21. Delete the onsets and all images to the left of the center dividing line.

22. Delete all lines.

23. Save the changes, using the same file name "Flip Book Base."

24. Print all Flip Card files and the "Flip Base."

25. Heat laminate all pages.

26. Line up all pages and comb bind them together.

27. Using scissors, cut along the center dividing line on all flip cards, removing the right side of the page.

28. Start flipping!

> **WHAT ARE ONSETS AND RIMES?**
>
> An "onset" is the letter or group of letters that come before the vowel in a word. The "rime" includes the vowel and all that follows. In the word "hat," h- is the onset and -at is the rime.

> **QUICK TIPS**
>
> **BINDING TIPS**
> - **Where to Go**
>   If you don't have access to a comb binder, run to a national office supply company (like Office Depot) or a national copying company (like Kinko's) and they will comb bind your flip book for you.
>
> - **Binding Smaller Documents**
>   Although plastic binding combs come in standard sizes, nothing says that you cannot bind smaller books. Bind the pages of a smaller book first and then cut off the excess plastic binding comb with a pair of scissors.

DESIGN VARIATIONS

Nothing says you cannot bind on either the right or left side of the page, or both! This example uses various prepositional phrases to create new sentences.

By binding on two sides you can create a flip book for past tense words. The left side is a stack of verbs. The right side is a single flip card with the -ed ending. When the card with the -ed ending is flipped back the word is present tense. When the card with the -ed ending is flipped forward the word becomes past tense.

The verbs chosen must be regular verbs: they cannot be irregular verbs or require more than an -ed ending to make the verb past tense (play and played, but not hop and hopped, teach and taught, or cry and cried).

You can pair text with images if you like. But I do not like using images when adding -ed endings to create past tense words because the image is a present tense image. Have you ever thought how to visually represent a past tense action? It isn't easy.

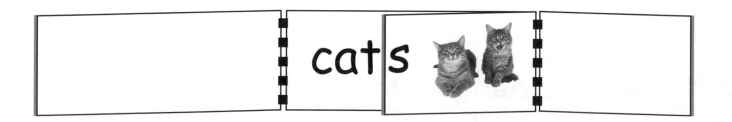

You can create a flip book to show plurals by adding text to a noun and by changing the image associated with it. The card with the word "cat" on it is paired with a single image of a cat (which is covered and does not show in the example above). The flip card makes the word plural by adding an -s which is also paired with an image of two cats.

SIMPLE SLIDER

What You'll Need

Materials
- White printer paper or printable card stock, 8½" x 11"
- Laminating pouches, 8¾" x 11¼"

Tools
- Scissors
- X-Acto knife
- Straight edge
- Heat laminator

Art
- Scanned image, computer graphic, or clip art

Software
- Graphics program

Hardware
- Color printer

Level of Difficulty
- Simple

In reinforcing the concept of word families, I was always experimenting with methods for Ashley to manipulate text. Sliders—made up of a rectangular base and a long card that slides up and down, exposing letters and images in the base's window—proved to be a great way for Ashley to do this. I especially wanted her to learn how changing the initial letters of words creates new words. I wanted her to understand "word families." Being able to identify new words with similar spelling patterns expanded Ashley's reading vocabulary.

Pairing an icon with each word gave meaning to the text to Ashley. She could look at one word and its icon at a time: the one appearing in the window. Presenting new words this way helped Ashley learn to decode letter and word patterns.

From a practical perspective, sliders are also great because they are compact, have no loose parts, and can be taken anywhere. If your child does not need the presence of the icons, by all means, leave them off.

If you are targeting a particular word family, or certain words, create exactly what you need. That's the beauty of making your own sliders on your computer: it is all up to you!

Skills to Teach

Visual perception
Math
● Language
Communication
● Reading
Handwriting
Self-help

Illustration 1

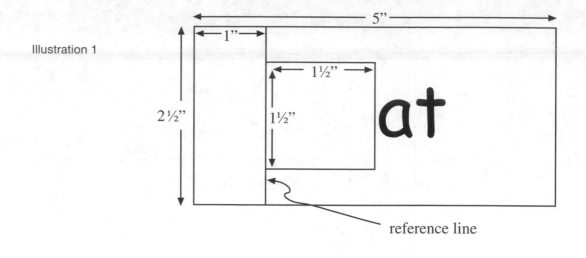

reference line

DIRECTIONS

Base

1. Open a new drawing document in a graphics program such as *AppleWorks®, FreeHand®,* or *Illustrator®.*

2. Turn on Grid and Rulers. (Refer to the previous section on **Grid and Rulers** in **Graphic Skills**.)

3. Using the Rectangle Tool, draw a 2½ x 5 inch rectangle.

4. Using the Line Tool, draw a vertical line 1 inch in from the left edge of the rectangle. (This line is only a reference line and will be deleted shortly.)

5. Using the Rectangle Tool, draw a 1½ x 1½ inch square. Using the Select Tool, select and move the square, placing it equidistant from the top and bottom of the rectangle and just to the right side of the vertical reference line. *(See Illustration 1.)*

6. Using the Select Tool, select the vertical reference line and now delete it.

7. Set the text size to 72 points.

8. Using the Text Tool, type the vowel and the letter(s) that follows the vowel of the chosen word family (called the "rime"). Using the Select Tool, select and move the text close to the right side of the square. *(See Illustration 1.)*

9. Save the Base with a distinct file name, such as "Simple Slider Base."

Slide Card

10. Open a new drawing document.

11. Turn on Grid and Rulers. (Refer to the previous section on **Grid and Rulers** in **Graphic Skills**.)

12. Using the Rectangle Tool, draw a 9 x 1½ inch rectangle.

13. Set the text size to 72 points.

14. Using the Text Tool, type the letter(s) before the vowel (called the "onset") of all the words to be created for the chosen word family. Using the Select Tool, select and move each onset along the right edge of the Slide Card, spacing them vertically at approximately 1½ inches apart or greater. (Note: If you space them closer together you run the risk of two onsets showing at the same time in the window.)

15. Copy a 1 x 1 inch image to the clipboard for the particular word represented by an onset on the slide card. (Or, be prepared to re-size a smaller or larger image once it has been pasted. Refer to the previous section on *Scale* in *Graphic Skills*.)

16. Paste the image into the Slide Card. Using the Select Tool, select and move the image to the left of the initial letter for the word it matches.

17. Copy and paste additional 1 x 1 inch images for each onset on the Slide Card. Using the Select Tool, select and move each image to the left side of its corresponding intial letter. *(See Illustration 2.)*

18. Save the Slide Card with a distinct file name, such as "Simple Slider Slide Card."

19. Print one copy of both the Base and Slide Card (preferably on printable card stock).

20. Heat laminate each copy.

21. Cut out the Base and Slide Card.

22. Using an X-Acto knife and a straight edge, make two horizontal slits in the Base along the top and bottom hortizontal lines of the interior square. *(See Illustration 3.)*

Illustration 2: Slide Card

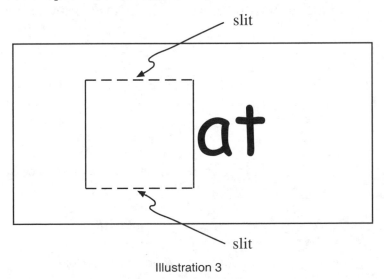

Illustration 3

23. Feed the Slide Card through the two slits.

WHAT ARE ONSETS AND RIMES?

An "onset" is the letter or group of letters that come before the vowel in a word. The "rime" includes the vowel and all that follows. In the word "hat," h- is the onset and -at is the rime.

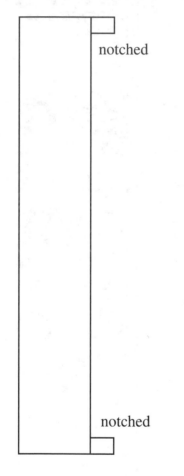

notched

notched

Illustration 4

DESIGN VARIATIONS

You may be wondering why there are only 4 onsets and images on the Slide Card, allowing the creation of only 4 words. That is because there are certain restrictions in the design and construction of Sliders that influence how they are created.

Problems occur when onsets and images are placed at the very top and bottom of the Slide Card. Often, the Slide Card is pulled out of the Base as you try to position the onsets and images within the window opening. If you want to increase the number of words to be created for a particular word family, here are three suggestions:

1. Reduce the height of the window on the Base and then space the onsets closer together on the Slide Card. The onsets should be no closer together than the height of the window (that is, if the window is 1½ inches in height, the spacing between the onsets on the slider must be 1½ inches or greater). Remember that reducing the size of the window may affect the size of the text that can be seen within the window opening.

2. Design your Slider on a document that is 8½ x 14 inches by changing the Document Setup and printing on legal sized paper.

3. Cut the Slide Card out with a notch at the top and bottom. *(See Illustration 4.)* This will keep the Slide Card from pulling out of the Base when more onsets and images are placed at the very top and bottom of the Slide Card.

QUICK TIPS

DESIGN TIP
■ **Sliders for Longer Words**
If you begin creating Sliders with onsets of blends rather than only one letter, such as sh-, ch-, or br-, enlarge the window of the Base and widen the dimension of the Slide Card to accommodate them.

POCKET SLIDER

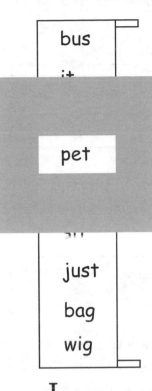

bus

it

pet

sit

just

bag

wig

I remember as a child using a ruler to help me read. Placed horizontally on the page of a book, I moved the ruler vertically down the page, reading each line of text just above the ruler's edge. For some reason, this seemed to help the ease and speed of my reading.

A somewhat similar concept (to a ruler) is the typoscope. Used by persons with low vision, it improves reading by allowing a reader (like Ashley) to focus on a single line of text.

Typoscopes are created by cutting a window in a small sheet of black mat board or plastic. The dimensions of the window correspond to the dimensions of one line of text. The typoscope is used like the ruler, isolating one line of text in the window as the typoscope is moved down the page.

A slider designed like the example above functions much the same as a typoscope. Ease of reading is improved because a single image is isolated and because there is high contrast between the color of the slider and the base. This is achieved by printing the base on colored paper, or by filling the square of the base with color in a graphics program so that the color is created from the inkjet printer (I'll show you how—it's easy). The slider is printed on white paper with black text.

The following pages will show you ways pocket sliders can be used, and fun ways in which they can be designed.

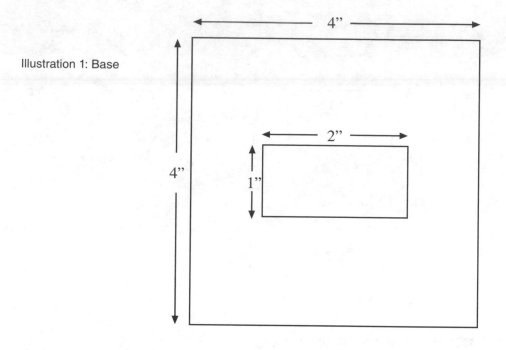

Illustration 1: Base

DIRECTIONS
Base

1. Open a new drawing document in a graphics program such as *AppleWorks®, FreeHand®,* or *Illustrator®*.

2. Turn on Grid and Rulers. (Refer to the previous section on **Grid and Rulers** in **Graphic Skills**.)

3. Using the Rectangle Tool, draw a 4 x 4 inch square for the Base. *(See Illustration 1. Also see Illustration 6, 7, and 8 for design ideas.)*

4. Using the Rectangle Tool, draw a 1 x 2 inch rectangle.

5. While selected, move and center the smaller rectangle in the middle of the Base. *(See Illustration 1.)*

6. Save the Base with a distinct file name, such as "Pocket Base."

Slide Card

7. Open a new drawing document.

8. Using the Rectangle Tool, draw a 9 x 2 inch rectangle.

9. Set the text size to 36 points.

10. Using the Text Tool, type the designated text so that each line of text is in a separate text frame. *(See Illustration 2, 3, and 4 for ideas.)*

11. Using the Select Tool, select and move each line of text, centering and spacing them vertically, and approximately 1 inch apart or greater.

12. Save the Slide Card with a distinct file name, such as "Pocket Slide Card."

QUICK TIPS

DESIGN TIP
■ **Spacing Images On the Slide Card**
The distance between images on a Slide Card should be greater than or equal to the height of the window in the Base. Otherwise, two images can show in the window of the Base at the same time.

CUTTING TIP
■ **Notching the Slide Card**
Consider cutting notches at the top and bottom of the Slide Card if text or images appear at the very top or very bottom. This will keep the Slide Card from being pulled out of the Base. (See **Simple Slider**.)

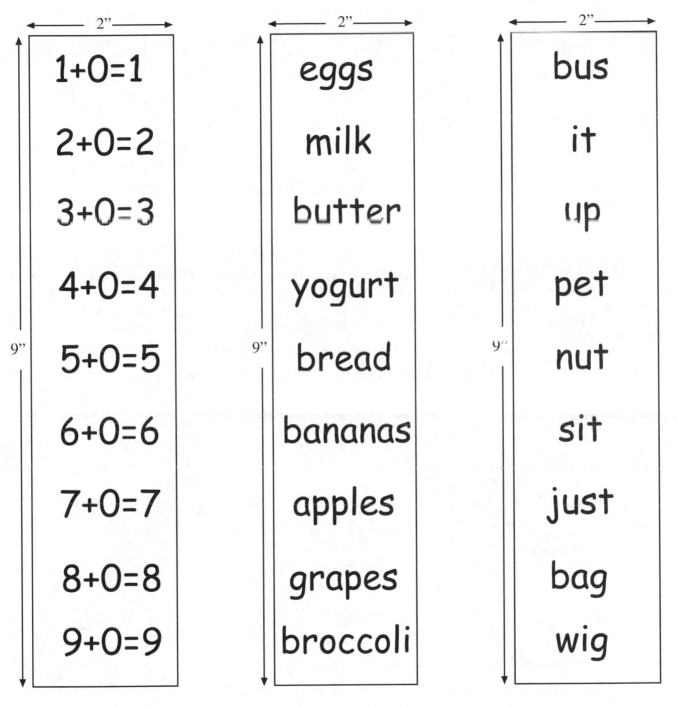

Illustration 2: Slide Card
Used for Math Facts

Illustration 3: Slide Card
Used for Grocery List

Illustration 4: Slide Card
Used for 1st Grade Spelling List

Illustration 5

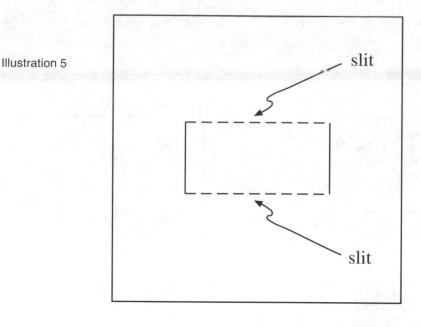

13. Print one copy of the Base on colored paper. Print one copy of the Slide Card on white paper (preferably on printable card stock).

14. Heat laminate each copy.

15. Cut out the Base and Slide Card.

16. Using an X-Acto knife and a straight edge, make two horizontal slits in the Base along the top and bottom hortizontal lines of the interior square. *(See Illustration 5.)*

17. Feed the Slide Card through the two slits.

DESIGN VARIATIONS

There are fun and creative ways to create the Base of the Pocket Slider. As long as design does not get in the way of function, be creative!

Illustration 6

Illustration 7

The Pocket Slider in *Illustration 6* was created in *AppleWorks*® by drawing a rectangle with rounded corners, filling it with a denim texture, and then creating a contrasting line to look like stitching.

Many graphics programs have the ability to create rectangles with rounded corners. For some programs, there is a completely separate tool. For others, it is a part of the Rectangle Tool—the radius of the corners can be selected. Many graphics programs also have pre-set fill textures, such as denim.

The contrast stitching was created by copying and pasting (or duplicating) the original exterior line and then resizing it to 90 percent (of its original size). The line color was then changed to a shade of orange (to mimic Levi's® jeans).

The Pocket Slider in *Illustration 7* was created with Adobe® *Illustrator*®. A rectangle was drawn using the Rounded Rectangle Tool. It was then filled with a dark blue color by selecting a color from the Color Palette and using the Paint Bucket tool, and dressed up with a contrasting dashed line to look like stitching.

Not all graphics programs have the ability to create a dashed line. Check the index of your software manual.

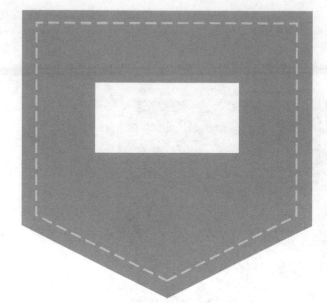

Illustration 8

The Pocket Slider in *Illustration 8* was created with Macromedia®
FreeHand®. The shape was created using 5 individual lines. The lines
were brought together at the intersections using the Join command. This
created a closed shape which was then filled with color by dragging a
color swatch from the Color Palette to the object.

Objects created using individual lines can appear closed, but if the
Join command is not used, the object cannot contain color or texture. It
is analogous to a box with four sides; the corners may be touching but
not glued. Therefore, the box will not hold anything.

DOUBLE SLIDER

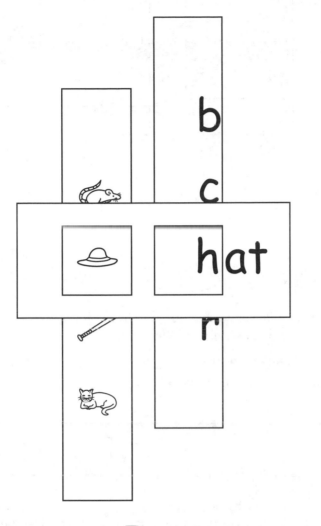

What You'll Need

Materials
- White printer paper or printable card stock, 8½" x 11"
- Laminating pouches, 8¾" x 11¼"

Tools
- Scissors
- X-Acto knife
- Straight edge
- Heat laminator

Art
- Scanned image, computer graphic, or clip art

Software
- Graphics program

Hardware
- Color printer

Level of Difficulty
- Moderate

Double sliders are a bit different from simple sliders. Simple sliders are designed without right or wrong answers. Nothing must be matched; information is only manipulated. Although simple sliders are useful, for teaching or reviewing, double sliders are more interactive. The two slide cards relate to one another and must be positioned so that images in both windows correspond. In the example above, children learn to match both the image for a specific word and its initial letter.

Double sliders are a great way to teach word families and to test that knowledge. This is a useful tool for Ashley since she does not have to utter a word to show her understanding.

Note: Since there is a right and wrong correspondence between the two windows, it is best to supervise their use so that the wrong information is not reinforced or self-taught incorrectly.

Skills to Teach

- Visual perception
- ● Math
- ● Language
- Communication
- ● Reading
- Handwriting
- Self-help

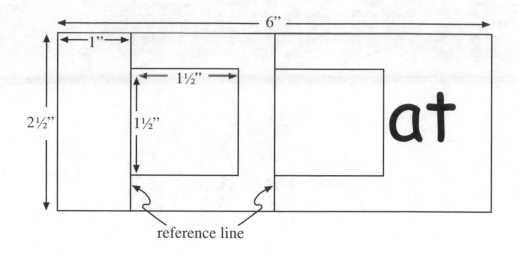

Illustration 1: Base

DIRECTIONS
Base

1. Open a new drawing document in a graphics program such as *AppleWorks®, FreeHand®,* or *Illustrator®.*

2. Turn on Grid and Rulers. (Refer to the previous section on **Grid and Rulers** in **Graphic Skills**.)

3. Using the Rectangle Tool, draw a 2½ x 6 inch rectangle.

4. Using the Line Tool, draw a vertical line 1 inch in from the left edge of the rectangle and another vertical line that divides the rectangle in half. (These lines are only reference lines and will be deleted shortly.)

5. Using the Rectangle Tool, draw two 1½ x 1½ inch squares. Using the Select Tool, select and move one square, placing it equidistant from the top and bottom of the rectangle and just to the right side of the first vertical reference line. Using the Select Tool, select and move the other square, placing it equidistant from the top and bottom of the rectangle and just to the right side of the second vertical reference line. *(See Illustration 1: Base.)*

6. Using the Select Tool, select and then delete both vertical reference lines.

7. Set the text size to 72 points.

8. Using the Text Tool, type the last two letters of the chosen word family (called the "rime"). Using the Select Tool, select and move the text close to the right side of the second square. *(See Illustration 1: Base.)*

9. Save the Base with a distinct file name, such as "Double Slider Base."

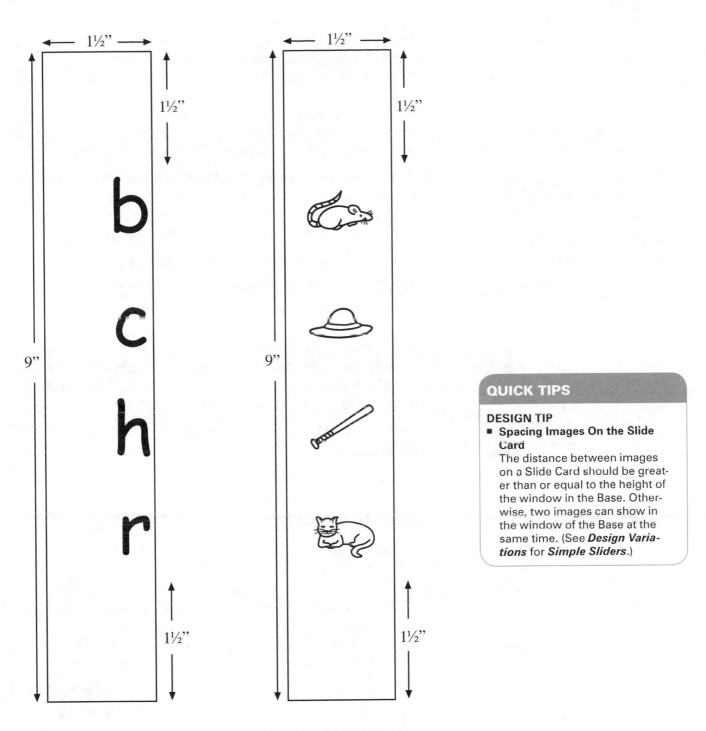

Illustration 2: Slide Card #1   Illustration 3: Slide Card #2

QUICK TIPS

DESIGN TIP
■ **Spacing Images On the Slide Card**
The distance between images on a Slide Card should be greater than or equal to the height of the window in the Base. Otherwise, two images can show in the window of the Base at the same time. (See *Design Variations* for *Simple Sliders*.)

Slide Cards

10. Open a new drawing document.

11. Turn on Grid and Rulers. (Refer to the previous section on *Grid and Rulers* in *Graphic Skills*.)

12. Using the Rectangle Tool, draw two 9 x 1½ inch rectangles.

13. Set the text size to 72 points.

14. Using the Text Tool, type the initial letter (called the "onset") of the four words to be created for the chosen word family so that each onset is in a separate text frame. Using the Select Tool, select and move each onset along the right edge of one of the Slide Cards, spacing them vertically at approximately 1½ inches apart or greater. Leave approximately 1½ inches at the top and bottom of the Slide Card. *(See Illustration 2: Slide Card #1.)*

15. Copy a 1 x 1 inch image to the clipboard for the particular word represented by an onset on the first Slide Card. (Or, be prepared to resize a smaller or larger image once it has been pasted. Refer to the previous section on *Scale* in *Graphic Skills*.)

16. Paste the image into the drawing document. Using the Select Tool, select and move the image to the second Slide Card.

17. Copy and paste additional 1 x 1 inch images for each onset on the Slide Card. Using the Select Tool, select and move each image, spacing them vertically at approximately 1½ inches apart or greater. Leave approximately 1½ inches at the top and bottom of the Slide Card. Do not place them in the same order as the initial letters in Slide Card #1. *(See Illustration 3: Slide Card #2.)*

18. Save the Slide Card with a distinct file name, such as "Double Slider Cards."

19. Print one copy of both the Base and Slide Cards (preferably on printable card stock).

20. Heat laminate each copy.

21. Cut out the Base and the two Slide Cards.

Illustration 4

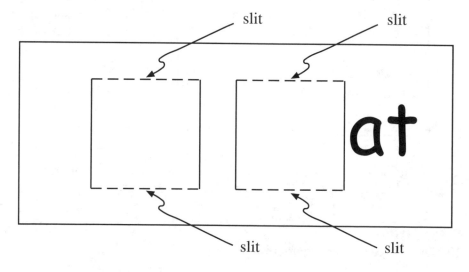

22. Using an X-Acto knife and a straight edge, make four horizontal slits in the Base along the top and bottom hortizontal lines of the two interior squares. *(See Illustration 4.)*

23. Feed the two Slide Card through the two sets of slits.

DESIGN VARIATIONS
Double Sliders for Longer Words

If you begin creating Sliders with onsets of blends, such as sh-, ch-, or br-, rather than only one letter, or rimes comprised of more than 2 letters, you can enlarge the window and the Base or widen the dimension of the Slide Card to accomodate them. *(See Illustration 5.)*

Double Sliders for Math Facts

Double sliders can be used for a set of math facts by reducing the size of the window of the Base and then placing more items on both Slide Cards. *(See Illustration 6.)*

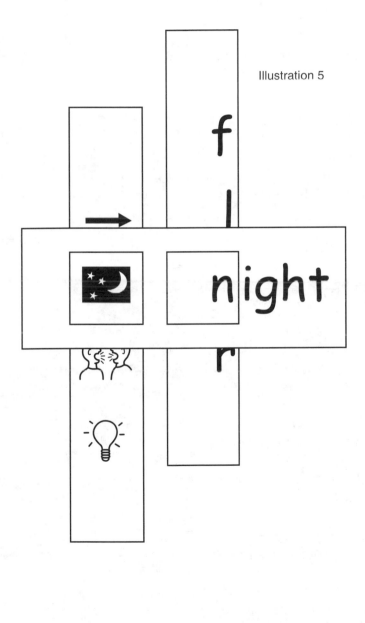

Illustration 5

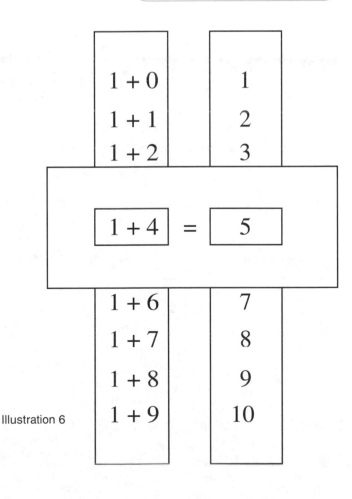

Illustration 6

BASIC WHEEL

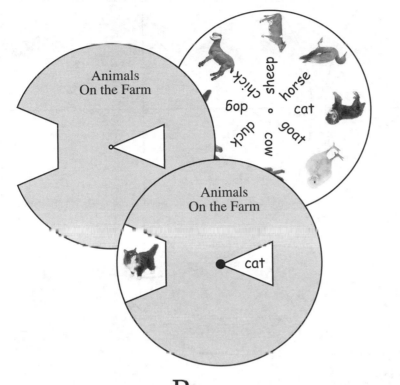

Animals On the Farm

Animals On the Farm

cat

Basic wheels are a great way to pack a lot of information into a small space. Their unique beauty is that images and text are isolated from surrounding visual clutter. The presentation is clean and straightforward. Basic wheels can be designed to be as simple or complicated as desired. And the font choice and image choice can be carefully controlled. Information can be grouped: family names and photographs; the pictures of the official bird, flower, and flag of a particular state and their corresponding names; or images of coins and their relative values.

For Ashley, wheels give her complete control over her selections. She can carry a wheel around anywhere, from the car to a restaurant, or to school. They are yet another interactive and innovative way to provide access to text and other information. They are foolproof—you don't have to supervise their use because they cannot be manipulated incorrectly—and fun!

The first time you try to create a basic wheel on the computer, you may find it moderately difficult. Orienting images and text correctly, and then properly placing them can seem tricky at first. But once you understand how the layout works, you'll be able to do them in your sleep, although I would not recommend it! I've made dozens of them, and will show you the easiest way to make them.

The following instructions provide the basic layout as well as variations of design options.

What You'll Need

Materials
- White printer paper or printable card stock, 8½" x 11"
- Laminating pouches, 8¾" x 11¼"
- Brass plated fastener

Tools
- Scissors
- Heat laminator
- X-Acto knife
- Straight edge

Art
- Scanned image, computer graphics, or clip art

Software
- Graphics program

Hardware
- Color printer

Level of Difficulty
- Moderate

Skills to Teach

Visual perception
- Math
- Language
- Communication
- Reading
Handwriting
- Self-help

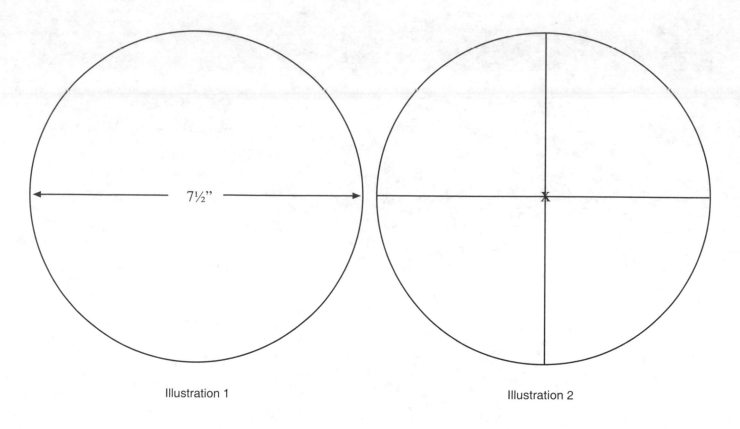

Illustration 1   Illustration 2

DIRECTIONS
Set-Up

1. Open a new drawing document in a graphics program such as *AppleWorks®, FreeHand®,* or *Illustrator®.*

2. Turn on Grid and Rulers. (Refer to the previous section on **Grid and Rulers** in **Graphic Skills**.)

3. Using the Ellipse Tool, draw a circle approximately 7½ inches in diameter. *(See Illustration 1.)*

4. Find the center of the circle. To do so, use the Line Tool to draw a horizontal reference line to divide the circle in half. Draw a vertical reference line to divide the circle in fourths. (These lines will be deleted later.)

5. Set the text size to 24 points or less.

6. Using the Text Tool, type a small "x." Place the "x" where the two reference lines intersect. *(See Illustration 2.)*

7. Using the Line Tool, draw two additional reference lines to divide the circle into 8 equal parts. *(See Illustration 3.)*

8. Using the Ellipse Tool, draw a second circle approximately 4 inches in diameter. Using the Select Tool, select and then move the second circle to the middle of the larger circle. *(See Illustration 4.)*

9. At this point, this image needs to be saved. Save it with a distinct file name, such as "Wheel Cover Template" (you'll work on the

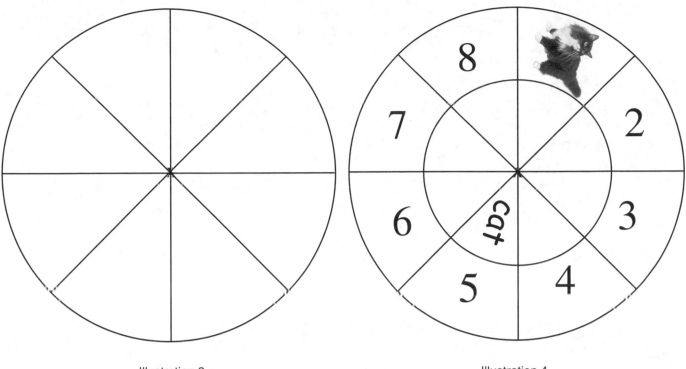

Illustration 3   Illustration 4

Wheel Cover a bit later). Now you will continue to work with the image you've created so far.

Wheel

10. Copy a 2 x 2 inch image to the clipboard. (Or, be prepared to re-size a smaller or larger image once it has been pasted. Refer to the previous section on *Scale* in *Graphic Skills*.)

11. Paste the image into the drawing document. While the image is selected, rotate the image 247 degrees. Drag and place the image within the section labeled "1" in *Illustration 4*, and move it to the outside edge of the circle.

12. Set the text size to 48 pts.

13. Using the Text Tool, type the name for the image that appears in section "1." While the text is selected, rotate it 247 degrees. Drag and place it within the inner circle of section 5.

14. Continue copying, pasting, rotating, and placing 7 more images into the last 7 sections as follows:

> section 2: rotate 202 degrees
> section 3: rotate 157 degrees
> section 4: rotate 112 degrees
> section 5: rotate 67 degrees
> section 6: rotate 22 degrees
> section 7: rotate 337 degrees
> section 8: rotate 292 degrees

QUICK TIPS

DESIGN TIP
▪ **Text Size**
   The font size often has to be adjusted up or down depending upon the font choice, the length of words, and the size of the area holding the text.

PRINTING TIP
▪ **The Size of Objects and the "Printable Area"**
   When drawing and printing larger objects that are close to the edge of the paper, "clipping" can occur if the object exceeds the "printable area." The "printable area" is a characteristic of each printer. To determine whether the size of an object exceeds the printable area of your printer, print a test copy once the object has been drawn.

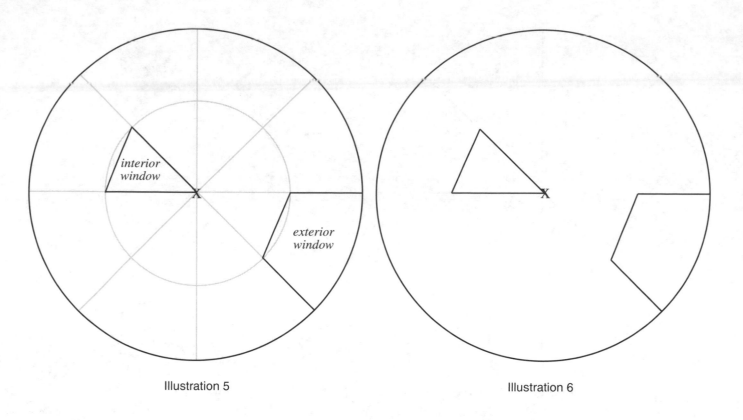

Illustration 5   Illustration 6

15. If the outer circle is partially covered by any pasted images, use the Select Tool to select and then Bring to Front the outer circle. (See *Arrange* in *Graphic Skills*.)

16. Continue typing the names of each image. While each name is selected, rotate it the same number of degrees as its corresponding image. Then drag and place the text to the section opposite the section holding its image. Each name should be placed in the interior portion of the middle (smaller) circle. *(See Illustration 4.)*

17. Save the image with a distinct file name, such as "Basic Wheel #1."

Cover

18. Open the previously saved document "Wheel Cover Template." This will serve as the image to create your cover.

19. Using the Line Tool, and utilizing the preexisting reference lines, draw three lines to create a triangle that will serve as the interior window of the cover. *(See Illustration 5.)*

20. Using the Line Tool, draw three lines to create the exterior window of the cover. *(See Illustration 5.)*

21. Delete all lines but those that create the interior and exterior windows and the large exterior circle. *(See Illustration 6.)*

22. Save the image with a distinct file name, such as "Basic Wheel Cover."

23. Print one copy of both the Basic Wheel Cover and the Wheel (preferably on printable card stock).

24. Heat laminate each copy.

25. Cut out the Cover and Wheel.

26. Using an X-Acto knife, a straight edge, and scissors, cut out the interior and exterior windows.

27. Using the X-Acto knife, poke a small hole in the middle of both the Cover and the Wheel where the "x" appears.

28. Line up the Cover and Wheel on top of one another and push a brass plated fastener through the center, and secure it.

DESIGN VARIATIONS

Basic wheels can also be used like Sliders. They can be created to teach word families. The onsets and their corresponding images are placed on the wheel while the rime is placed on the cover just next to the interior window. *(See Illustration 7.)*

This particular wheel is divided into four sections. The reference lines are rotated 45 degrees from horizontal and vertical to create these sections. *(See Illustration 8.)* A smaller circle is drawn and the reference lines are again

Illustration 7

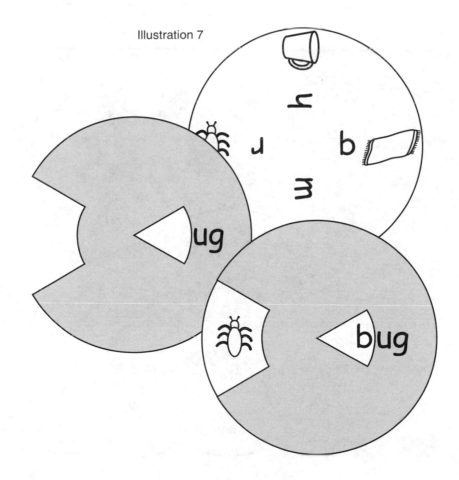

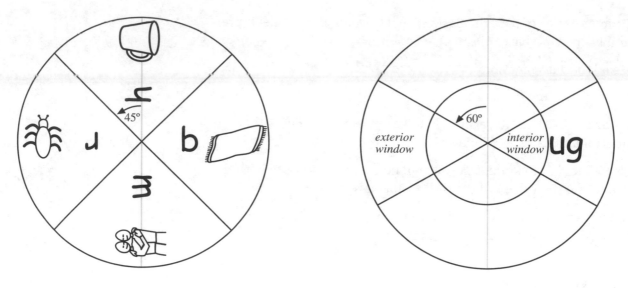

Illustration 8

Illustration 9

rotated an additional 15 degrees and -15 degrees (to 60 degrees and 30 degrees) to create the interior and exterior windows. *(See Illustration 9.)*

Basic wheels can be easily customized. The size, shape, and location of windows can be manipulated to convey more complex information. This is another example of a simple wheel for the official symbols of a state. *(See Illustration 10.)* This exterior window works well for text that

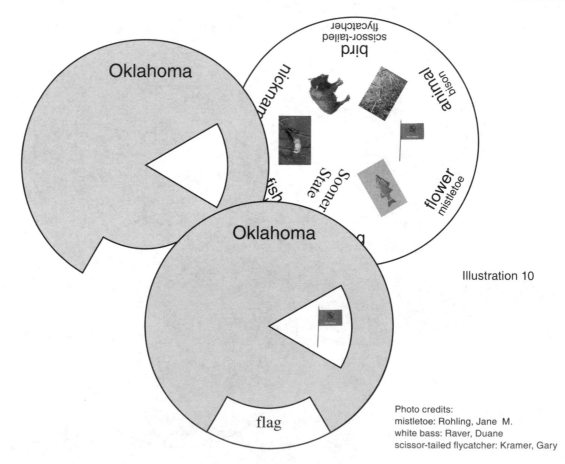

Illustration 10

Photo credits:
mistletoe: Rohling, Jane M.
white bass: Raver, Duane
scissor-tailed flycatcher: Kramer, Gary

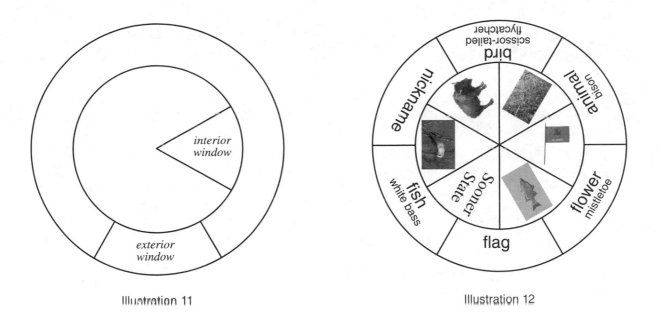

Illustration 11   Illustration 12

is long and narrow. *(See Illustration 11.)* The wheel is divided into 6 sections with text and images slightly offset. *(See Illustration 12.)*

Images of official symbols of a state are easy to locate and download from the Internet. Low resolution images (72 dpi) are readily available and are satisfactory for this purpose. The images I used are high resolution (300 dpi) from Hemera *Photo-Objects*® and the National Image Library (http://images.fws.gov/), a government site with downloadable public domain images. See the ***Resources*** section for a listing of these and other photo sources.

COMPLEX WHEEL

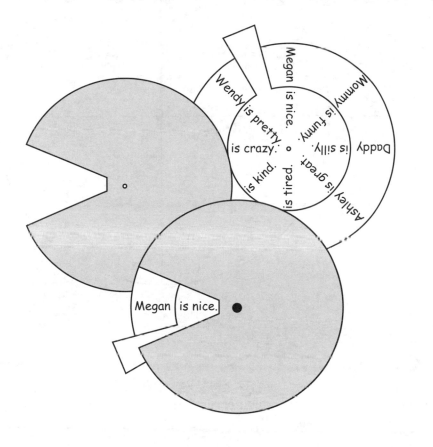

What You'll Need

Materials
- White printer paper or printable card stock, 8½" x 11"
- Laminating pouches, 8¾" x 11¼"
- Brass plated fastener

Tools
- Scissors
- Heat laminator
- X-Acto knife
- Straight edge

Art
- Scanned images, computer graphics, or clip art

Software
- Graphics program

Hardware
- Color printer

Level of Difficulty
- High

After creating a simple word wheel the first time, my brain went into overdrive as I began thinking of ways I could pack more and more information in an organized fashion onto a wheel (or wheels!). I realized I could create a more complex wheel with 2, or maybe even 3 wheels, joined together.

With more complex wheels, Ashley could manipulate text to create unique sentences with different parts of speech on each of the wheels. She could select a meal at a restaurant with a menu made from a complex wheel consisting of the lowest wheel with main dish selections, the middle wheel with side dish selections, and the top with drink selections.

Be creative and think of ways you can use complex wheels for your child to manipulate 2 or 3 sets of information at one time. With complex wheels, there is really no limit to the sophistication of the information you convey.

I'll show you how to create a wheel with two interior wheels and a cover. And I'll even show you how to add a handle to make manipulating the different wheels easy. But I would recommend that you first get comfortable with creating Basic Wheels before attempting to tackle a Complex Wheel.

Skills to Teach

Visual perception
Math
● Language
● Communication
● Reading
Handwriting
● Self-help

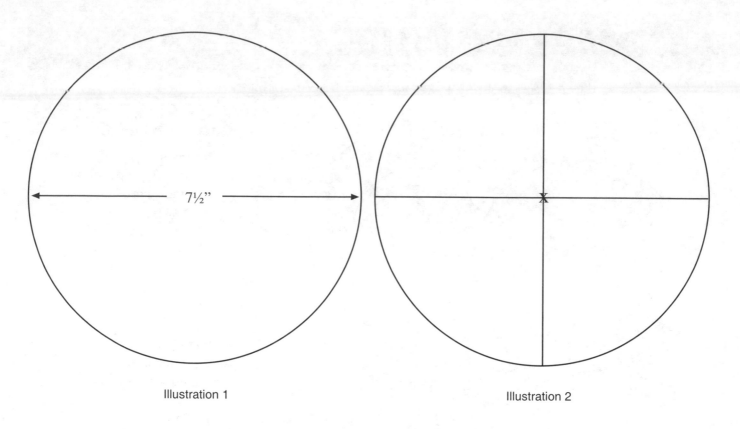

Illustration 1   Illustration 2

DIRECTIONS
Set-Up

1. Open a new drawing document in a graphics program such as *AppleWorks*®, *FreeHand*®, or *Illustrator*®.

2. Turn on Grid and Rulers. (Refer to the previous section on **Grid and Rulers** in **Graphic Skills**.)

3. Using the Ellipse Tool, draw a circle approximately 7½ inches in diameter. *(See Illustration 1.)*

4. Find the center of the circle. To do so, use the Line Tool to draw a horizontal reference line to divide the circle in half. Draw a vertical reference line to divide the circle in fourths. (These lines will be deleted later.)

5. Set the text size to 24 points or less.

6. Using the Text Tool, type a small "x." Place the "x" where the two reference lines intersect. *(See Illustration 2.)*

7. Using the Line Tool, draw two additional reference lines to divide the circle into 8 equal parts. *(See Illustration 3.)*

8. Using the Ellipse Tool, draw a second circle approximately 4½ inches in diameter. Using the Select Tool, select and drag the second circle to the middle of the larger circle. *(See Illustration 3.)*

9. At this point, this image needs to be saved. Save it with a distinct file name, such as "Complex Wheel Cover Template" (you'll go

QUICK TIPS

DRAWING TIPS

■ **Drawing Lines**
To simplify drawing lines horizontally, vertically, or at constrained angles, hold down the Shift key while dragging the Line Tool.

■ **Drawing Circles**
To simplify drawing circles, hold down the Shift key while dragging the Ellipse Tool.

■ **Drawing Perfectly Sized Circles**
To draw circles of a specific dimension, use Grid and Rulers as a guide as you drag the pointer to create a circle of a desired size. Or, hold down the Alt (Windows) or Option (Mac OS) key to draw a circle from its center outward, available in many graphics programs.

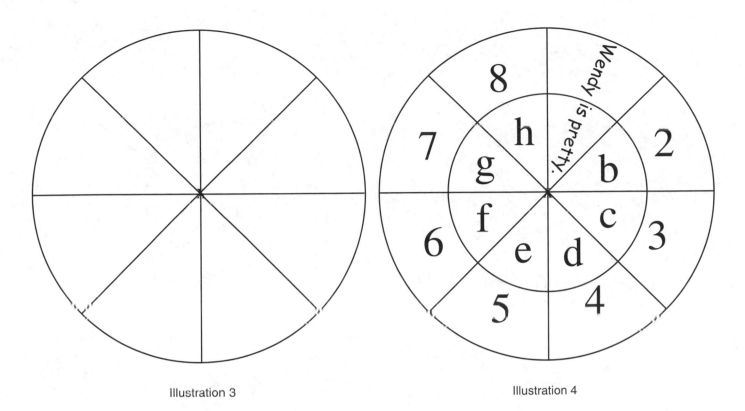

Illustration 3   Illustration 4

back to work on the Wheel Cover a bit later). Now you will continue to work with the image you've created so far.

Wheel #1 (Bottom Wheel)

10. Set the text size to 24 pts.

11. Using the Text Tool, type the name of one meaningful individual. While the text is selected, rotate it 247 degrees. Drag, center, and place it within section "1" *(where "Wendy" appears in Illustration 4),* moving it toward the line of the smaller circle.

12. Continue typing, rotating, and placing up to 7 more names as follows:

> section 2: rotate 202 degrees
> section 3: rotate 157 degrees
> section 4: rotate 112 degrees
> section 5: rotate 67 degrees
> section 6: rotate 22 degrees
> section 7: rotate 337 degrees
> section 8: rotate 292 degrees

13. At this point, this image needs to be saved. Save it with a distinct file name, such as "Wheel #2 Template" (you'll work on the Wheel #2 in a moment). Now you will continue to work with the image you've created so far.

14. Delete all lines except the line for the large exterior circle.

15. Save image using a distinct name, such as "Complex Wheel #1."

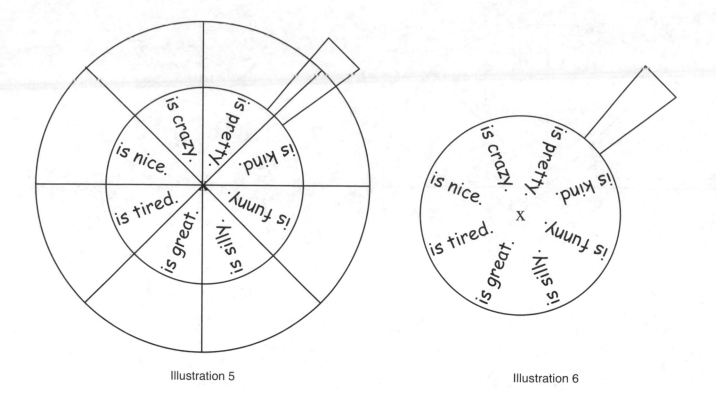

Illustration 5   Illustration 6

Wheel #2 (Top Wheel)

16. Open the previously saved document "Wheel #2 Template." This will serve as the image to create Wheel #2.

17. With the text size still 24 pts., use the Text Tool to type a very short phrase describing one of the individuals named on Wheel #1. While the text is selected, rotate it 247 degrees. Drag, center, and place it within section "a" *(where "is pretty" appears in Illustration 4)*, moving it toward the outside edge of the smaller circle.

18. Continue to type, rotate, and place up to 7 more phrases as follows:
    section b: rotate 202 degrees
    section c: rotate 157 degrees
    section d: rotate 112 degrees
    section e: rotate 67 degrees
    section f: rotate 22 degrees
    section g: rotate 337 degrees
    section h: rotate 292 degrees

Handle (Wheel #2)

19. Using the Line Tool, draw two lines from the outside edge of the smaller circle beyond the outside edge of the larger circle. Be sure to place these lines between two phrases appearing on the smaller circle. Connect the two lines with a smaller line to complete the handle. *(See Illustration 5.)*

20. Delete all lines except the smaller interior circle and the lines that comprise the handle. Delete all names. *(See Illustration 6.)*

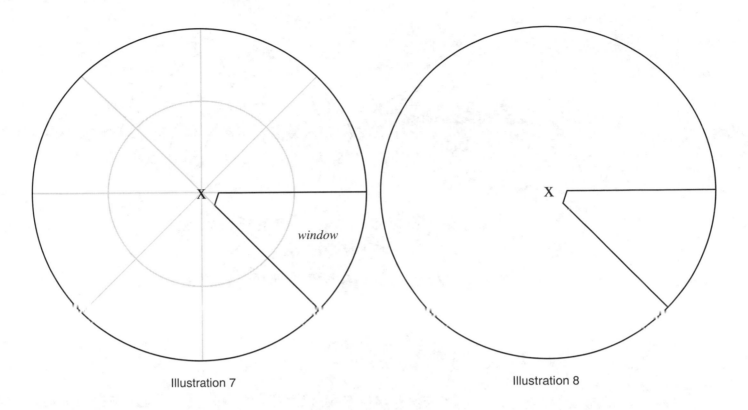

Illustration 7   Illustration 8

21. Save the image using a distinct name, such as "Complex Wheel #2."

Cover

22. Open the previously saved document "Complex Cover Template." This will serve as the image to create your cover.

23. Using the Line Tool, and utilizing the preexising reference lines, draw three lines to create the interior window of the cover. *(See Illustration 7.)*

24. Delete all lines except those that create the window and the large exterior circle. *(See Illustration 8.)*

25. Save the image with a distinct file name, such as "Complex Wheel Cover."

26. Print one copy of the Cover, Wheel #1, and Wheel #2 (preferably on printable card stock).

27. Heat laminate each copy.

28. Cut out the Cover, Wheel #1, and Wheel #2.

29. Using an X-Acto knife, straight edge, and scissors, cut the window out of the Cover.

30. Using the X-Acto knife, poke a small hole in the middle of the Cover, Wheel #1, and Wheel #2 where each "x" appears.

31. Line up the Cover, Wheel #1, and Wheel #2 on top of one another and push a brass plated fastener through the center, and secure it.

QUICK TIPS

DESIGN TIP
■ **Revealing the Mystery Behind Creating Complex Products with Multiple Parts!**
Although these directions ultimately produce the various pieces necessary to create your final product, you may be looking for the logic in how everything seems to come together. Rest assured, it is not random! "Reverse engineering" is the key.

The process typically requires creating the entire object as a single image, as if you were looking at it all put together—let's call this the "Whole." This image is saved and then the various pieces unnecessary for Part #1 are removed. Then it's back to the Whole again and now all the parts unnecessary for Part #2 are removed.

By creating everything in this way, the process is fluid and all your images end up where they need to be! And, in the end, the final product is greater than the Whole or its Parts!

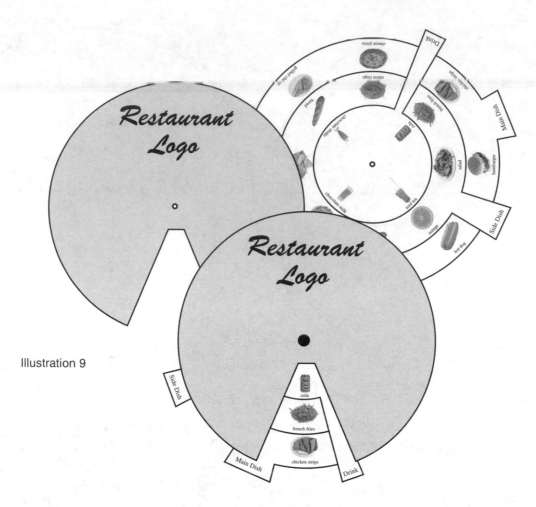

Illustration 9

DESIGN VARIATIONS

Complex wheels can also be used to create a menu for your child for a favorite restaurant. *(See Illustration 9.)* This particular complex wheel is comprised of three separate wheels: one for main dishes, one for side dishes, and one for drinks. *(See Illustrations 10-12.)*

Many national chain restaurants have copies of their adult and children's menus on their website, as well as images of the food they serve.

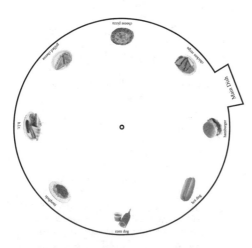

Illustration 10

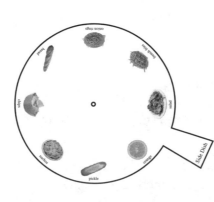

Illustration 11

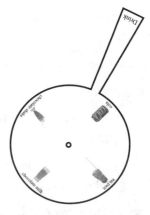

Illustration 12

CLOCK FACES

11:10

For Ashley, the concept of time has been one of the most elusive and challenging to teach. It has not been for lack of trying; however, the concept of time is so incredibly abstract and difficult to comprehend.

In searching for materials to help Ashley understand time, I realized I needed to attach meaning to the hands on the face of an analog clock and the numerals on a digital one. I tied time to daily activities, classroom schedules, or favorite TV programs. This gave Ashley the opportunity to connect a familiar activity occurring at a predictable time with the appearance of a clock face. But, believe it or not, I could not find images of clock faces with the appropriate times, if I could find images of clock faces at all. So I was left to create my own teaching materials, and even my own clock faces.

A clock face is comprised of a circle, numerals 1 through 12, and "hands." The hands are created by drawing lines: a long line for the minutes and a shorter line for the hours. Arrowheads are added to the appropriate end. (Many graphics programs provide the ability to easily add arrowheads to either end of the selected line; if this feature is unavailable, triangles can be used instead.) The longer line (the minute hand) is rotated 30 degrees for each 5 minute interval on a clock face. The shorter line (the hour hand) is rotated 30 degrees for each 1 hour interval.

Create a visual schedule for your child by using these clock faces paired with images related to time that are meaningful to your child—her lunch box, his favorite Sesame Street character, or her bathtub—to help your child attach real meaning to this challenging concept. Help your child learn to tell time by designing your own interactive materials and worksheets. I'll show you some on the following pages.

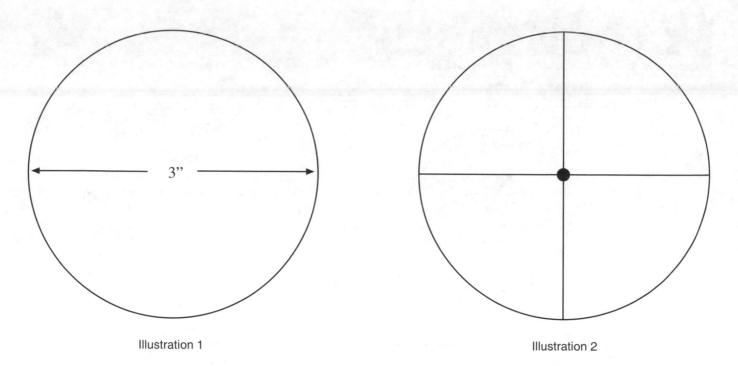

Illustration 1   Illustration 2

DIRECTIONS

1. Open a new drawing document in a graphics program such as *AppleWorks®, FreeHand®,* or *Illustrator®.*

2. Turn on Grid and Rulers. (Refer to the previous section on **Grid and Rulers** in **Graphic Skills**.)

3. Using the Ellipse Tool, draw a 3 inch diameter circle. *(See Illustration 1.)*

4. To find the center of the clock face, use the Line Tool to draw one vertical reference line and one horizontal reference line through the center of the circle.

5. Using the Ellipse Tool, draw a small circle to mark the center of the clock face and place it where the two lines intersect. *(See Illustration 2.)*

6. Fill the circle with the color black from the Color Palette.

7. Delete the horizontal reference line only (the vertical line will be deleted later).

8. Set the text size to 24 points.

9. Using the Text Tool, type the numbers "12" and "6" so that each number is in a separate text frame. Using the Select Tool, select and move the "12" to its position at the top of the vertical reference line. Select and move the "6" to its position at the bottom of the vertical reference line.

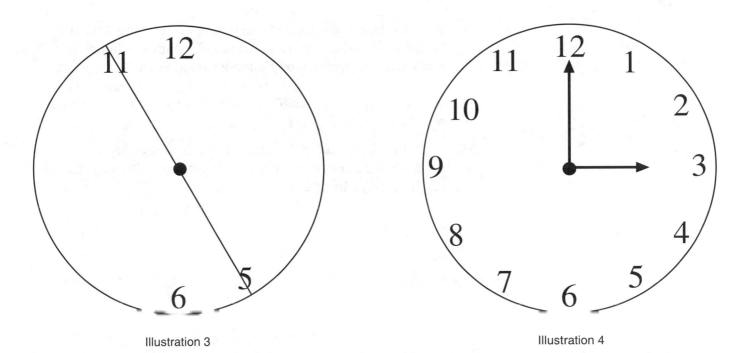

Illustration 3   Illustration 4

10. Using the Select Tool, select the reference line and rotate it counter-clockwise 30 degrees. (Remember: rotating lines is the same as rotating any other object or image. Refer to **Rotate** in **Graphic Skills**.)

11. Using the Text Tool, type the numbers "11" and "5" so that each number is in a separate text frame. Using the Select Tool, select and move both numbers to their proper position on the clock face using the reference line as a guide. *(See Illustration 3.)*

12. Continue rotating the reference line at intervals of 30 degrees, placing the rest of the clock face numbers in their proper location.

13. Delete the reference line.

14. Using the Line Tool, draw a vertical line beginning at the center of the clock to just below the number "12." This is the "minute hand." *(See Illustration 4.)*

15. While the "minute hand" is selected, add an arrowhead to the end of the line. (If the graphics program does not have this feature, draw a triangle and place it on the end of the line.)

16. Using the Line Tool, draw a horizontal line beginning at the center of the clock half the distance to the "3." This is the "hour hand." *(See Illustration 4.)*

17. While the "hour hand" is selected, add an arrowhead to the end of the line. (If the graphics program does not have this feature, draw a triangle and place it on the end of the line.)

18. To set the hands of the clock face to times other than 3:00, use the Select Tool to select the "hour hand" or "minute hand" lines. While selected, use the rotation tool to change the hand position to the desired time, rotating the line 30 degrees for each 1 hour interval for the "hour hand" or 30 degrees for each 5 minute interval for the "minute hand."

19. To change the size of the clock face, use the Select All command and Scale the image to the desired size. (See the *Drawing Tip* for **Scaling Vector Images**.)

VISUAL SCHEDULE

Ashley's Visual Schedule

lunch
11:00

art
9:00

A visual schedule is a way to teach the abstract concept of time in a concrete form while representing a sequence of activities that occur throughout a child's day. Although often used for children with autism, visual schedules can be extremely helpful for any student struggling with transitioning from one activity to another. And because schedules can be associated with clock faces, they can help teach telling time.

There are a number of ways to create visual schedules. They can be designed using objects, photographs, symbols, or text, or a combination of all four. They can also show an entire day's worth of activities as a series of cards, or just one or two activities and cards at a time.

Over the years, I have made a number of different visual schedules for Ashley. I will show you how to create two versions. The first one is a flip schedule that sat on Ashley's desk in her elementary classroom. I took a digital camera to school and used these "real world images" to represent various activities in her day. I copied and pasted these images onto 4 x 6 inch cards and then placed them in a photo stand. Ashley flipped each card as one activity was finished and the next activity was to begin. The second visual schedule traveled with Ashley around high school in a binder. The binder was created with two pockets so that she could move a card from one pocket to another as she moved from class to class.

In the following examples, I have incorporated clock faces that I have already shown you how to create, allowing the association of time with a specific activity. But don't feel you must incorporate clock faces into your child's visual schedule if it is not appropriate.

Whether the visual schedule is posted on a wall or sits on a desk, uses pockets, VELCRO®, or a photo stand, utilizes photographs or symbols, or represents an entire day in an array of images (from top to bottom or left to right) or just one activity at a time, it is most important to create something that is meaningful and appropriate for your child.

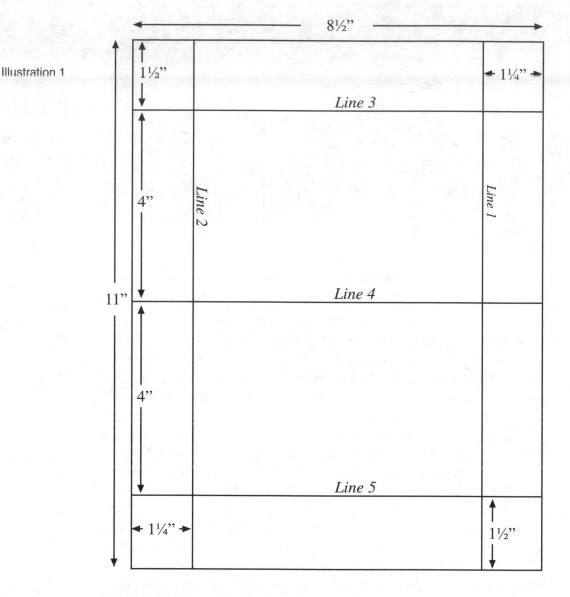

Illustration 1

DIRECTIONS FOR FLIP SCHEDULE

1. Open a new drawing document in a graphics program such as *AppleWorks*®, *FreeHand*®, *or Illustrator*®.

2. Turn on Grid and Rulers. (Refer to the previous section on **Grid and Rulers** in **Graphic Skills**.)

3. Using the Line Tool, draw the following lines:
   - **Line 1:** a vertical line the length of the page located 1¼ inches from the right edge of the page
   - **Line 2:** a vertical line the length of the page located 1¼ inches from the left edge of the page
   - **Line 3:** a horizontal line the width of the page located 1½ inches from the top edge of the page
   - **Line 4:** a horizontal line the width of the page located 4 inches below Line 3
   - **Line 5:** a horizontal line the width of the page located 1½ inches above the bottom edge of the page *(See Illustration 1.)*

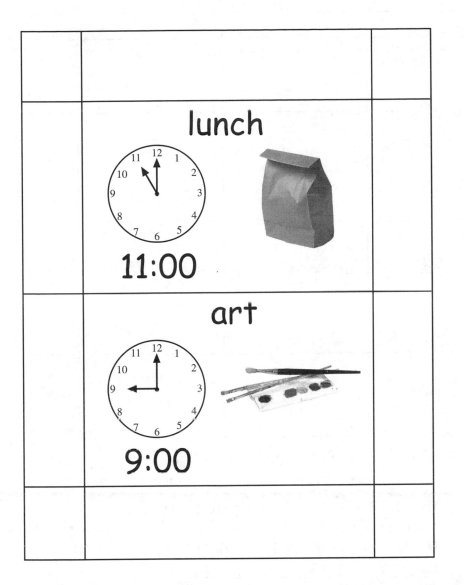

Illustration 2

4. Copy a 2 x 2 inch clock face image to the clipboard. (Or, be prepared to resize a smaller or larger image once it has been pasted. Refer to the previous section on *Scale* in *Graphic Skills*.)

5. Paste the image into the drawing document. While the image is selected, drag and place it within the left half of the top large rectangle. *(See Illustration 2.)*

6. Set the text size to 48 pts.

7. Using the Text Tool, type the time that corresponds with the clock face image. While the text frame is selected, drag and place it beneath the clock face.

8. Copy a 2 x 2 inch image to the clipboard that corresponds with an activity that occurs at the time set on the clock face. (Or, be prepared to resize a smaller or larger image once it has been pasted. Refer to the previous section on *Scale* in *Graphic Skills*.)

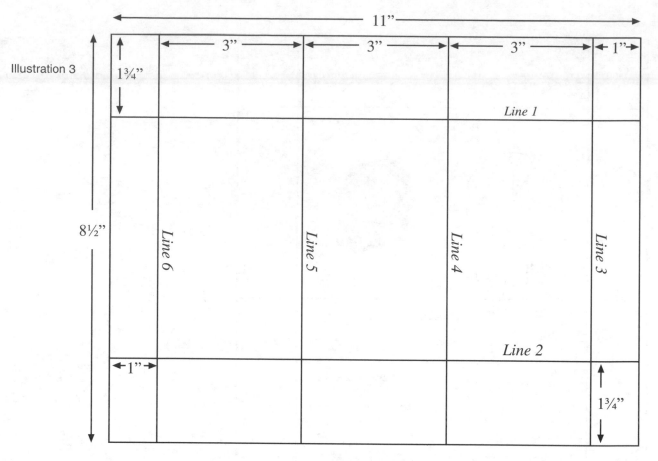

Illustration 3

9. Paste the image into the drawing document. While the image is selected, drag and place it to the right of the clock face.

10. Using the Text Tool, type the name of the activity represented by the image. While the text frame is selected, drag and place it above the clock face and the image. *(See Ilustration 2 on previous page.)*

11. Repeat steps #4-10 for the second rectangle.

12. Save the document with a distinct file name, such as "Visual Schedule 1."

13. Delete all lines (or read the *Drawing Tip* for **Making Lines Disappear Without Deleting Them**) leaving the text and images.

14. Print a test copy on standard printer paper. (See *Printing Tip* for **Printing a Test Copy.**)

15. Print a final copy on a sheet of 4 x 6 inch inkjet index cards.

16. Fold the paper back and forth along the perforations and remove the cards.

17. Place the index cards into two 4 x 6 inch clear photo sleeves.

18. Create additional index cards for various activities throughout the day, place them in clear photo sleeves, and put them in time order.

19. Place the photo sleeves in the photo stand.

QUICK TIPS

DRAWING TIPS
■ **Drawing Lines**
To simplify drawing lines horizontally, vertically, or at constrained angles, hold down the Shift key while dragging the Line Tool.

■ **Making Lines Disappear Without Deleting Them**
You can make lines not appear when printed yet have them remain in a document. This can be accomplished by changing the line width to "None" or the line color to "white." Why bother? If you ever want to use an old file as a template, the lines will guide you as to where to properly place new images or text.

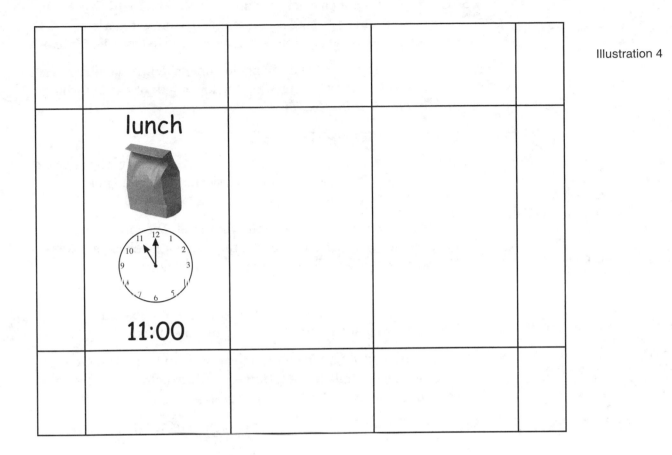

Illustration 4

DIRECTIONS FOR BINDER SCHEDULE

1. Open a new drawing document in a graphics program such as *AppleWorks®, FreeHand®,* or *Illustrator®.*

2. In the File Menu, select Page Setup. Change paper Orientation to Landscape. (Refer to the previous section on ***Document Settings*** in ***Graphic Skills.***)

3. Turn on Grid and Rulers. (Refer to the previous section on ***Grid and Rulers*** in ***Graphic Skills.***)

4. Using the Line Tool, draw the following lines:
   - **Line 1:** a horizontal line the width of the page located 1¾ inches below top edge of the page
   - **Line 2:** a horizontal line the width of the page located 1¾ inches above the bottom edge of the page
   - **Line 3:** a vertical line the length of the page located 1 inch from the right edge of the page
   - **Line 4:** a vertical line the length of the page located 3 inches to the left of Line 3
   - **Line 5:** a vertical line the length of the page located 3 inches to the left of Line 4
   - **Line 6:** a vertical line the length of the page located 1 inch from the left edge of the page *(See Illustration 3.)*

5. Copy a 1½ x 1½ inch clock face image to the clipboard. (Or, be prepared to resize a smaller or larger image once it has been pasted. Refer to the previous section on *Scale* in *Graphic Skills*.)

6. Paste the image into the drawing document. While the image is selected, drag and place it within the lower half of one of the large rectangles. *(See Illustration 4.)*

7. Set the text size to 36 pts.

8. Using the Text Tool, type the time that corresponds with the clock face image. While the text frame is selected, drag and place it beneath the clock face.

9. Copy a 1½ x 1½ inch image to the clipboard that corresponds with an activity that occurs at the time set on the clock face. (Or, be prepared to resize a smaller or larger image once it has been pasted. Refer to the previous section on *Scale* in *Graphic Skills*.)

10. Paste the image into the drawing document. While the image is selected, drag and place it directly above the clock face.

11. Using the Text Tool, type the name of the activity represented by the image. While the text frame is selected, drag and place it above the clock face and the image. *(See Ilustration 4.)*

12. Repeat steps #5-11 for the other two large rectangles.

13. Save the document with a distinct file name, such as "Visual Schedule 2."

14. Delete all lines (or read the *Drawing Tip* for **Making Lines Disappear Without Deleting Them**) leaving the text and images.

15. Print a test copy on standard printer paper. (See *Printing Tip* for **Printing a Test Copy**.)

16. Print a final copy on a sheet of 3 x 5 inch inkjet index cards.

17. Fold the paper back and forth along the perforations and remove the cards.

18. Adhere one self-adhesive data diskette pocket to the left side of the open binder and another to the right side of the binder.

19. Create an inkjet label for the binder cover. (See *Design Tip* for **Create an Inkjet Label for the Binder Cover of Your Visual Schedule**.)

20. Adhere the inkjet label to the binder cover.

QUICK TIPS

DRAWING TIP

▪ **Scaling Vector Images**
Scaling a vector image can change the way an image appears, not only by its size but by the prominence of the lines comprising the image. An image scaled to 50% of its original size will have a line thickness that is half the width of the original image. Pay attention to the appearance of lines and adjust the line thickness when you significantly reduce the size of an image. (See *Adjusting Line Thickness When Scaling Vector Images* in *Graphic Skills: Extras*.)

DESIGN TIP

▪ **Create an Inkjet Label for the Binder Cover of Your Visual Schedule**
By using an 8½ x 11 inch inkjet sticker sheet and an image of your child, it is easy to create a cover label for your visual schedule. Just copy and paste the image into a new document, add text, print and you're done!

PRINTING TIP

▪ **Printing a Test Copy**
When using specialty papers, it is always best to run a test copy on standard printer paper first. Place the test copy on top of the specialty paper, hold both up to the light to determine whether all images and text are properly aligned. This is a good habit when printing such things as labels, decals, and pre-perforated papers. Specialty papers are significantly more expensive than standard printer paper, therefore, it is worth the effort to take the time to run a test before printing your final copy.

TELLING TIME

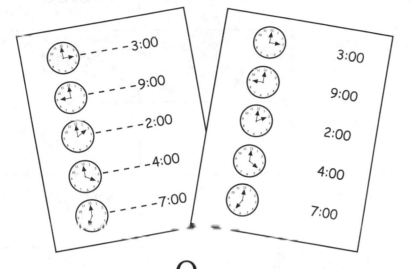

What You'll Need

Materials
- White printer paper, 8½" x 11"

Tools
- None

Art
- Clock faces

Software
- Graphics program with dashed line

Hardware
- Color printer

Level of Difficulty
- Simple

Once I had a ready supply of the clock faces by drawing them myself, I began creating materials to help teach Ashley what the appearance of a clock meant. To do this, I created a series of worksheets.

I'll be honest: I am not a big fan of worksheets. They are flat, static pieces of paper that can be a visual challenge. They don't talk. They don't move. They aren't easy to adapt except for simple text changes. And, like tissue, once they are used, they are pitched. I've been told "they have their place," but it's probably not the place I have in mind! Trust me: there are some awesome "high tech" educational approaches that make static worksheets all but obsolete. But that's another book!

But if students are going to use worksheets, by gosh, the layout needs to be just right. And the images should be meaningful and engaging. Most importantly, students need to be taught the skills necessary to complete them. For example, if they need to draw a line from an image to a corresponding one, then they need to be taught that skill. If they need to circle the correct answer, then they need to be taught to do that as well. The following instructions provide ideas for making worksheets using clock faces, utilizing a dashed line found in most graphics programs. To begin, provide the information in a pre-dictable order, first with a dashed line from the clock face to the correct time, and then without. Have your child trace over the dashed line, and then draw a line, from the clock face to the correct text. Then mix things up, changing the order of the presentation, first with a dashed line, and then again without. Its presence is faded as your child learns to draw lines by him or herself.

If you have followed the previous instructions and learned to draw clock faces, you now have the opportunity to create some very useful materials. But don't use your new skills to create only materials for telling time. Think about creating materials that use this same "step wise" process for teaching other skills.

Skills to Teach

- Visual perception
- ● Math
- Language
- Communication
- Reading
- Handwriting
- ● Self-help

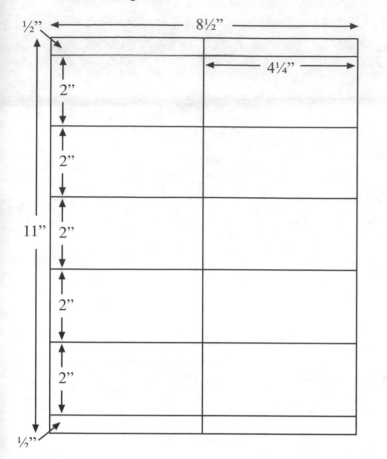

Illustration 1

Illustration 2

DIRECTIONS

1. Open a new drawing document in a graphics program such as *AppleWorks®, FreeHand®,* or *Illustrator®*.

2. Turn on Grid and Rulers. (Refer to the previous section on **Grid and Rulers** in **Graphic Skills**.)

3. Using the Line Tool, draw 6 horizontal lines at 2 inch intervals beginning ½ inch below the top of the page. *(See Illustration 1.)*

4. Using the Line Tool, draw a vertical line the length of the page located 4¼ inches from the right edge of the page.

5. Copy a 1½ x 1½ inch clock face image to the clipboard. (Or, be prepared to resize a smaller or larger image once it has been pasted. Refer to the previous section on **Scale** in **Graphic Skills**.)

6. Paste the image into the drawing document. Using the Select Tool, select and move the clock face image between the top two horizontal lines and center it within the rectangle along the left side of the page. *(See Illustration 2.)*

7. Copy and paste 4 additional 1½ x 1½ inch clock face images showing different times. Using the Select Tool, select, move,

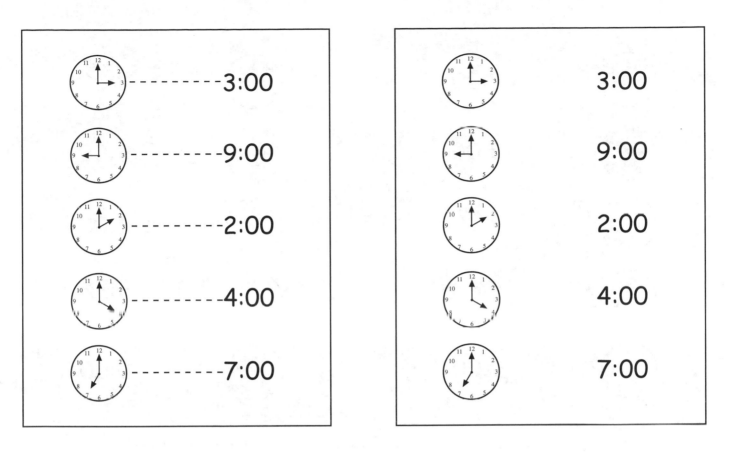

Illustration 3   Illustration 4

and center the images within each rectangle vertically down the page. *(See Illustration 2.)*

8. Set the text size to 48 points. Using the Text Tool, type the text that corresponds with the time that appears on each clock face image. Using the Select Tool, select and move the text to the right of each image and center it within the rectangle to the right of the clock face image. *(See Illustration 2.)*

9. Using the Line Tool, draw a horizontal line from the clock face to the text of the corresponding time. Change the line characteristic to "dashed." *(See Illustration 3.)*

10. Continue using the Line Tool to draw dashed horizontal lines from each clock face to the corresponding time.

11. Delete all horizontal and vertical lines but the horizontal dashed lines.

12. Print one copy of the document.

13. Save it with a distinct file name, such as "Time Worksheet #1." Now you will continue to work with the image you've created so far.

14. Delete all the horizontal dashed lines. *(See Illustration 4.)*

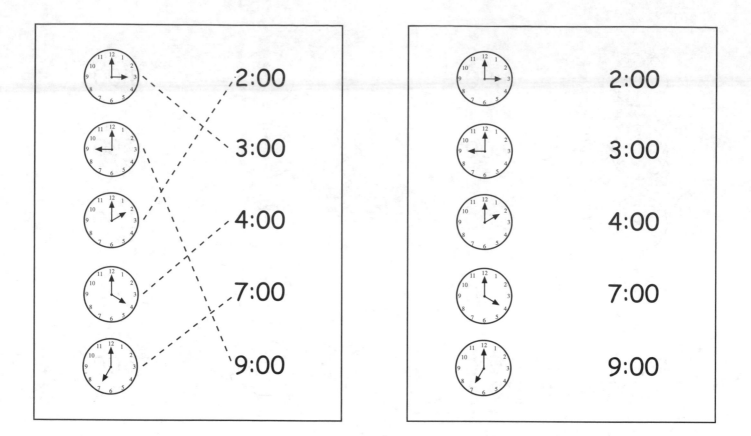

Illustration 5   Illustration 6

15. Print one copy of the document.

16. Save it with a distinct file name, such as "Time Worksheet #2." Now you will continue to work with the image you've created so far.

17. Mix up the order of the text by selecting and moving each text frame.

18. Draw the necessary horizontal and diagonal dashed lines to connect the clock face images to the corresponding times. *(See Illustration 5.)*

19. Print one copy of the document.

20. Save it with a distinct file name, such as "Time Worksheet #3." Now you will continue to work with the image you've created so far.

21. Delete all horizontal or diagonal dashed lines. *(See Illustration 6.)*

22. Print one copy of the document.

23. Save it with a distinct file name, such as "Time Worksheet #4."

24. Create new Telling Time worksheets by simply altering the clock faces and changing the text.

DESIGN VARIATIONS

The same process can be used for creating telling time worksheets where the answer needs to be circled. Using the Ellipse Tool, draw a circle around the correct answer and change the line characteristic to "dashed." *(See Illustration 7.)*

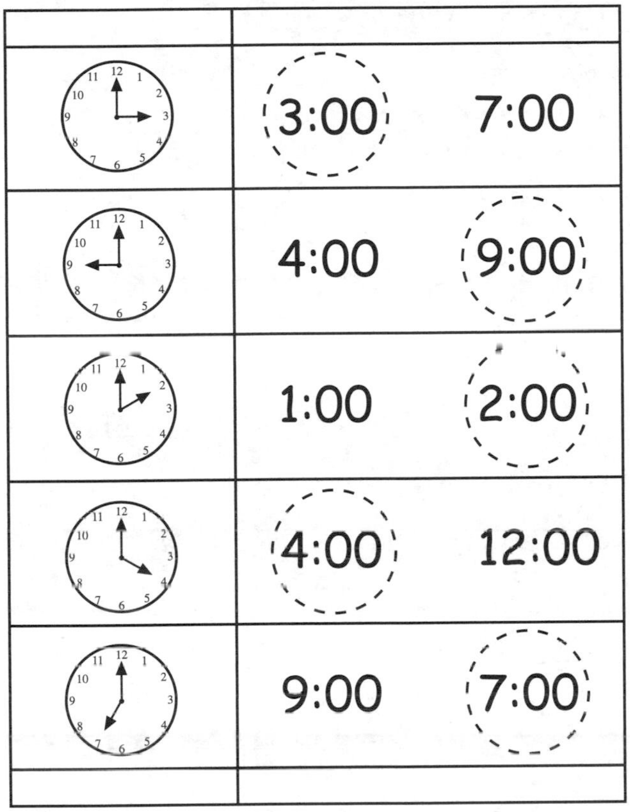

🕒	(3:00)	7:00
🕘	4:00	(9:00)
🕛	1:00	(2:00)
🕓	(4:00)	12:00
🕖	9:00	(7:00)

Illustration 7

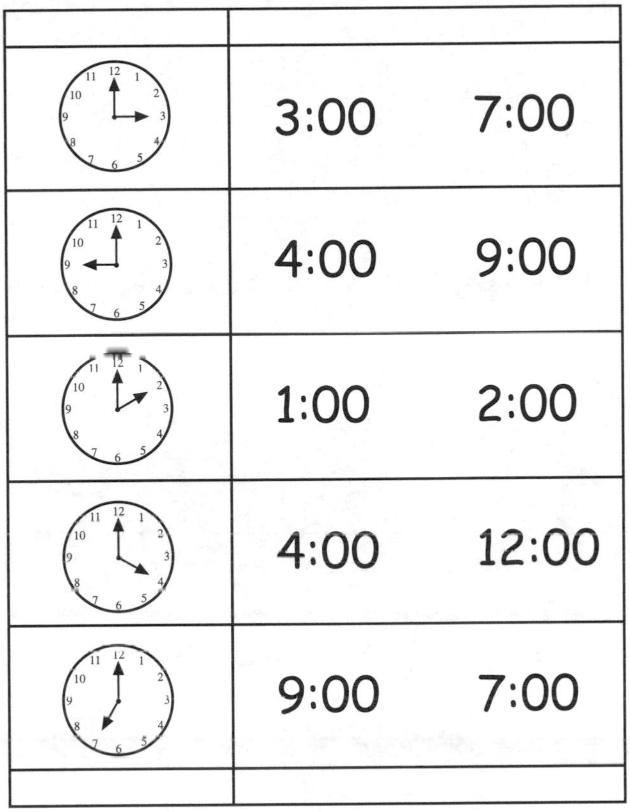

🕒	3:00	7:00
🕘	4:00	9:00
🕛	1:00	2:00
🕓	4:00	12:00
🕖	9:00	7:00

Illustration 8

But don't feel limited by the presentation I have provided. Use fewer clock face images on a page if 5 are too many. Limit the possible answers to one (only the correct answer!) or increase the possible answers to more than 2. The complexity is up to you.

Remove the dashed circle around the correct answer, leaving the job of selecting and circling the correct answer to your child. *(See Illustration 8.)*

ROTARY CARDS

bananas

To provide Ashley as much independence at the grocery store as possible, I created an organized box of Rolodex® cards with images of the different food items we purchase regularly. The images are paired with text with the goal that she eventually learns to follow a "text only" grocery list. Before we begin our excursion, we sit down together and go over intended purchases. We remove the cards from the file for the items we will be shopping for. Ashley then uses these cards at the grocery store as her "list."

Once I created the grocery list, I quickly realized that Rolodex® cards can be used in many other ways. For children (or adults) who like to write, a collection of cards can become a personal word bank or dictionary, with their own personal words (like favorite sports teams or the names and images of best friends). It can contain words or phrases to keyboard in a high school keyboarding class, or words and images of leisure activities to choose from after school. The possibilities are endless.

I use a Rolodex® file to organize the cards and Rolodex® Necessities™ Printer Cards, designed for use in laser and inkjet printers, photo copiers, and typewriters. They are manufactured in two sizes: 8½ x 11 inch sheets, perforated with 8 cards (each 2¼ x 4 in.) per sheet or 4 cards (each 3 x 5 in.) per sheet. Once printed, they tear apart easily and can be placed in clear plastic card protectors to extend their life, shielding the cards from dirty hands and the ink from exposure to the elements. The cards can then be stored in a variety of Rolodex® card files.

Consider creating a box such as this for your child or student. But don't limit yourself to only grocery shopping. Check out the other neat ways you can apply this concept.

Illustration 1

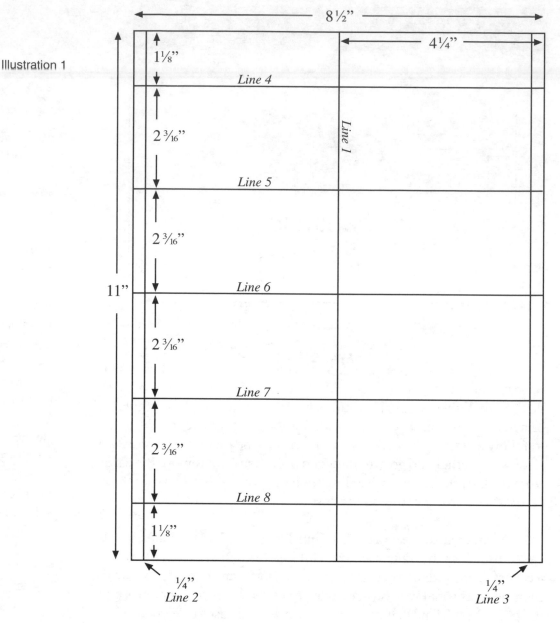

BOARDMAKER™ TIP
■ **Image Size**
When using *Boardmaker*™ prior to version 5.0, and copying a symbol to another program, setting the Picture Size to 50% automatically sets the image size to approximately 1 x 1 inches.

When using *Boardmaker*™ version 5.0 and higher, and copying a symbol to another program, the image is automatically set to approximately 2 x 2 inches. Be prepared to resize the image to the desired size.

DIRECTIONS

1. Open a new drawing document in a graphics program such as *AppleWorks*®, *FreeHand*®, or *Illustrator*®.

2. Turn on Grid and Rulers. (Refer to the previous section on **Grid and Rulers** in **Graphic Skills**.)

3. Using the Line Tool, draw the following lines:
   - **Line 1:** a vertical line the length of the page located 4¼ inches from the right edge of the page
   - **Line 2:** a vertical line the length of the page located ¼ inch from the left edge of the page
   - **Line 3:** a vertical line the length of the page located ¼ inch from the right edge of the page
   - **Line 4:** a horizontal line the width of the page located 1⅛ inches from the top edge of the page

Illustration 2

eggs	bananas
bread	toilet paper
steak	Swiss cheese
doughnuts	avocado

- **Line 5:** a horizontal line the width of the page located 2³/₁₆ inches below Line 4
- **Line 6:** a horizontal line the width of the page located 2³/₁₆ inches below Line 5
- **Line 7:** a horizontal line the width of the page located 2³/₁₆ inches below Line 6
- **Line 8:** a horizontal line the width of the page located 2³/₁₆ inches below Line 7 (or 1¹/₈ inches from the bottom edge of the paper) *(See Illustration 1.)*

4. Copy a 1 x 1 inch image to the clipboard. (Or, be prepared to re-size a smaller or larger image once it has been pasted. Refer to the previous section on **Scale** in **Graphic Skills**.)

5. Paste the image into the drawing document. While the image is selected, drag it within one of the 8 large rectangles, placing it close to the top line of the rectangle.

6. Continue this process of copying, pasting, and centering 7 additional 1 x 1 inch images into the last 7 empty rectangles. *(See Illustration 2.)*

7. Set the text size to 24 pts.

8. Using the Text Tool, type the name that corresponds with each of the 8 images so that each name is in a separate text frame.

9. Using the Select Tool, select, move, and center the text beneath each image within the 8 rectangles. Place the text close to the image, leaving room for the perforated notches at the bottom of the rotary cards. *(See Illustration 2.)*

10. Delete all lines (or read the *Drawing Tip* for **Making Lines Disappear Without Deleting Them)** leaving the text and images.

11. Print a test copy on standard printer paper. (See *Printing Tip* for **Printing a Test Copy**.)

12. Print a final copy on a blank Rolodex® Necessities™ Printer Card.

13. Fold the paper back and forth along the perforations and remove the cards.

14. Slip the cards into the plastic card protectors and place in a Rolodex® file box.

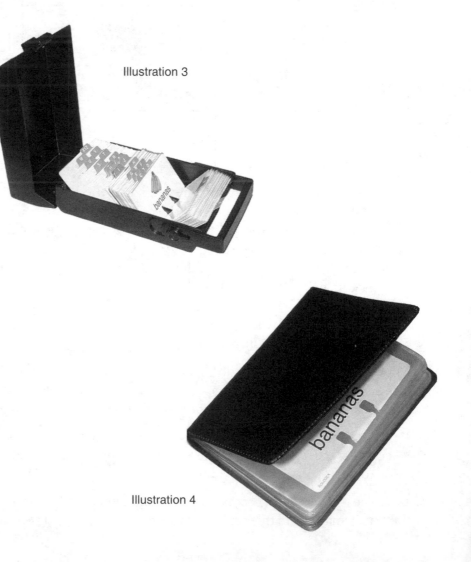

Illustration 3

Illustration 4

DESIGN VARIATIONS

▪ Create a "phone bank" with pictures of friends and their telephone numbers.

▪ Create an "image bank" of leisure activities for your child to choose from.

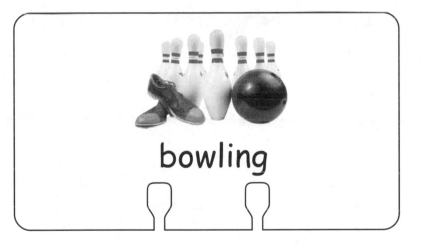

▪ Create a word bank of "favorite things," such as college or professional sports teams.

■ Create a word bank for keyboarding. Provide text on one side and the corresponding image on the other. Show the text side for simple keyboarding, or the image side for a word retrieval and spelling activity.

Remove them from the card file as needed and use the process of returning them for practice in alphabetization.

RECIPE CARDS

Ashley's Easy Tuna Sandwich
1 can · 1 Tbs. · 1 Tbs. · 2 slices

...en can of tuna.
...tuna.
...a into a bowl.
...relish and mayonnaise.
...ork.
...ad on bread.
...ich in half.

Unfortunately, recipes or cookbooks for visual learners are not abundant. But creating your own collection of favorite recipes on index cards is a reasonable and simple alternative. Printable index cards come in two sizes: 3 x 5 and 4 x 6 inches. The cards are card stock so it is possible to print on both sides of the card. My preference, however, is to use the larger 4 x 6 inch cards (two to a sheet), printing the ingredients on one card and the instructions on the other.

You can easily tailor the size of the text and the content of the recipe to your child's learning needs. And with access to food images from a variety of sources, it is quick and easy to design some awesome visual tools. Even better, on the Internet, it is possible to grab images of recipe ingredients that look the way they are packaged and found in the grocery store. Rather than an image of a generic bag of shredded cheese, your child will know exactly what ingredient to use by the appearance of the packaging. (If you can't find a picture of an ingredient on the manufacturer's website, take your own photograph and create your own image.)

Invest in a set of measuring cups and measuring spoons whose handles are color coded, and match the color of your text to the handles of the measuring cups and spoons:

> yellow: ¼ cup or teaspoon
> green: ⅓ cup or ½ teaspoon
> red: ½ cup or 1 teaspoon
> blue: 1 cup or 1 tablespoon

Print the recipes on inkjet index cards and store them in clear photo pocket pages. Place the pages in a 3-ring easel binder and you've got a wonderful visual tool protected from spills and splatters.

Bon appetit!

What You'll Need

Materials
- Oxford inkjet index cards, 4" x 6", plain
- Photo pocket pages for 4" x 6" photos or post cards
- Three-ring easel binder

Tools
- Color-coded measuring cup and spoons

Art
- Scanned image, computer graphic, or clip art

Software
- Graphics program

Hardware
- Color printer

Level of Difficulty
- Simple

Skills to Teach

Visual perception
Math
Language
Communication
● Reading
Handwriting
● Self-help

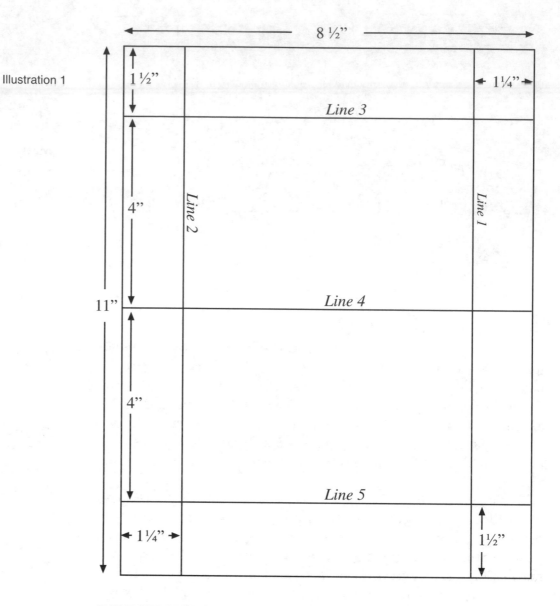

Illustration 1

DIRECTIONS

1. Open a new drawing document in a graphics program such as *AppleWorks®, FreeHand®,* or *Illustrator®.*

2. Turn on Grid and Rulers. (Refer to the previous section on **Grid and Rulers** in **Graphic Skills**.)

3. Using the Line Tool, draw the following lines:
   - **Line 1:** a vertical line the length of the page located 1¼ inches from the right edge of the page
   - **Line 2:** a vertical line the length of the page located 1¼ inches from the left edge of the page
   - **Line 3:** a horizontal line the width of the page located 1½ inches from the top edge of the page
   - **Line 4:** a horizontal line the width of the page located 4 inches below Line 3
   - **Line 5:** a horizontal line the width of the page located 1½ inches above the bottom edge of the page. *(See Illustration 1.)*

Illustration 2

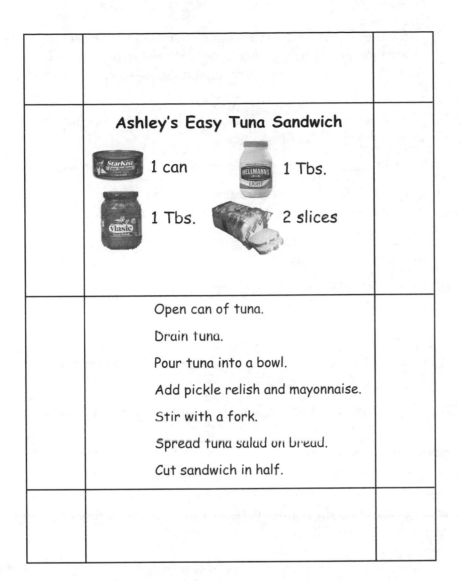

4. Copy a small image (approximately 1 x 1 inch) of a recipe ingredient to the clipboard. (Or, be prepared to resize a smaller or larger image once it has been pasted. Refer to the previous section on **Scale** in **Graphic Skills**.) Depending on the number of ingredients, the images will be approximately 1 x 1 inch or smaller.

5. Paste the image into the drawing document. While the image is selected, drag it into place within the top large rectangle.

6. Continue this same process of copying, pasting, and moving additional 1 x 1 inch images. *(See Illustration 2.)*

7. Set the text size to 24 pts.

8. Using the Text Tool, type the recipe title. Using the Select Tool, select and move the recipe title to the top of the large rectangle.

9. Using the Text Tool, type the amount of each ingredient so that each one is in a separate text frame. Using the Select Tool, select and move the ingredient amount to the right of each image.

10. Using the Text Tool, drag the cursor over the measurements related to measuring cups and spoons. Change the text color to match the corresponding color coded measuring cups and spoons.

11. Using the Text Tool, type the recipe directions. Using the Select Tool, select and move the recipe directions within the bottom large rectangle. *(See Illustration 2.)*

12. Save the document using a distinct name, such as "Tuna Sandwich."

13. Delete all lines (or read the *Drawing Tip* for **Making Lines Disappear Without Deleting Them**) leaving the text and images.

14. Print a test copy on standard printer paper. (See *Printing Tip* for **Printing a Test Copy**.)

15. Print a final copy on a sheet of index cards.

16. Fold the paper back and forth along the perforations and remove the cards.

17. Place the index cards in the two horizontal windows of the photo pocket page.

18. Place the photo pocket page in the 3-ring easel binder.

DESIGN VARIATION

Using the Text Tool, you can change the text color to match the corresponding color coded measuring cups and spoons. Or, you can create rectangles around the text for each spoon or cup measurement, filling each rectangle with the corresponding color.

Also, consider creating an index card showing images of the necessary utensils and cooking equipment. *(See Illustration 3.)* The card can be removed from the photo pocket page so that your child can look at the images and carry it around the kitchen as she gathers the necessary tools.

Illustration 3

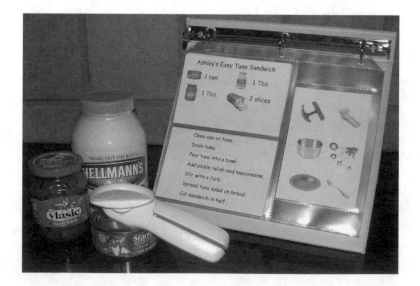

MENU

I am all for Ashley making as many choices in her life as possible. And, like everyone else, what she chooses to eat when she is out should be her decision, if at all possible, and not somebody else's. When we go to a restaurant, I prefer she choose her meal rather than follow a consensus among family members of what we think Ashley might like to eat. Her disability makes expressing her preferences harder, but, thanks to some simple, easy-to-make materials, far from impossible.

Menus at some restaurants like IHOP® and Denny's® are great for kids unable to select from a regular text menu—their picture menus are full of wonderful photographs of the selections. Ashley can easily point to exactly what she wants. But most national chains do not have images of their food on their menus (surprisingly, even on their children's menus). And the text is typically so small that it is difficult to read even for those considered to have "normal vision."

For Ashley to have something she can order from, it takes planning. I gather copies of the menus from the restaurants we frequent to preview their choices. Images are found or pictures taken of the food selections she might like to choose from. The picture menu is then created on the computer with appropriately sized text and images. This can be easily modified and adapted for different restaurants, or as her likes and dislikes change over time.

Check the Internet sites of your favorite restaurants, especially national chains (usually www.restaurantname.com). Most have adult and kid's menus posted, and many have pictures of their menu items on their site. Either capture images from the Internet or screen capture the food images and their restaurant logos. (See *Capturing Images from the Internet* and *Screen Capture* in the section *Controlling Variables: Images*.) Or take a digital camera along to take pictures of not only what you think your child wants to eat but of what others order, too.

This is well worth the effort if it provides your child the dignity of choosing for herself. And you may find out she is tired of macaroni & cheese and has been coveting your choice of eggplant parmesan!

What You'll Need

Materials
- White printer paper or printable card stock, 8½" x 11"
- Laminating pouches, 8¾" x 11¼"
- VELCRO® coins, self-adhesive

Tools
- Heat laminator
- Write-on/wipe-off pen

Art
- Scanned images, computer graphics, or clip art

Software
- Graphics program

Hardware
- Color printer

Level of Difficulty
- Simple

Skills to Teach

Visual perception
Math
Language
Communication
Reading
Handwriting
● Self-help

Illustration 1

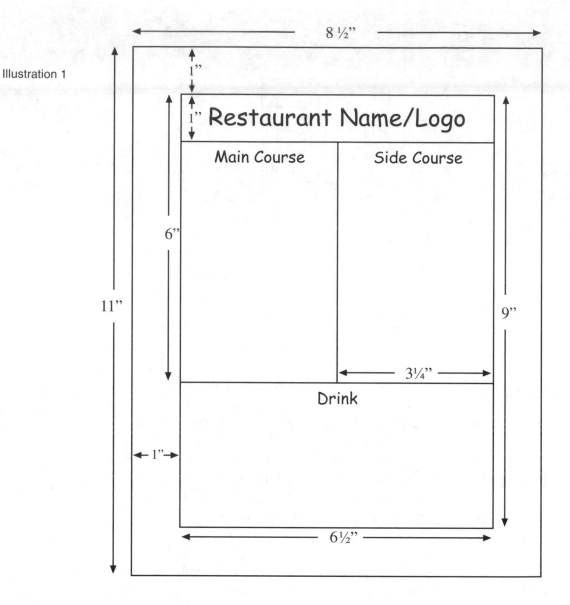

DIRECTIONS

1. Open a new drawing document in a graphics program such as *AppleWorks®, FreeHand®,* or *Illustrator®.*

2. Turn on Grid and Rulers. (Refer to the previous section on **Grid and Rulers** in **Graphic Skills**.)

3. Using the Rectangle Tool, draw a 9 x 6½ inch rectangle. *(See Illustration 1.)*

4. Select and move the rectangle 1 inch below the top edge of the page and 1 inch from the left side of the page. *(See Illustration 1.)*

5. Using the Line Tool, draw a horizontal line the width of the rectangle and 1 inch below the top edge of the rectangle.

6. Using the Line Tool, draw a horizontal line the width of the rectangle and 6 inches below the top edge of the rectangle.

Illustration 2

7. Using the Line Tool, draw a vertical line between the two horizontal lines 3¼ inches from the right side of the rectangle.

8. Set the font size to 24 pts.

9. Using the Text Tool, type the names of your choice of categories so that each line of text is in a separate text frame.

10. Using the Select Tool, select and move the text to the three large rectangles.

11. Copy and paste an appropriately sized logo (approximately ¾ x ¾ inches) for the upper most section. *(See Illustration 1.)*

12. Copy and paste appropriately sized images into the drawing document. (Or, be prepared to resize an image once it has been pasted. Refer to the previous section on *Scale* in *Graphic Skills*.)

13. Using the Select Tool, select and move the logo and images to their designated sections, grouping images together according to your choice of categories (that is, main course, side course, drink, dessert, etc.).

QUICK TIPS

DESIGN TIPS

▪ **Looking for High Quality Logo Images?**
A great source of high quality vector drawn (that is, smooth line and scaleable) logos is Lots O'Logos (www.lots-o-logos. com). Their collection provides over 14,000 black & white and full-color corporate logos and trademarks. Although not free, it is a huge timesaver. But you must still obtain permission for anything other than your personal use.

▪ **Providing Menus for Person with Visual Impairments**
While some restaurants provide accommodations for persons with visual impairments, it is the exception rather than the rule to find Braille or large print versions of menus. It is rather simple to create your own large print menu with Optical Character Recognition software (OCR) and a scanner, and there may be an organization in your community that can translate a menu into Braille. But if you do not find the accommodations you require, or cannot create them yourself, explain the need by talking with management. We seldom get what we don't ask for!

14. Print (preferably on printable card stock).

15. Heat laminate.

DESIGN VARIATIONS

Once Ashley reached high school, the cafeteria food was relatively consistent from day to day, making it easier to create a menu for her to choose what she wanted to eat. Ashley generally took her lunch, but on Fridays she was given the opportunity to select from the typical fare provided in most high school cafeterias: pizza, chicken nuggets, roast beef sandwich, chips, salad, and the like. This gave her the opportunity to make choices and manage money.

Using photos I took of the various food items or the containers they are served in, I added check boxes next to each image, and then printed and laminated the menu. A write-on/wipe-off pen was adhered to the menu with a self-adhesive VELCRO® coin fastener. Ashley was able to take her time checking off what she wanted long before arriving at the cafeteria. *(See Illustration 2 on previous page.)*

Another presentation we have used for Ashley to communicate her selections at a restaurant is one-sided flash cards. (See ***Flash Cards***.) Photographs of restaurant items are collected and each choice is individually placed on separate flash cards with text requesting her selection ("I would like a turkey sandwich on wheat, please"). She can then show the text and food image to the server when she is ordering. *(See Illustration 3.)*

Illustration 3

All the cards for a particular restaurant are placed on a loose-leaf ring, the first card holding the logo for the corresponding restaurant. Each group of cards are placed on a hook in our home so that Ashley can easily retrieve them before walking out the door.

TEACHING ASHLEY TO READ

There is nothing simple about teaching a nonverbal child to read, especially one with significant visual impairments. It is always assumed that a reader can speak...and see! We instruct and listen; the child looks and speaks.

But these are not options for Ashley, and many other children. Because of her disabilities, I did not find educators interested in taking on this daunting task of teaching Ashley to read, or able to direct me to materials I could use to do so.

We live in a print rich world and I was determined to provide Ashley access to it. She will be faced with many challenges throughout her life that relate to text: reading the "Men" and "Women" signs on public restrooms, handling menus when she eats out, managing labels on food items in the grocery store, receiving e-mails or letters from her sisters away at college. And she will be reading books and magazines for leisure and pleasure. If it were possible to provide her access to text, how could I deny her that skill?

Although I found little to encourage me to attempt teaching a child like Ashley to read, I found nothing that said it could not be done. I ignored that she was supposed to speak to communicate her comprehension of the collection of letters in front of her and, instead, found other ways for her to communicate her understanding.

Like lots of people, Ashley requires a very systematic approach to learning, and reading was no different. Students don't have to have expressive language deficits or visual impairments to be challenged by the process of learning to read. Many children without identifiable disabilities have a difficult time. The methods I used are not dissimilar to the methods used to teach any child to read. But the materials were customized to meet Ashley's needs.

Unfortunately, everything I used to teach Ashley to read had to be created from scratch. But, fortunately none of it is difficult to do. Whether you follow every step I used, or you pick and choose what might help your child, there will hopefully be something I have created that will be of assistance.

I used the following methods:
- create materials to build a sight word vocabulary comprised of familiar and motivating words

- create a font that exactly matches a set of plastic letters that makes text kinesthetic
- create materials using that font for teaching Ashley to spell her name
- create materials using that font for teaching Ashley to spell words
- create materials using that font for teaching word families and learning to decode text
- create a dashed font to trace over for kinesthetic and tactile input
- create a set of materials for taking inventory of the words Ashley could read
- create materials and decals for Ashley to "fill in the blank," labeling familiar objects and images
- create interactive books for Ashley to move from seeing and reading words in isolation to reading words in sentences
- create color coded materials to teach Ashley parts of speech, allowing her to create sentences of her own

And finally, I had created enough magnets and had acquired plenty of know-how to generate sentences and utilize magnets for her to answer comprehension questions for simple books she had read.

I often begin teaching a new skill by matching: matching images, matching colors, matching text, matching plastic letters, and so on. Matching is a simple strategy to determine the recognition of sameness. Because Ashley is nonverbal, matching is a very efficient way for her to tell me that she can recognize the similarity of a letter, an image, or a word. You may find it helpful with your child to begin by using this same approach. This not only gives your child the opportunity to demonstrate their ability to visually discriminate, but it also provides a simple method for acquiring new information.

Read on and find out how you can quickly create motivating materials to assist your child with learning to read.

SIGHT WORDS

What You'll Need

Materials
- White printer paper or printable card stock, 8½" x 11"
- Glue stick (optional)

Tools
- None

Art
- Scanned image, computer graphic, or clip art

Software
- Graphics program

Hardware
- Color printer

Level of Difficulty
- Simple

When Ashley was quite young, I had the good fortune to attend a workshop Patricia Oelwein gave before her book, *Teaching Reading to Children with Down Syndrome* (Woodbine House, 1995), was published. Her technique began by following a three-step progression (matching, selecting, and naming), and was very visual, initially teaching sight words rather than phonics or text decoding. Pat suggested starting off by playing simplified Lotto type games (see pages 97-116), matching text to text, for example, putting the word "Daddy" on "Daddy." After that was mastered, Pat suggested matching text to an image and then selecting the correct word from a set of different word choices. We would ask "Give me the card that says 'Daddy.'" This approach worked very well for Ashley.

For Ashley, teaching sight words held real potential. Because of her complex speech problems, Ashley could not verbally describe what letters she was seeing or what words she was reading, making it even more of a challenge to teach her to read. But Pat's approach of matching words and selecting words required no speech at all. Using these methods, Ashley was quickly able to learn to read a number of meaningful sight words, matching text to text, matching text to image, and then selecting a requested word from a set. Over time, she significantly increased her sight word vocabulary and eventually completed the final step of naming: expressively communicating her identification of many words using sign language. As she began to read and sign, lo and behold, along came speech.

Sight word cards really show the advantages to designing the materials by computer, including the opportunity to customize the word choices, and to keep it constantly fresh and new. And the computer enables uniformity. If the words are to be matched, it is best if they are an exact copy of one another (so that they are truly visually the same) which they cannot be if handwritten. It is quick and easy to accomplish this using a computer.

Skills to Teach

Visual perception
Math
● Language
Communication
● Reading
Handwriting
Self-help

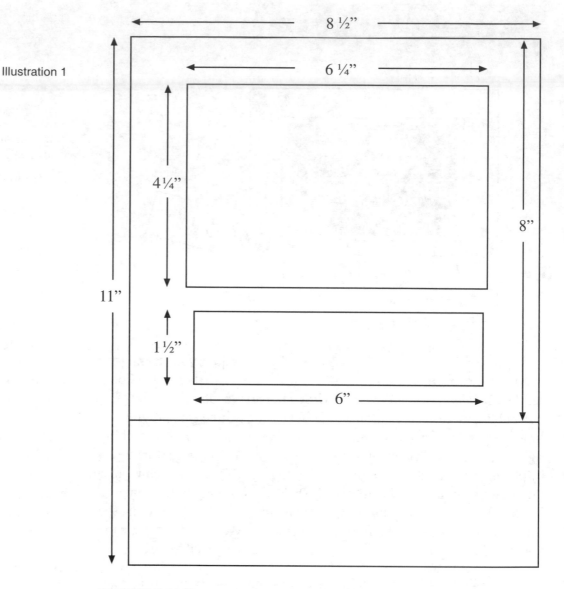

Illustration 1

DIRECTIONS

1. Open a new drawing document in a graphics program such as *AppleWorks*®, *FreeHand*®, or *Illustrator*®.

2. Turn on Grid and Rulers. (Refer to the previous section on **Grid and Rulers** in **Graphic Skills**.)

3. Using the Line Tool, draw a horizontal line the width of the page 8 inches below the top of the page.

4. Using the Rectangle Tool, draw a 4¼ x 6¼ inch rectangle. While the rectangle is selected, move it to the center of the page and place it approximately 1 inch from the top of the page.

5. Using the Rectangle Tool, draw a 1½ x 6 inch rectangle. While the rectangle is selected, move it to the center of the page and place it equally spaced between the larger rectangle and the horizontal line. *(See Illustration 1.)*

6. Set the text size to 72 pts.

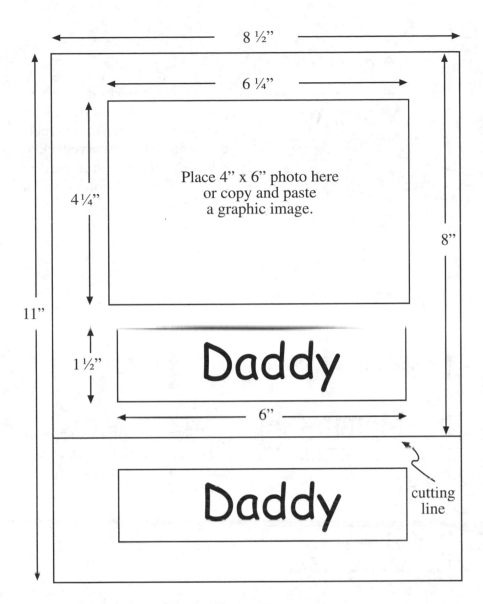

Illustration 2

7. Using the Text Tool, type the name of the image that corresponds with the image on the page.

8. Using the Select Tool, select, move, and center the text inside the smaller rectangle. *(See Illustration 2.)*

9. Using the Select Tool, simultaneously select both the smaller rectangle and the text inside it by dragging the pointer over both images. (See ***Making An Exact Copy*** on page 220.)

10. Copy to the clipboard and paste (or use Duplicate).

11. While selected, move them together below the previously drawn horizontal line. *(See Illustration 2.)*

12. Print (preferably on printable card stock).

13. Laminate.

14. Cut along the 8½ inch horizontal line. Then cut out the smaller rectangle that was placed below the horizontal line.

Once your child learns to place a word card on the text of the same word (like the example on the first page), have your child select the correct word card to match to the text from a set of two cards.

Then have your child select the correct word card to match the text from a set of three or more cards.

Move onto matching the word card to an image.

Next, have your child select the correct word card to match the image from a set of two cards.

Mommy

Daddy

Then have your child select the correct word card to match the image from a set of three or more cards. And so on.

Mommy

Daddy

Granny

And, have your child select the appropriate card from a simple set by asking, "Give me the one that says Daddy" or asking your child to read the text on a given card.

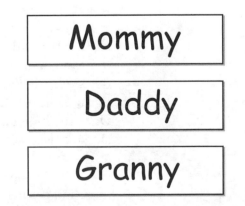

Mommy

Daddy

Granny

You can also have your child select a word and match it with a picture from a set of words and a set of pictures.

MAKING AN EXACT COPY: USING THE GROUP COMMAND

When text is placed inside a rectangle, the overall image is comprised of two separate components: the rectangle and the text frame. By selecting the rectangle with the Select Tool, the rectangle can be moved. By selecting the text frame, the text can be moved. Each one can move independently from the other.

But to make an *exact copy* of an entire image that is comprised of two or more items, you want the relative placement of objects to stay the same. In this example, you want the text to remain in the same location within the rectangle. To accomplish this, you have two choices:

1. Using the Select Tool, simultaneously select the rectangle and text by dragging the pointer over both components at the same time. Then use the Copy and Paste, or Duplicate, command, and an exact copy is achieved. Or,

2. Using the Select Tool, simultaneously select the rectangle and text, and then use the Group command found in the pull down menu under Modify in *FreeHand*®, under Object in *Illustrator*®, or under Arrange in *CorelDraw*®. Grouping objects maintains their relative placement. Once the individual images are grouped, they can then be treated as a single object, copied to the clipboard, and then pasted.

The Group command is useful in lots of situations: when two or more images need to be moved relative to one another, copied, pasted, or scaled. The Ungroup command will reverse the process, allowing you to independently manipulate images.

MAKING TEXT TACTILE & KINESTHETIC

TEXT WITH A DIFFERENT PURPOSE

MAKING TEXT LESS ABSTRACT AND MORE TACTILE & KINESTHETIC: THE CREATION OF THE HANDS ON FONT

For many children with a variety of disabilities, including Ashley, text is incredibly abstract, appearing at first as a collection of random flat shapes on a piece of paper. Text has no meaning until the child learns the meaning assigned to each symbol. This is true for many early readers. For them, and for Ashley, this may mean pairing this collection of shapes called "words" with photos and icons.

By using methods described by Patricia Oelwein in *Teaching Reading to Children with Down Syndrome* (Woodbine House, 1995), Ashley was able to quickly learn to read a number of meaningful sight words, matching text to text, matching words to images, and then selecting a requested word from a given set. She "expressed" identification of many words through sign language and by speaking the few words she could say. But, as we began to introduce more and more sight words, Ashley's ability to read surpassed her ability to sign or speak. She was able to correctly match and select from a set of choices many more word cards than she could either say or sign.

Additionally, as her sight word vocabulary increased, we encountered words that were more and more visually similar. It became increasingly difficult for Ashley to visually discriminate between them. Words with the same beginning letter (such as "Daddy" and "Derek"), words with similar configurations (such as "Ashley" and "Asbury"), and words with the same beginning and ending letters (such as "hat" and "hot") were often incorrectly identified. Because the first letter of a word is perceived best, and the final letter second best, the problem she was having was evident, but the strategy to address it was not. She needed an approach that would help her attend not just to the first and last letter of a word, or the word's configuration (the shape of the word), but to all the letters. Although I wanted Ashley ultimately to become a fluid reader—not necessarily needing to sound out every letter of a word—she first needed to learn that changing an individual letter can completely change the meaning of a word.

Ashley had successfully used an educational product from Lakeshore® Learning Materials. It was called the *Ready to Read Box*™ and consisted of the following:

- a set of plastic letters
- 26 miniature three dimensional objects, and
- 26 word cards, one card for each letter of the alphabet, comprised of a word in text that matches the plastic letter set, and an image that matches one of the three-dimensional objects.

The object of the activity was for Ashley to spell the word by placing the plastic letters on top of the text and to select the correct miniature object that matched the image on the card.

Ashley successfully placed the letters on top of the matching text for each word card. She attended to each letter of a word as she placed the plastic letters from left to right, as I cued her, on the corresponding text. She also successfully paired the miniature object with the corresponding image on each word card by selecting the correct object from the 26 miniature objects provided. But, although the process of matching the plastic letters to the text worked beautifully, once we completed the 26 cards and objects, we were done!

I liked the *Ready to Read Box*™, and wanted to keep going with it, but I wanted complete control over the word selection and choice of images. In addition to the limited number of cards, I would have chosen other words and images for the word cards since there seemed to be no reason for their selection (words like "frog" and "dolphin"). I needed a more systematic approach to teach Ashley to read. All I was really lacking were more word cards filled with words of my choosing.

I realized that if I could design a font that exactly matched this same set of plastic letters I could create a tactile and kinesthetic method to reading, taking something flat and abstract (text) and connecting it to something that could be handled and manipulated (the plastic letters). This approach could help Ashley to see all the letters of a word and visually discriminate between them. By designing educational materials with this font, I could create personalized educational materials for Ashley to assist her in learning to read and spell.

This tactile and kinesthetic approach could assist Ashley in making an abstract concept concrete, providing her the opportunity to physically interact with text so that she could learn by touching and doing rather than by only seeing or hearing. She could be actively engaged rather than only passively attending. By working side by side with Ashley—available to read the words to her and verbally identify the letters—I could involve all four styles of learning: visual, auditory, tactile, and kinesthetic.

Driven by Ashley's need for this font, I spent hours and hours creating it. I went to great lengths to precisely match the design of the font to the set of plastic letters, while experimenting with the spacing between the letters to reduce the chance of bumping the plastic letters as they are placed on top of the text. The process took over a year. Called Hands On, this font was subsequently published by Mayer-Johnson, Inc. in 1997 as part of *School Fonts for Beginning Writing*, a series of fonts I created for designing customized educational materials. Loaded into a computer's system folder like other fonts, such as Helvetica or Geneva, it can be used in any word processing or graphics programs, or any other software program that uses text.

The set of plastic letters, by Lakeshore® Learning Materials, is manufactured with all uppercase letters in red and all lowercase letters in blue. This is quite different from many other plastic letter sets on the market that assign the color for each letter of the alphabet randomly. With Lakeshore® letters, each letter does not have a unique "value" based on its color since all uppercase letters are the same color, as are all lowercase letters. This directs the attention of the child to the letter's shape rather than to its color.

Using the Hands On font, educational materials can be quickly and consistently designed on a computer to match the plastic Lakeshore® letters. With a color printer, the uppercase letters can be printed in a comparable red, and lowercase letters printed in blue. This consistency in color helps kids quickly visually discriminate between upper and lowercase letters.

Utilizing materials I created on the computer using this font, Ashley has learned to pay attention to every letter of a word. She has also learned to spell her name (see *Spelling Your Name*) and uses the same method to participate in lots of spelling activities (see *Interactive Spelling Cards*) at school and at home. Unable to independently write or verbally spell words, she has learned to spell many words using the plastic letters, first matching the plastic letters to the corresponding text, and then independently spelling words with no prompt at all. Even better, she has learned to decode text using educational materials to teach word families (see *Decoding Text with Word Families*), and has become phonemically aware, a necessary skill to move beyond a purely sight word reading vocabulary.

This method does not require speech, nor does it require handwriting. What it does require is the ability to match, a skill most children learn with ease and one they have typically mastered long before they begin to learn to read. And, unlike using pencil and paper for spelling, using the plastic letters allows for easy self-correction.

So, whether your child is nonverbal or verbal, has learning challenges or not, making text tactile and kinesthetic can be of benefit to all children learning to read and spell. Teachers may choose to use these methods as part of their normal repertoire for teaching children to read. This allows the creation of materials containing meaningful words like your child's name, the names of their siblings and classmates, spelling words related to the school curriculum. What child would not benefit from that?

TRACING OVER MEANINGFUL TEXT: PROVIDING MOTOR INPUT FOR THE SHAPE OF LETTERS

For years following her stroke (and brain damage), Ashley struggled terribly with drawing and handwriting. Unable to color or write, she mostly pounded the paper with whatever writing instrument she was given. She eventually learned to hold a marker or crayon perfectly in her hand, but what she was able to produce with her beautiful tripod grasp was anything but beautiful. And what's worse, Ashley knew it. Her brain was not correctly telling her hand what to do because of motor apraxia, but her eyes and brain were capable of assessing the product. She knew it wasn't right.

Ashley not only had all but lost her ability to speak due to the brain damage, but she had lost her ability to write as well. By definition she was agraphic.

Keyboarding was a viable alternative, but Ashley had to first learn the necessary skills to successfully keyboard: learn the shapes that represent the letters of the alphabet, learn the uppercase letters and their lowercase equivalents, isolate a finger, scan a keyboard, and spell. This long list of educational objectives needed to reach the goal of keyboarding would take some time.

While we tackled these skills, I ran across a software program that piqued Ashley's interest and mine. It was called *Touch 'n Write* by Sunburst Technology and utilized a TouchWindow® by Edmark. Attached to the front of the computer's monitor, the TouchWindow® allowed Ashley to access the computer by pointing and touching the screen directly. The *Touch 'n Write* program used a stylus to trace the letters of the alphabet on the TouchWindow® as the program prompted her strokes with animation, color, and sound.

It was a hit! Her first time using this program was nothing short of amazing. She sat for hours and hours, not wanting to get up from the computer. She did not want to stop tracing, as she would self-correct, get angry at herself, and sign "wrong" when the computer emitted a noise indicating that she had drawn the letter incorrectly. It was difficult to watch Ashley being so hard on herself, but it was also inspiring to see her determination.

Unfortunately, Sunburst did not continue to support this program so, as new computers and new operating systems emerged, the program became obsolete. It was time to design an alternative for Ashley to practice writing her letters.

Ashley had done such a beautiful job tracing over the strokes comprising the letters of the alphabet using the *Touch 'n Write* software that it gave me an idea: What if I could create a dashed font that I could use to prompt Ashley to write? Unfortunately, it was not an easy task. I first had to determine the overall shape of each letter before creating the individual pieces that comprised its dashed version. The first set I designed was published by Mayer-Johnson, Inc. as part of *School Fonts for Beginning Writing*. This set is in the Palmer manuscript style of handwriting, similar to simple printing. A subsequent set is in the slanted D'Nealian style, called *Transitional Fonts for Emerging Writers*.

Ashley could not independently write her words using paper and pencil but, given the dashed text, she could trace them. Tracing over the words in the dashed text was a great method of input. Her performance showed that words she traced over were more likely to be remembered, and spoken! As I began teaching Ashley to read and spell, I remembered my school days when teachers would have me write my spelling words three times each. Surely there was something to this and not just busy work since teachers are still using this method today. Well, there is! Using your hands to write words engages a different type of memory than just seeing them.

Each set of fonts includes 12 dashed fonts, in 6 different design variations, either with or without a dashed line.

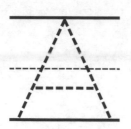

dashed letters
on a dashed line

dashed letters
without a dashed line

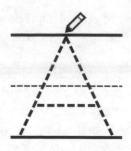

dashed letters with pencil
prompts on a dashed line

dashed letters with pencil
prompts without a dashed line

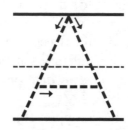

dashed letters with directional
arrows on a dashed line

dashed letters with directional
arrows without a dashed line

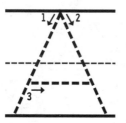

dashed letters with numbered directional
arrows on a dashed line

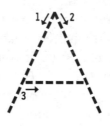

dashed letters with numbered
directional arrows without a dashed line

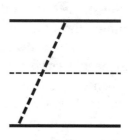

dashed letter strokes
on a dashed line

dashed letter strokes
without a dashed line

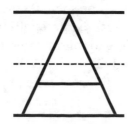

solid letter
on a dashed line

solid letter
without a dashed line

I have often seen teachers dashing letters by hand in an attempt to provide meaningful text for students to trace. But the image of each letter changes each day since no one writes the same letter the exact same way twice, and no two people write the same letter identically. And I guarantee they do not dash it the same way twice. The process is inconsistent, not to mention labor intensive. A keystroke takes a split second to execute and the size of the letters is easy to modify by changing the size of the font. Now when I see or hear of teachers hand dashing letters, I absolutely cringe. Not only is this poor form, it is of poor quality. I'd like to say, "This child deserves better. Please use this font."

For Ashley, these "dashed fonts" became the bridge from scribbling to producing beautiful horizontal, vertical, diagonal, and curved lines. She has learned to meticulously trace over dashed text with proper directionality to create the letters of the alphabet. Although Ashley now colors beautifully, unfortunately the dashed fonts have not completely remediated her agraphia. She traces her letters, creating the various strokes with the proper direction. But she continues to struggle with handwriting. We have long ago moved to keyboarding on a computer as a viable alternative to written language. But we have not given up. And that does not diminish the impact tracing over text of meaningful words has had for her as she learned to attend to the individual shapes of each letter while she traces over them.

Once the fonts are loaded into the computer's system folder, it is quick and easy to create pages of meaningful materials for your child to trace over. Many ideas are included in the pages that follow.

SPELLING YOUR NAME

What You'll Need

Materials
- White printer paper or printable card stock, 8½" x 11"
- Laminating pouches, 8¾" x 11¼"

Tools
- Scissors
- Heat laminator
- Lakeshore® plastic letters

Art
- None

Software
- Graphics program
- *School Fonts for Beginning Writing*

Hardware
- Color printer

Level of Difficulty
- Simple

Not surprisingly, one of the first words Ashley was able to identify was her name. She could read it and quickly learned to sign it as well: the "A" sign touched to her chest twice for the two syllables of her name. She even learned to say her version of her name: "La La." So when I would show Ashley her name, I could ask her, "Who is this?" and get a heart-warming response. "La La!" But, could she spell her name? Could she properly order the letters: A-s-h-l-e-y? And if not, could I teach her how?

Once I created the Hands On font, part of *School Fonts for Beginning Writing*, I had a way to teach her. I could create materials with text that exactly matched the set of plastic letters by Lakeshore® Learning Materials. First, I created a page of text using the Hands On font comprised of all the letters necessary to spell her name and in the proper order. She matched the plastic letters with one to one correspondence to the text on the page by placing the plastic letters on top of the text. By initially verbally cueing her, she also learned to place the plastic letters from left to right. Then I created additional materials, leaving out some letters of her name and replacing those letters with an underscore character. Given only the letters of her name, Ashley matched with one to one correspondence those letters that were present, and "filled in the blank" with plastic letters for those letters represented by the underscore. Next, I gave Ashley only the plastic letters necessary to spell her name and asked her to "spell Ashley." And, finally, I gave her a pile of letters comprised of more than just the letters in her name and asked her again to spell her name. Could she do it? You bet! Maybe she couldn't clearly articulate her name, and maybe she couldn't write the letters with pencil and paper, but, by gosh, she could spell it!

You can easily create these materials for your child. Depending upon the length of your child's name, this may be harder or easier than it was for Ashley, but give it a shot. Consider adding a photo of your child to make the materials engaging and meaningful and, by all means, use this same process for teaching other words.

Skills to Teach

- Visual perception
- Math
- ● Language
- Communication
- ● Reading
- Handwriting
- Self-help

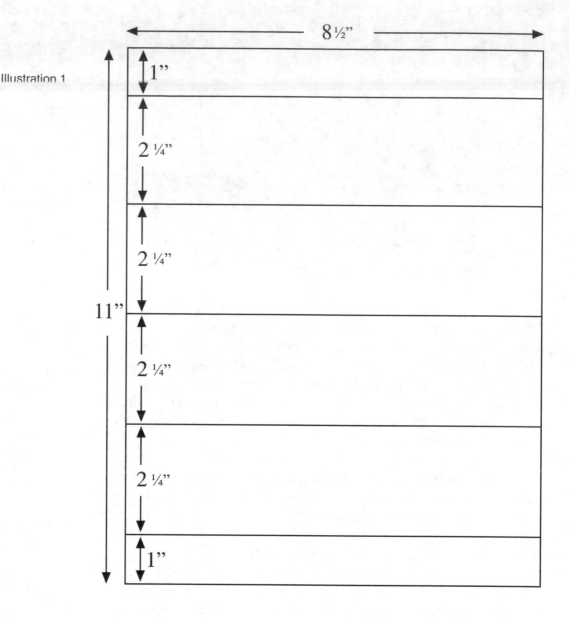

Illustration 1

DIRECTIONS

1. Open a new drawing document in a graphics program such as *AppleWorks®, FreeHand®,* or *Illustrator®.*

2. Turn on Grid and Rulers. (Refer to the previous section on **Grid and Rulers** in **Graphic Skills**.)

3. Using the Line Tool, draw 5 horizontal lines the width of the page and at 2¼ inch intervals, drawing the first line 1 inch below the top edge of the page. *(See Illustration 1.)*

4. Select the Hands On font from the font pull down menu.

5. Set the text size to 120 points.

6. Using the Text Tool, type all the letters of the child's name. While the name is selected, drag and place the text between the first two horizontal lines.

QUICK TIPS

ORIENTATION TIP
■ **Portrait or Landscape?**
Depending upon the length of your child's name, it may be necessary to change the paper Orientation to Landscape (Refer to previous section on ***Document Settings****.)*

Illustration 2

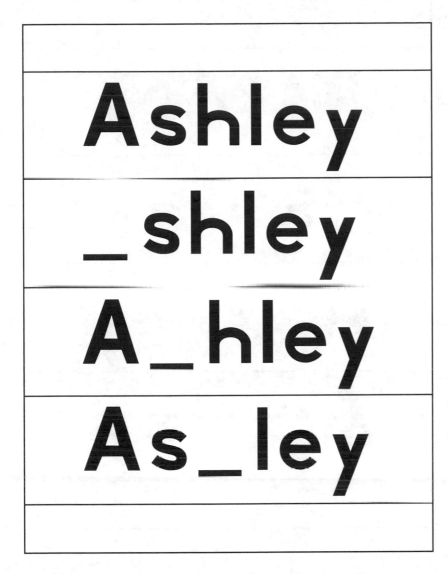

7. Using the Text Tool, type an underscore character in place of the first letter of the child's name and then type the rest of the letters in the name. While the name is selected, drag and place the text between the next two horizontal lines.

8. Continue this process of using the Text Tool and typing the letters of the child's name, replacing some of the letters of the child's name with an underscore character. While the text is selected, drag and place the text between the other horizontal lines. *(See Illustration 2.)*

9. Once the page is filled, use the Text Tool to select the first letter of the child's name by dragging the cursor over the letter. Change the text color to a red that closely matches the uppercase letter of the Lakeshore® plastic letters. *(See Illustration 3.)*

QUICK TIPS

DESIGN TIP
■ **Matching Text Color to the Colors of the Lakeshore® Plastic Letters**
Unlike newspaper print, text color does not have to appear only black. Text color can be selected from a Color Palette of a word processing or graphics program just like the color of any other graphic image.

Lakeshore® plastic letters come in two colors: red for uppercase letters and blue for lowercase letters. Through a bit of trial and error, you can find just the right red and blue in the Color Palette to match the colors of the Lakeshore® plastic letters. Printing the Hands On font in these colors provides one additional clue to your child about whether the letter is upper or lowercase.

Illustration 3

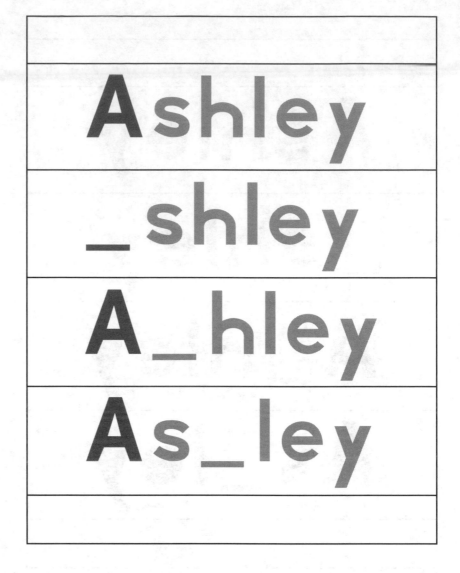

10. Using the Text Tool, select the rest of the letters in the child's name by dragging the cursor over the letters. Change the text color to a blue that closely matches the lowercase letter of the Lakeshore® plastic letters. *(See Illustration 3.)*

11. Print one copy of the page (preferably on printable card stock).

12. Heat laminate the page.

13. Cut the page apart into 4 cards. Do so by cutting just inside all printed lines, removing all the black lines on each name card.

INTERACTIVE SPELLING CARDS

Once Ashley was able to identify the letters of the alphabet, match a copy of a word to another copy of the same word, select a requested word from a set, and spell her own name, I wondered whether she could spell less familiar words. Unable to spell words aloud because of her expressive language disorder, unable to fingerspell using sign language because of fine motor deficits, and unable to write her spelling words because of handwriting difficulties, I had to devise a system that would allow Ashley to demonstrate her understanding of the order in which letters must appear to spell a unique word.

After a bit of trial and error, I created interactive spelling cards using a font, called Hands On, from a set of fonts I designed called *School Fonts for Beginning Writing* published by Mayer-Johnson, Inc. Designed to exactly match a common set of plastic letters made by Lakeshore® Learning Materials, the font allowed me to create a tactile and kinesthetic activity in which Ashley matched the plastic letters with one to one correspondence to printed text. By verbally cueing her, Ashley learned to place the plastic letters, from left to right, on top of the text. This helped Ashley to attend to all the letters of the word in left to right progression. For Ashley, pairing the text with an image gave the word meaning.

How does this prove she can spell? It doesn't until the prompt is removed. Given only a pile of plastic letters—initially only the ones necessary to make a particular word—and no interactive spelling card, Ashley must place the letters in the proper order to spell the requested word.

Yes, she could do it! She's even been known to spell a few words backwards to drive home the point: that given the proper presentation and proper tools, there is often more there than meets the eye.

Illustration 1

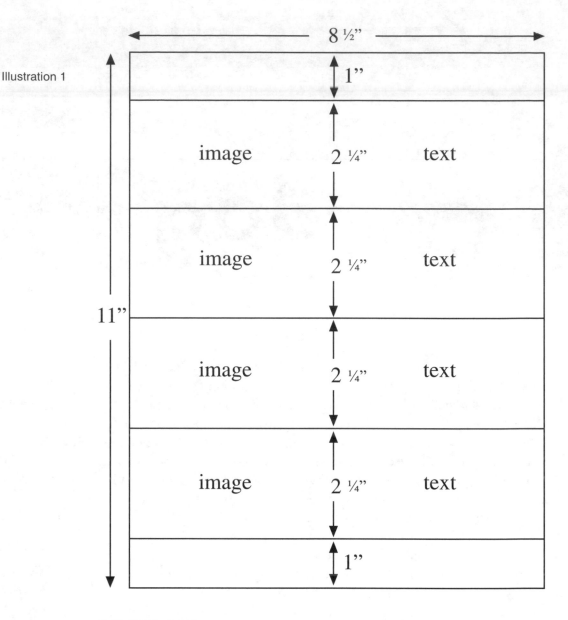

QUICK TIPS

BOARDMAKER™ TIP
■ IMAGE SIZE
When using *Boardmaker*™ prior to version 5.0, and copying a symbol to another program, setting the Picture Size to 100% automatically sets the image size to approximately 2 x 2 inches.

When using *Boardmaker*™ version 5.0 and higher, and copying a symbol to another program, the image is automatically set to approximately 2 x 2 inches.

DIRECTIONS

1. Open a new drawing document in a graphics program such as *AppleWorks*®, *FreeHand*®, or *Illustrator*®.

2. Turn on Grid and Rulers. (Refer to the previous section on **Grid and Rulers** in **Graphic Skills**.)

3. Using the Line Tool, draw 5 horizontal lines the width of the page and at 2¼ inch intervals, drawing the first line 1 inch below the top edge of the page. *(See Illustration 1.)*

4. Copy a 2 x 2 inch image to the clipboard. (Or, be prepared to re-size a smaller or larger image once it has been pasted. Refer to the previous section on **Scale** in **Graphic Skills**.)

5. Paste the image into the drawing document. While the image is selected, drag and place it about 1 inch in from the left edge of the page and between the top two horizontal lines.

Illustration 2

6. Continue this same process of copying, pasting, and placing 3 additional 2 x 2 inch images between the last 3 sets of horizontal lines, lining up all images vertically. *(See Illustration 2.)*

7. Select the Hands On font from the font pull down menu.

8. Set the text size to 120 points.

9. Using the Text Tool, type the name of the first image. While the name is selected, drag and place it to the right of the image.

10. Continue this same process, typing the names of the last 3 images so that each name is in a separate text frame, and placing them to the right of their corresponding image.

11. Print one copy of the page (preferably on printable card stock).

12. Heat laminate the page.

13. Cut the page apart into 4 cards. Do so by cutting just inside all printed lines, removing all the black lines on each spelling card.

DECODING TEXT WITH WORD FAMILIES

Although Ashley's sight word vocabulary grew enormously over time, she had to decode the text of unfamiliar words to truly become a competent reader. Word families (also referred to as phonograms and "chunks"), which are often used to teach the predictable patterns within many words, make that challenge easier. Learning these patterns helps to decode new words.

Like many times before, I could find nothing commercially that was appropriate to teach Ashley this important skill. So, I began designing my own materials. I needed a method for her to see the predictable pattern and visual similarities among words within the same word family. So, I carefully watched Ashley use trial materials and then edited the presentation, finally aligning words within a word family vertically and changing the text color of the onset and rime. This yielded a presentation that worked. She could see the pattern and quickly understood that changing the initial letter created an entirely new word!

Initially I made materials for only the "high utility phonograms." These thirty-seven phonograms can be found in almost five hundred primary grade words (Wylie & Durrell, 1970). Once Ashley mastered these, I created additional materials for less frequently occurring word families that she might run across, reinforcing the concept of predictable patterns. I did this in a deliberate progression:

- providing meaning to the word by pairing it with an image or icon
- color coding the "onset" and "rime"
- matching the text with the Lakeshore® plastic letters by placing the letters on top of the text with one to one correspondence
- filling in the blank with plastic letters for those letters represented by the underscore
- using dashed text to trace the words for motor reinforcement of the letter pattern

Create your materials and then sit side by side with your child, providing verbal instruction and tons of great reinforcement. These materials are well worth the time spent to create them.

What You'll Need

Materials
- White printer paper or printable card stock, 8½" x 11"
- Laminating pouches, 8¾" x 11¼"

Tools
- Scissors
- Heat laminator
- Lakeshore® plastic letters
- Write-on/wipe-off pen

Art
- Scanned image, computer graphic, or clip art

Software
- Graphics program
- *School Fonts for Beginning Writing*

Hardware
- Color printer

Level of Difficulty
- Simple

Skills to Teach

Visual perception
Math
● Language
Communication
● Reading
Handwriting
Self-help

Illustration 1

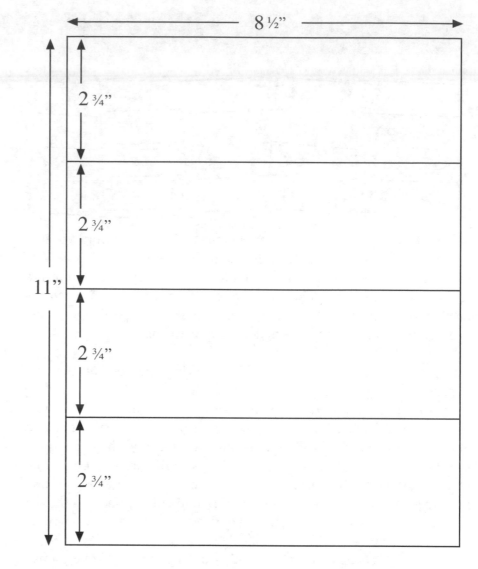

DIRECTIONS

1. Open a new drawing document in a graphics program such as *AppleWorks*®, *FreeHand*®, or *Illustrator*®.

2. Turn on Grid and Rulers. (Refer to the previous section on **Grid and Rulers** in **Graphic Skills**.)

3. Using the Line Tool, draw 3 horizontal lines the width of the page and at 2¾ inch intervals, starting from the top of the page. *(See Illustration 1.)*

4. Select the Hands On font from the font pull down menu.

5. Set the text size to 120 points.

6. Using the Text Tool, type one of four words for the selected word family.

7. Using the Select Tool, select and move the word to the right half of the page, close to the right edge and below the top of the page, and above the first horizontal line. *(See Illustration 2.)*

WHAT ARE ONSETS AND RIMES?

An "onset" is the letter or group of letters that come before the vowel in a word. The "rime" includes the vowel and all that follows. In the word "hat," h- is the onset and -at is the rime.

Illustration 2

8. Continue this process of using the Text Tool to type three more words for the selected word family so that each word is in a separate text frame. While the text is selected, drag and place it between the other horizontal lines, aligning all the rimes verti-cally. *(See Illustration 2.)*

9. Once all four words have been placed, use the Text Tool to select the onset of each word by dragging the cursor over the letter(s). Change the text color to a blue that closely matches the lowercase letter of the Lakeshore® plastic letters. Leave the letters of the rime black. *(See Illustration 2.)*

10. Copy a 2 x 2 inch image to the clipboard for the first word. (Or, be prepared to resize a smaller or larger image once it has been pasted. Refer to the previous section on *Scale* in *Graphic Skills*.)

11. Paste the image into the document. Using the Select Tool, select and move the image to the left of the word it matches.

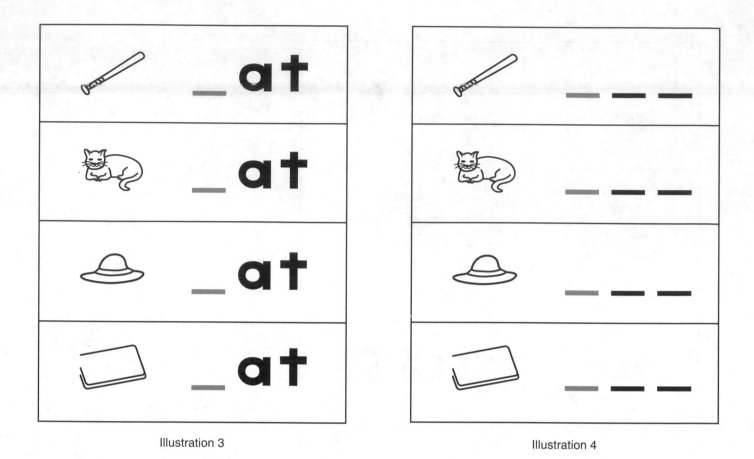

Illustration 3   Illustration 4

12. Copy and paste additional 2 x 2 inch images for the other three words. Using the Select Tool, select and move each image to the left side of its corresponding word, aligning the images vertically. *(See Illustration 2.)*

13. At this point, this image needs to be saved. Save it with a distinct file name, such as "Word Family Page 1." Now you will continue to work with the image you've created so far.

14. Using the Text Tool, select the onset of each word by dragging the cursor over the letter(s) and type an underscore character in place of the letter(s), keeping the text color of the underscore(s) blue. *(See Illustration 3.)*

15. At this point, this image needs to be saved. Save it with a distinct file name, such as "Word Family Page 2." Continue working with the image.

16. Using the Text Tool, select the rime of each word by dragging the cursor over the letters and type underscore characters in place of the letters, keeping the text color of the underscores black. *(See Illustration 4.)*

17. Save this image with a distinct file name, such as "Word Family Page 3."

Illustration 5

Illustration 6

18. Open the document "Word Family Page 1." Using the Text Tool, select each word by dragging the cursor over the letters. Change the font to a version of dashed text. *(See Illustration 5.)*

19. Save this image with a distinct file name, such as "Word Family Page 4."

20. Open the document "Word Family Page 4." Using the Text Tool, select each word by dragging the cursor over the letters. Change the text to a series of underscore keystrokes to create a blank line next to each image. *(See Illustration 6.)*

21. Save this image with a distinct file name, such as "Word Family Page 5."

22. Print one copy of each of the five pages (preferably on printable card stock).

23. Heat laminate all five pages.

24. DO NOT cut the pages apart.

25. Use pages 1-3 with the Lakeshore® plastic letters. Use pages 4-5 with a write-on/wipe-off pen.

QUICK TIPS

DESIGN TIP
■ **Matching Text Color to the Colors of the Lakeshore® Plastic Letters**
Unlike newspaper print, text color does not have to appear only black. Text color can be selected from a Color Palette of a word processing or graphics program just like the color of any other graphic image.

Lakeshore® plastic letters come in two colors: red for uppercase letters and blue for lowercase letters. Through a bit of trial and error, you can find just the right red and blue in the Color Palette to match the colors of the Lakeshore® plastic letters. Printing the Hands On font in these colors provides one additional clue to your child about whether the letter is upper or lowercase.

HIGH-UTILITY PHONOGRAMS

Here is the list of the thirty-seven high-utility phonograms ("word families") which can be found in almost five hundred primary grade words (Wylie and Durrell, 1970):

ack	ap	est	ing	ot
ail	ash	ice	ink	uck
ain	at	ick	ip	ug
ake	ate	ide	it	ump
ale	aw	ight	ock	unk
ame	ay	ill	oke	
an	eat	in	op	
ank	ell	ine	ore	

READING INVENTORY WORD MAGNETS & DECAL

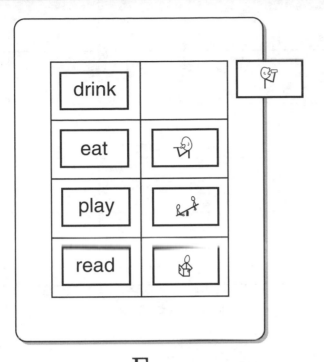

Far too often I have had to convince Ashley's teachers that she could learn to read. Even though I took responsibility for teaching Ashley to read, I nevertheless had to debunk the myth that a child who cannot speak can read. What I needed was a method requiring no speech to demonstrate the words she could read.

Using lists of basic vocabulary and word families as a guide, I created a large set of magnets. Each magnet had the text of words Ashley could read, and each word had a corresponding magnet with an icon or image of that word. I also created a grid using an inkjet decal. The grid was comprised of two columns, each column containing four rectangles. The decal stuck to the magnetic board using static-cling. The magnetic board was then placed in a stand that oriented it vertically. This was the ideal presentation for Ashley with the materials "front and center."

With video camera rolling, Ashley was given magnetic words and the corresponding magnetic icons, four at a time. She was to match the word with the image by placing their magnets in the grid, communicating her understanding of each word. She filled the grid with word after word after word!

I hope you do not have to go to these extreme measures to prove your child can read. If you do—even if your child can read but cannot articulate well—this is a great way to take inventory. Follow these instructions and you will know how to create magnets and decals that can be put to all sorts of uses.

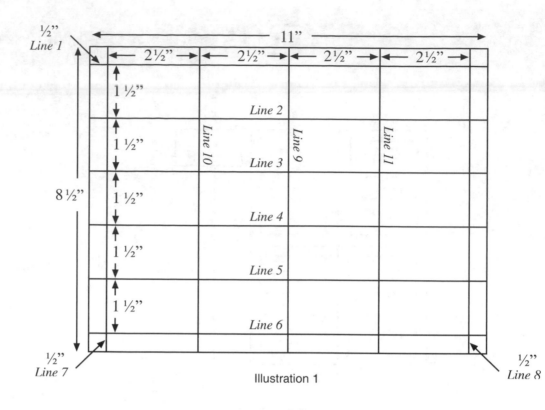

Illustration 1

DIRECTIONS: WORD MAGNETS

1. Open a new drawing document in a graphics program such as *AppleWorks®, FreeHand®,* or *Illustrator®.*

2. In the File Menu, select Page Setup. Change paper Orientation to Landscape. (Refer to the previous section on *Document Settings* in *Graphic Skills.*)

3. Turn on Grid and Rulers. (Refer to the previous section on *Grid and Rulers* in *Graphic Skills.*)

4. Using the Line Tool, draw the following lines:
   - **Line 1:** a horizontal line the width of the page located ½ inch below the top edge of the page
   - **Line 2:** a horizontal line the width of the page located 1½ inches below Line 1
   - **Line 3:** a horizontal line the width of the page located 1½ inches below Line 2
   - **Line 4:** a horizontal line the width of the page located 1½ inches below Line 3
   - **Line 5:** a horizontal line the width of the page located 1½ inches below Line 4
   - **Line 6:** a horizontal line the width of the page located 1½ inches below Line 5
   - **Line 7:** a vertical line the length of the page located ½ inch from the left edge of the page
   - **Line 8:** a vertical line the length of the page located ½ inch from the right edge of the page

> - **Line 9:** a vertical line the length of the page located 5½ inches from the right edge of the page
> - **Line 10:** a vertical line the length of the page located 2½ inches to the left of Line 9
> - **Line 11:** a vertical line the length of the page located 2½ inches to the right of Line 9 *(See Illustration 1.)*

5. Using the Rectangle Tool, draw a rectangle within one of the twenty rectangles in the grid, drawing it slightly smaller in dimension than the rectangle holding it (approximately 2¼ by 1¼ inches). (If your graphics program allows you to change the thickness of the line, set the line thickness to approximately 2 pts.)

6. While the rectangle is selected, copy it to the clipboard, paste it within the document (or use the Duplicate command), and center it within one of the other nineteen rectangles. Continue this process until all 20 rectangles of the grid are filled. Adjust the placement of the rectangles so that they are aligned vertically and horizontally. *(See Illustration 2.)*

7. Delete all lines in the document, leaving only the twenty rectangles. *(See Illustration 3.)*

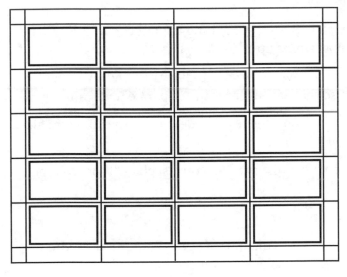

Illustration 2

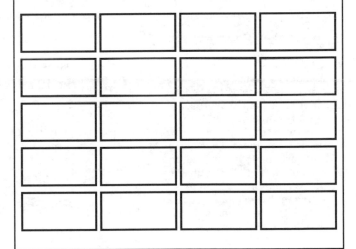

Illustration 3

8. Copy a 1 x 1 inch image to the clipboard. (Or, be prepared to resize a smaller or larger image once it has been pasted. Refer to the previous section on *Scale* in *Graphic Skills*.)

9. Paste the image into the drawing document. While the image is selected, drag and center it within one of the 5 rectangles in the second column from the left. *(See Illustration 4.)*

10. Continue this same process of copying, pasting, and centering 4 additional 1 x 1 inch images into the last 4 empty rectangles within this column. *(See Illustration 4.)*

Illustration 4

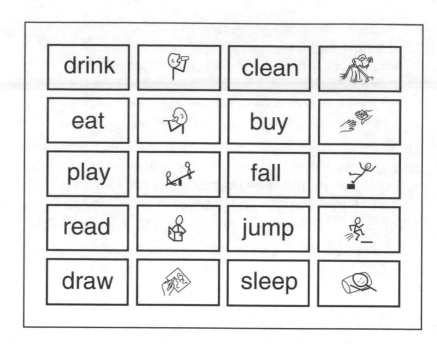

11. Repeat the same process, copying and pasting 1 x 1 inch images, and placing them in the 5 rectangles in the far right column. *(See Illustration 4.)*

12. Set the text size to 48 pts. (Depending upon the font, this will accommodate most words up to 5 characters.)

13. Using the Text Tool, type the word that corresponds with each of the 10 images so that each word is in a separate text frame.

14. Select, move, and center the text inside each of the 10 rectangles. *(See Illustration 4.)*

15. Save the image with a distinct file name, such as "Word Magnet Template."

16. Print one copy of the page.

17. Adhere to a magnetic media. (See ***Types of Magnetic Media: Choosing the Right One*** later in this section.)

18. Cut the page apart into 20 magnets. Do so by cutting just outside all printed lines, leaving each magnet with a black border.

DIRECTIONS: DECAL

19. Open a new drawing document in a graphics program such as *AppleWorks®, FreeHand®,* or *Illustrator®.*

20. Turn on Grid and Rulers. (Refer to the previous section on ***Grid and Rulers*** in ***Graphic Skills.***)

21. Using the Rectangle Tool, draw a rectangle 6 x 8 inches. While the rectangle is selected, drag and center it within the document, 1¼

QUICK TIPS

SOURCE TIP
■ **Vocabulary Lists**
Word lists, such as the Dolch list or Fry's Instant Words, are a great source of sight word vocabulary for high frequency words for readers. These lists can easily be found by searching the Internet. Although some words are more difficult to represent by an image (such as *or* and *if*), many can be. Sign language images are also a wonderful option. Along with their Picture Communication Symbols, Mayer-Johnson, Inc. also has libraries of sign language symbols that are used in *Boardmaker™*.

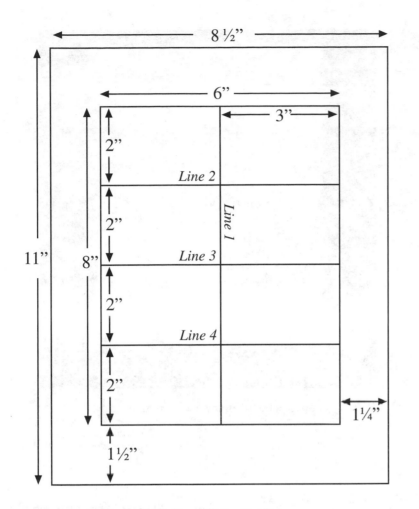

Illustration 5

inches from the right edge of the page and 1½ inches above the bottom edge of the page. *(See Illustration 5.)*

22. Using the Line Tool, draw the following lines:
    - **Line 1:** a vertical line the length of the rectangle located 3 inches from the right edge of the rectangle
    - **Line 2:** a horizontal line the width of the rectangle located 2 inches below the top edge of the rectangle
    - **Line 3:** a horizontal line the width of the rectangle located 2 inches below Line 2
    - **Line 4:** a horizontal line the width of the rectangle located 2 inches below Line 3

23. Save the image with a distinct file name, such as "Word Decal."

24. Print a test copy on standard printer paper. (See *Printing Tip* for **Printing a Test Copy.**)

25. Choose Transfer, Glossy, Photo, or Transparency mode of your printer.

26. Load the decal in your inkjet printer so that the image is printed on the proper side of the decal.

27. Allow the decal to completely dry before removing the backing from the decal and adhering it to the magnetic board.

QUICK TIPS

PRINTING TIP
▪ **Printing a Test Copy**
When using specialty papers, it is always best to run a test copy on standard printer paper first. Place the test copy on top of the specialty paper, hold both up to the light to determine whether all images and text are properly aligned. This is a good habit when printing such things as labels, decals, and pre-perforated papers. Specialty papers are significantly more expensive than standard printer paper, therefore, it is worth the effort to take the time to run a test before printing your final copy.

magnetic board, stand, decal, and magnets

TEACHING STRATEGY

One of the things I like most about magnets and decals is that I have the ability to mix things up. Ashley can quickly bore of activities. She can also learn the order in which things appear. So, after she has done something once, I can never be completely sure whether she is really looking at all her choices and making the correct selection or has merely memorized the proper order of the answers (no small feat). What I am after, however, is determining whether she has looked at all her choices and whether she truly understands the selection she has made. So, by mixing things up, I can keep things fresh and interesting, and be assured that she is providing the proper response.

Ashley's responses are a lesson in probabilities. In the examples shown, she has a 1:4 chance of matching the first response correctly. If she gets that one correct, she has a 1:3 chance of matching the second one correctly. If she gets the first two correct, she has a 1:2 chance of matching the third one correctly. And, finally, if she gets 3 correct, then by process of elimination she will match the final one correctly.

Since Ashley cannot say the words aloud and may not be able to sign them all, I can only assume she knows all four words when she correctly matches the words in various orders. I can have her match icons to words (*see Illustration 6*) or words to icons (*see Illustration 7*).

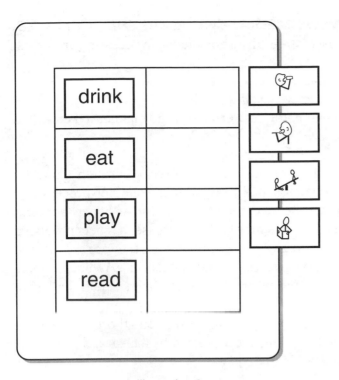

Illustration 6

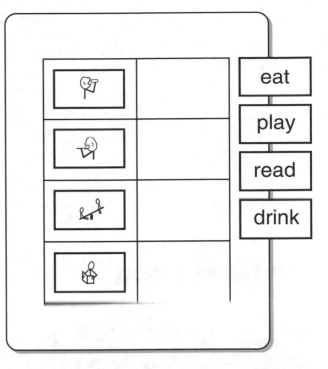

Illustration 7

I can mix up the order in which the word magnets appear *(see Illustrations 7 and 8)*. I can also mix up the order in which the icon magnets appear, and I can also mix up the word magnets and icon magnets at the same time.

But there's a twist: If Ashley consistently leaves the same word for last, I still cannot be completely sure she knows this word since the probability of getting the last word correct is 100% after the first 3 words have been properly placed (a sophisticated standardized test taking technique). But the beauty of using magnets is that I can remove the word that may be least familiar (the one she places last) from the first set and include it in a new set of 4 words until I am convinced she can truly identify the word.

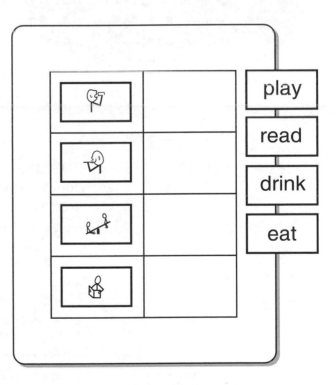

Illustration 8

TYPES OF MAGNETIC MEDIA: CHOOSING THE RIGHT ONE

There are at least three different media for creating magnets. They include:

- white printable magnetic sheets
- magnetic sheets with self-adhesive
- a heat-free laminator, stickermaker, and magnetmaker, called a Xyron®

White printable magnetic sheets run directly through an inkjet printer. This is advantageous since production is a one step process. But the disadvantage is that the media is nearly as thin as paper (approximately 11 mils); therefore, it is more difficult to use magnets produced from this media as a manipulative since they are a challenge to pick up or remove from a magnetic surface. White printable magnetic sheets are readily available at most national office supply stores in 8½ x 11 inch sheets, but their size limits the production of any larger magnets beyond those dimensions. And since the ink is not protected by a clear laminate, it is more susceptible to damage.

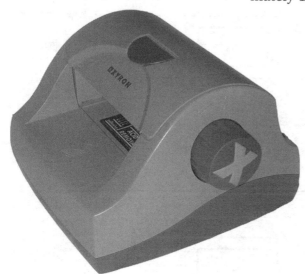

Xyron® Model 500

Documents printed from an inkjet printer are easily adhered to magnetic sheets with self-adhesive. The advantage of magnetic sheets with self-adhesive is that they come in nearly limitless sizes. They are also quite thick (25-35 mils), making them ideal for the production of magnets as manipulatives. The surface of the inkjet printed document is not protected by a laminate, although this can be applied as a separate process (by either using a clear acrylic spray or applying a self-adhesive laminate). Magnetic sheets with self-adhesive are not readily available, although they can sometimes be found at national craft stores as small sheets or rolls, and on the Internet in numerous sizes.

The Xyron® machine (www.xyron.com) laminates on one side and simultaneously applies a magnet to the other of materials printed from an inkjet printer. The laminate protects the ink. Depending upon the model of Xyron®, the magnet cartridge can come in lengths up to 10 feet, accommodating just about any size of magnet. However, the width of the magnet is somewhat limited by the Xyron® model, from 5 inches to 12 inches in width. The magnet is not quite as thick as the self-adhesive magnetic sheets, but is quite satisfactory, making it an excellent choice for creating a manipulative. The disadvantage of the Xyron® is the initial cost of the machine and magnetic cartridge. Depending upon the model you choose, full retail for a Xyron® machine ranges from $35 to $200 for the most common consumer models. But they are an excellent investment. You will turn to the Xyron® time and time again for laminating, creating stickers, and producing magnets. The Xyron® and their replacement cartridges are readily available at most national craft stores.

FILL IN THE BLANK WORD MAGNETS & DECAL

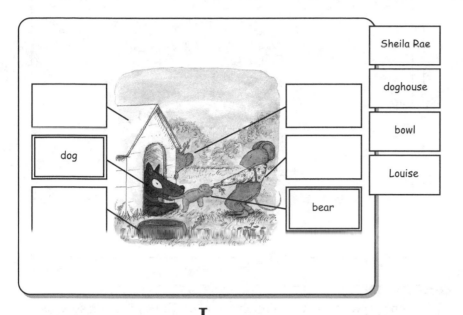

Sheila Rae

doghouse

bowl

Louise

dog

bear

What You'll Need

Materials
- White printer paper, 8½" x 11"
- Magnetic media
- Inkjet clear decal, 8½" x 11"

Tools
- Scissors
- Magnetic board
- Stand

Art
- Scanned images, computer graphics, or clip art

Software
- Graphics program

Hardware
- Color printer

Level of Difficulty
- Moderate

I made my first "fill in the blank" decal and magnets set because I wanted to try to determine what fascinated Ashley about a single image of a computer program, a Broderbund® *Living Book*® called *Sheila Rae, the Brave*. Sheila Rae is a spunky little mouse who is afraid of nothing, including "the big black dog at the end of the block." Sheila Rae pulls and pulls at her sister Louise's stuffed bear clamped in the dog's mouth. As if Ashley feels responsible for the stuffed bear's fate, she interacts with this page again and again as Sheila Rae struggles to free the toy from the dog's teeth.

In an effort to figure out what fascinates her about this page, I took a "picture" of the image using the computer's screen capture function and turned it into a "fill in the blank" decal. I made text magnets for all the different images: Sheila Rae, Louise, the bear, and so on. Presented on a magnetic board and after only a few minutes of instruction, Ashley correctly labeled the parts of the decal by placing the magnets in their respective empty rectangles. Did I figure out what it was about that image that enthralls her? Nope. But I used something motivating that taught her how to fill in a blank! Now she can label all sorts of images: the parts of a face, the parts of a bee, the parts of a skeleton.

The following instructions will show you how to properly lay out a "fill in the blank" decal and how to create the magnets to use with it. By creating everything yourself on the computer, you can create materials using motivating images (such as the parts of Daddy's face), and materials that match the academic content of the classroom (such as the parts of a grasshopper during the study of insects). And, what a relief for the kids challenged by handwriting: all materials test reading and knowledge without testing handwriting.

Skills to Teach

Visual perception
Math
● Language
Communication
● Reading
Handwriting
Self-help

Illustration 1

8½"

11"

DIRECTIONS: DECAL

1. Open a new drawing document in a graphics program such as *AppleWorks®, FreeHand®,* or *Illustrator®.*

2. In the File Menu, select Page Setup. Change paper Orientation to Landscape. (Refer to the previous section on **Document Settings** in **Graphic Skills**.)

3. Turn on Grid and Rulers. (Refer to the previous section on **Grid and Rulers** in **Graphic Skills**.)

4. Copy a 5 x 5 inch image to the clipboard. (Or, be prepared to resize a smaller or larger image once it has been pasted. Refer to the previous section on **Scale** in **Graphic Skills**.)

5. Paste the image into the drawing document. While the image is selected, drag and center it within the document. *(See Illustration 1.)*

6. Using the Rectangle Tool, draw a 1⅜ x 2⅜ inch rectangle.

7. While the rectangle is selected, copy it to the clipboard, paste it within the document (or use the Duplicate command), and move it to the left side of the previously pasted image. Continue this process until there are 3 rectangles on the left side of the image and 3 rectangles on the right side of the image. Make adjustments to the placement of the rectangles so that they are lined up vertically and horizontally. *(See Illustration 2.)*

8. Using the Line Tool, draw a line from each rectangle to the image that is to be identified. *(See Illustration 3.)*

9. Save the image with a distinct name, such as "Fill In the Blank Decal."

10. Print a test copy on standard printer paper. (See *Printing Tip* for **Printing a Test Copy**.)

Illustration 2

Illustration 3

11. Choose Transfer, Glossy, Photo, or Transparency mode of your printer.

12. Load the decal in your inkjet printer so that the image is printed on the proper side of the decal.

13. Print.

14. Allow the decal to completely dry before removing the backing from the decal and adhering it to the magnetic board.

DIRECTIONS: WORD MAGNET

15. Open a new drawing document in a graphics program such as *AppleWorks*®, *FreeHand*®, or *Illustrator*®.

QUICK TIPS

PRINTING TIP
▪ **Printing a Test Copy**
When using specialty papers, it is always best to run a test copy on standard printer paper first. Place the test copy on top of the specialty paper, hold both up to the light to determine whether all images and text are properly aligned. This is a good habit when printing such things as labels, decals, and pre-perforated papers. Specialty papers are significantly more expensive than standard printer paper, therefore, it is worth the effort to take the time to run a test before printing your final copy.

Illustration 4

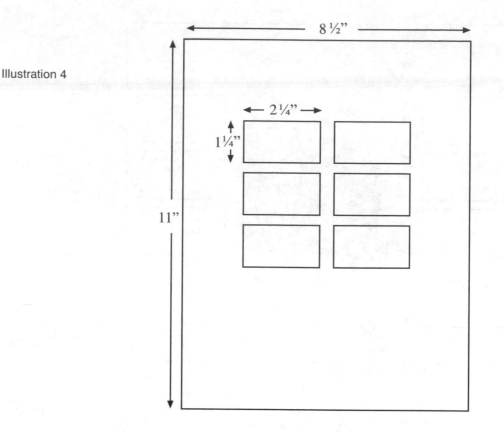

16. Turn on Grid and Rulers. (Refer to the previous section on **Grid and Rulers** in **Graphic Skills**.)

17. Using the Rectangle Tool, draw an individual rectangle approximately 1¼ by 2¼ inches.

18. While the rectangle is selected, copy it to the clipboard, and paste it within the document (or use the Duplicate command). Continue this process until there are 6 rectangles. Adjust the placement of the rectangles so that they are lined up vertically and horizontally. (See Illustration 4.)

19. Set the text size to 24 pts. (Depending upon the font, this will accommodate most words up to 12 characters.)

20. Using the Text Tool, type the words that correspond with each of the 6 images in the 6 separate text frames.

21. Using the Select Tool, select, move, and center the text frame inside each of the 6 rectangles.

22. Save using a distinct file name, such as "Fill In the Blank Magnets."

23. Print one copy of the page.

24. Adhere to a magnetic media. (See **Types of Magnetic Media: Choosing the Right One**.)

25. Cut the page apart into 6 magnets. Do so by cutting just outside all printed lines, leaving each magnet with a black border.

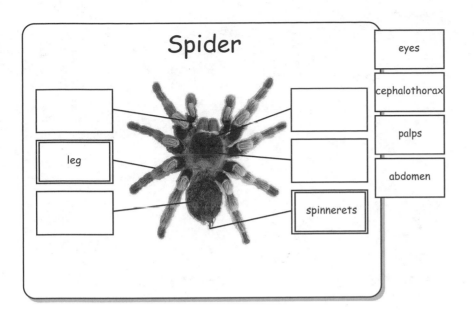

Create a decal to label the parts of a spider,

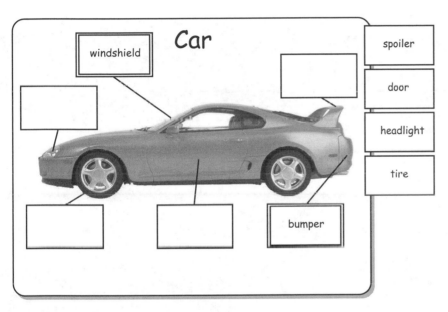

or the parts of a car,

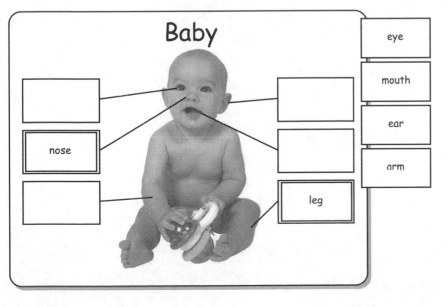

or the body parts of a baby.

INTERACTIVE BOOKS

I see a b...
I see a ball.
...ee a bat
...a cat.

What You'll Need

Materials
- White printer paper or printable card stock, 8½" x 11"
- Laminating pouches, 8¾" x 11¼"
- VELCRO® coins, self-adhesive
- White index cards, 3" x 5" and 4" x 6"
- Self-adhesive 3½" diskette pockets
- Sheet protectors
- Three-ring binder
- Plastic binding comb

Tools
- Scissors
- X Acto knife
- Straight edge
- Heat laminator
- Comb binder

Art
- Scanned images, computer graphics, or clip art

Software
- Graphics program

Hardware
- Color printer

Level of Difficulty
- Moderate

At the point where Ashley had built a significant sight word vocabulary, had learned to spell many words (including her name), could decode text, and was phonemically aware, I was thrilled. She had proven, despite all the naysayers, that she could read a large body of words although she might not be able to speak them.

Nevertheless, that was not enough. Reading words in isolation needed to lead to reading words within sentences, and sentences within pages of text. I began thinking about ways to create meaningful books for Ashley.

One of Ashley's favorite early books was *There's A Mouse About the House* by Richard Fowler (Usborne, 1984). As the book is read, a cardboard mouse is passed through a slot on each page. Ashley's attention was held as she passed the mouse through the book. That gave me the idea that I could create books with parts, that could test her comprehension as she manipulated what went with each page.

I set about creating a number of styles of interactive books. Interactive books are more than just static pages of text. They include something for the child to do: velcro an image to the page of appropriate text, slip a card into a pocket that corresponds with a sentence, or place the correct character into a slit on the page.

It is easy to create a page of text, but an interactive book is a whole lot more engaging and a whole lot more fun. And it's not that much more difficult to create an interactive book just by knowing a few tricks of layout, lamination, and materials.

And even if your child cannot speak or articulate clearly, it is possible to recognize her understanding of the text on the page by the way she uses her interactive books.

Skills to Teach

- Visual perception
- Math
- ● Language
- Communication
- ● Reading
- Handwriting
- Self-help

Illustration 1

DIRECTIONS FOR INTERACTIVE BOOK TYPE ONE—
Interactive Book with Pockets and Prompt

1. Open a new drawing document in a graphics program such as *AppleWorks*®, *FreeHand*®, or *Illustrator*®.

2. Turn on Grid and Rulers. (Refer to the previous section on **Grid and Rulers** in **Graphic Skills**.)

3. Using the Line Tool, split the page in half by drawing a horizontal reference line the width of the page located 5½ inches from the top edge of the page.

4. Using the Rectangle Tool, draw a 3½ x 3 ½ inch square.

5. Using the Select Tool, select and move the square, 2½ inches from the right side of the page and resting on top of the horizontal ref-erence line. *(See Illustration 2.)*

6. Set the text size to 72 points.

7. Using the Text Tool, type a simple "I see..." sentence.

8. Select and move the text to approximately 1 inch below the horizon-tal reference line and centered under the square. *(See Illustration 1.)*

9. Copy the 2 x 2 inch image to the clipboard for the noun that cor-responds with the sentence. (Or, be prepared to resize a smaller or

Illustration 2   Illustration 3

larger image once it has been pasted. Refer to the previous section on *Scale* in *Graphic Skills*.)

10. Paste the image from the clipboard into the document. Using the Select Tool, select, move, and center the image within the 3½ x 3½ inch square.

11. Save the document with a distinct file name, such as "Book With Pocket Prompt Page 1."

12. Delete the horizontal reference line that splits the page in half and the square (but only the lines, not the image).

13. Print one copy.

14. Slip the page into a sheet protector.

15. Adhere the self-adhesive data diskette pocket onto the sheet protector directly over the image. *(See Illustration 1.)*

16. Open the file you saved in Step 11 called "Book With Pocket Prompt Page 1." Change the sentence and then replace the image to correspond with the new sentence.

17. Save the document with a distinct file name, such as "Book With Pocket Prompt Page 2."

QUICK TIPS

DRAWING TIP
■ **Drawing Squares**
To simplify drawing squares, hold down the Shift key while dragging the Rectangle Tool.

BOARDMAKER™ TIP
■ **Image Size**
When using *Boardmaker™* prior to version 5.0, and copying a symbol to another program, setting the Picture Size to 100% automatically sets the image size to approximately 2 x 2 inches.

When using *Boardmaker™* version 5.0 and higher, and copying a symbol to another program, the image is automatically set to approximately 2 x 2 inches.

18. Delete the horizontal reference line that splits the page in half and the square (but only the lines, not the image).

19. Print one copy.

20. Slip the page into a sheet protector.

21. Adhere the self-adhesive data diskette pocket onto the sheet protector directly over the image. *(See Illustration 1.)*

22. Repeat steps 16-21 for each new page of your book, assigning a new page number to each new file name.

Directions for Pocket Cards

23. Open a new drawing document in a graphics program such as *AppleWorks®, FreeHand®,* or *Illustrator®.*

24. Turn on Grid and Rulers. (Refer to the previous section on *Grid and Rulers* in *Graphic Skills.*)

25. Using the Rectangle Tool, draw 4 squares, each 3 x 3 inches. *(See Illustration 3 on previous page.)*

26. Copy the 2 x 2 inch image to the clipboard for the noun associated with one of the sentences of your book. (Or, be prepared to resize a smaller or larger image once it has been pasted. Refer to the previous section on *Scale* in *Graphic Skills.*)

27. Paste the image from the clipboard into the document. Using the Select Tool, select, move, and center the image within one of the 3 x 3 inch squares.

28. Repeat steps 26-27 for 3 additional images.

29. Print one copy.

30. Laminate.

31. Cut the page apart into 4 cards. Do so by cutting just outside all printed lines.

Illustration 4

DIRECTIONS FOR INTERACTIVE BOOK TYPE TWO—
Interactive Book with Pockets and No Prompt

1. Open a new drawing document in a graphics program such as *AppleWorks®, FreeHand®,* or *Illustrator®.*

2. Turn on Grid and Rulers. (Refer to the previous section on *Grid and Rulers* in *Graphic Skills*.)

3. Using the Line Tool, split the page in half by drawing a horizontal reference line the width of the page located 5½ inches from the top edge of the page.

4. Set the text size to 72 points.

5. Using the Text Tool, type a simple "I see..." sentence.

6. Using the Select Tool, select and move the text to approximately 1 inch below the horizontal reference line and centered on the page. *(See Illustration 4.)*

7. Delete the horizontal reference line that splits the page.

8. Print one copy.

9. Slip the page into a sheet protector.

10. Adhere the self-adhesive data diskette pocket onto the sheet protector centered and approximately 1 inch above the sentence. *(See Illustration 4.)*

11. Create pocket cards the same as for Book Type One.

Illustration 5

DIRECTIONS FOR INTERACTIVE BOOK TYPE THREE—
Interactive Book with Two Pockets

1. Open a new drawing document in a graphics program such as *AppleWorks®, FreeHand®,* or *Illustrator®.*

2. Turn on Grid and Rulers. (Refer to the previous section on **Grid and Rulers** in **Graphic Skills**.)

3. Using the Line Tool, split the page in half by drawing a horizontal reference line the width of the page located 5½ inches from the top edge of the page.

4. Set the text size to 72 points.

5. Using the Text Tool, type a simple "I see..." sentence using the conjunction "and."

6. Using the Select Tool, select and move the text to approximately 1 inch below the horizontal reference line and centered on the page. *(See Illustration 5.)*

7. Delete the horizontal reference line that splits the page.

8. Print one copy.

9. Slip the page into a sheet protector.

10. Adhere two self-adhesive data diskette pockets onto the sheet protector approximately 1 inch above the sentence. *(See Illustration 5.)*

11. Create pocket cards the same as for Book Type One.

Illustration 6

DIRECTIONS FOR INTERACTIVE BOOK TYPE FOUR—
Interactive Book with Pockets with Prepositional Phrases

1. Open a new drawing document in a graphics program such as *AppleWorks®*, *FreeHand®*, or *Illustrator®*.

2. Turn on Grid and Rulers. (Refer to the previous section on **Grid and Rulers** in **Graphic Skills**.)

3. Using the Line Tool, split the page in half by drawing a horizontal reference line the width of the page located 5½ inches from the top edge of the page.

4. Set the text size to 72 points.

5. Using the Text Tool, type a simple "The noun is + prepositional phrase." sentence.

6. Using the Select Tool, select and move the text to approximately 1 inch below the horizontal reference line and centered on the page. (See Illustration 6.)

7. Delete the horizontal reference line that splits the page.

8. Print one copy.

9. Slip the page into a sheet protector.

10. Adhere the self-adhesive data diskette pocket onto the sheet protector centered and approximately 1 inch above the sentence. (See Illustration 6.)

11. Create pocket cards the same as for Book Type One.

Illustration 7

INTERACTIVE BOOK TYPE FIVE

Book Type Five uses simple sentences with adjectives. Sentences can be created using adjectives for number, size, and color:

I see one cat.
I see two cats.
I want a large drink.
I want a small drink.
I have a black cat.
I have a white cat.

Pocket cards can be created by easily duplicating images for number, scaling for size, or modifying for color to represent a number of different adjectives.

DIRECTIONS FOR INTERACTIVE BOOK TYPE FIVE— Interactive Book with Pockets with An Adjective

1. Open a new drawing document in a graphics program such as *AppleWorks*®, *FreeHand*®, or *Illustrator*®.

2. Turn on Grid and Rulers. (Refer to the previous section on **Grid and Rulers** in **Graphic Skills**.)

3. Using the Line Tool, split the page in half by drawing a horizontal reference line the width of the page located 5½ inches from the top edge of the page.

4. Set the text size to 72 points.

5. Using the Text Tool, type a simple sentence using an adjective.

6. Using the Select Tool, select and move the text to approximately 1 inch below the horizontal reference line and centered on the page. *(See Illustration 7.)*

7. Delete the horizontal reference line that splits the page.

8. Print one copy.

9. Slip the page into a sheet protector.

10. Adhere the self-adhesive data diskette pocket onto the sheet protector centered and approximately 1 inch above the sentence. *(See Illustration 7.)*

11. Create pocket cards the same as for Book Type One.

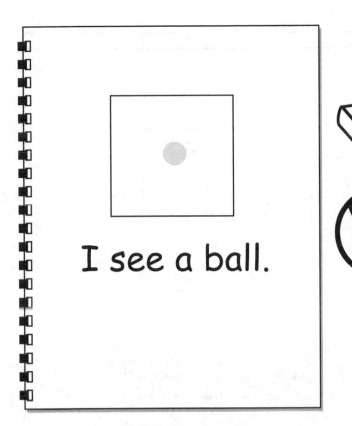

Illustration 8

I see a ball.

DIRECTIONS FOR INTERACTIVE BOOK TYPE SIX—
Interactive Book with VELCRO® Coins

1. Open a new drawing document in a graphics program such as *AppleWorks®, FreeHand®,* or *Illustrator®.*

2. Turn on Grid and Rulers. (Refer to the previous section on **Grid and Rulers** in **Graphic Skills**.)

3. Using the Line Tool, split the page in half by drawing a horizontal reference line the width of the page located 5½ inches from the top edge of the page.

4. Using the Rectangle Tool, draw a square 3½ x 3½ inches.

5. Using the Select Tool, select and move the square, 2½ inches from the right side of the page and resting on top of the horizontal reference line. *(See Illustration 9.)*

6. Set the text size to 72 points.

7. Using the Text Tool, type a simple sentence.

8. Using the Select Tool, select and move the text to approximately 1 inch below the horizontal line and centered on the page. *(See Illustration 9.)*

9. Delete the horizontal reference line that splits the page in half (but not the square). *(See Illustration 8.)*

10. Print one copy.

11. Laminate.

INTERACTIVE BOOK TYPE SIX

Book Type Six is a different presentation than Types One through Five. Items are placed in the book using self-adhesive VELCRO® coins (little round VELCRO® circles). A shape is drawn to hold the velcroed image and to serve as a "target." (Otherwise, your child may have a difficult time bringing the two pieces of VELCRO® together.)

Rather than placing the page in a sheet protector and adding a data diskette pocket, the pages are laminated and then comb bound. Items to be placed on the page are cut out in their natural shape. *(See Illustration 8.)*

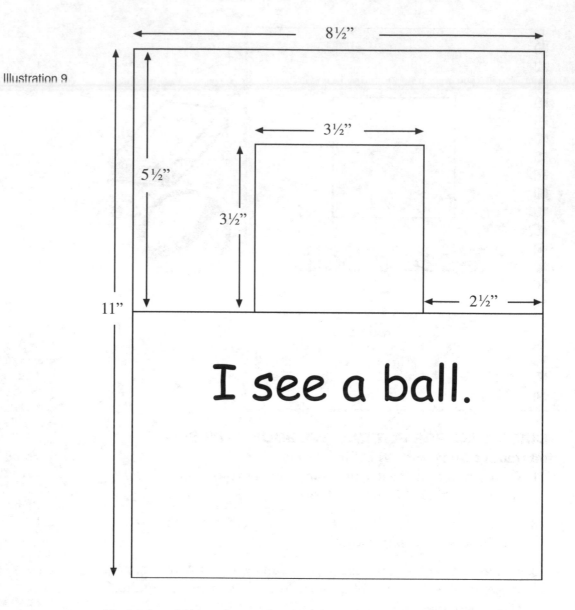

Illustration 9

12. Make additional pages by changing the sentence, dragging the cursor of the Text Tool over the sentence and then typing a new sentence.

13. Print and laminate additional pages.

14. Comb bind the pages together.

Directions for Response Objects

15. Open a new drawing document in a graphics program such as *AppleWorks®, FreeHand®,* or *Illustrator®.*

16. Turn on Grid and Rulers. (Refer to the previous section on **Grid and Rulers** in **Graphic Skills**.)

17. Copy the 3 x 3 inch image to the clipboard for the noun that corresponds with the sentence. (Or, be prepared to resize a smaller or larger image once it has been pasted. Refer to the previous section on **Scale** in **Graphic Skills**.)

18. Paste the image from the clipboard into the document. Using the Select Tool, select and move the image on the page to allow room for pasting other images.

19. Continue copying and pasting all necessary images.

20. Print one copy.

21. Laminate.

22. Cut the images out by cutting along the outside edge of each image.

23. Stick two opposing pieces of the self-adhesive VELCRO® coins together. Remove the paper backing to expose the adhesive on both pieces. While the two pieces are still stuck together, adhere one side to the back of the response object. Then attach the response object to the middle of the square by adhering the other side of the VELCRO® coin to the page.

Illustration 10

Cows live on a farm.

INTERACTIVE BOOK TYPE SEVEN

Book Type Seven uses a slit cut in the page to create a pocket to place a correct reponse. The trick to cutting a slit in the page is to laminate an unlined index card (3 x 5 or 4 x 6 inch) directly behind the spot where the slit is going to be cut. This creates a pocket.

This book type is great for learning to place animals in their appropriate habitats, for placing packages under a Christmas tree, or food inside a refrigerator.

DIRECTIONS FOR INTERACTIVE BOOK TYPE SEVEN—
Interactive Book with Slits

1. Open a new drawing document in a graphics program such as *AppleWorks®, FreeHand®,* or *Illustrator®.*

2. Turn on Grid and Rulers. (Refer to the previous section on **Grid and Rulers** in **Graphic Skills**.)

3. Using the Line Tool, split the page in half by drawing a horizontal reference line the width of the page located 5½ inches from the top edge of the page.

4. Set the text size to 72 points.

5. Using the Text Tool, type a simple sentence.

6. Using the Select Tool, select and move the text to approximately 1 inch below the horizontal reference line and centered on the page. *(See Illustration 10.)*

7. Copy a large image to the clipboard that relates to the sentence. (Or, be prepared to resize a smaller or larger image once it has been pasted. Refer to the previous section on **Scale** in **Graphic Skills**.)

8. Paste the image from the clipboard into the document. Using the Select Tool, select, move, and center the image above the horizontal reference line.

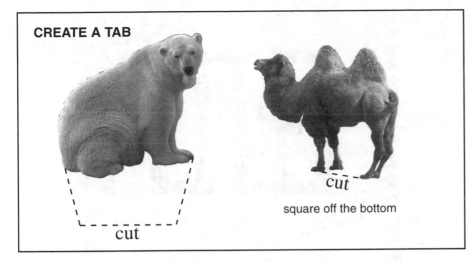

CREATE A TAB

cut

square off the bottom

cut

Illustration 11

QUICK TIPS

CUTTING TIP
■ **Creating a Tab**
In order to make it easier to handle the pocket cards, you may want to create tabs on the bottom of objects you intend to place into the slit of your Interactive Book. Cut below the object to create a tab. Or, square off the bottom of the object when you cut it out. This will make it easier to slip your objects in and out of the slit. *(See Illustration 11.)*

9. Delete the horizontal reference line that splits the page.

10. Print one copy.

11. Slip the page into a laminating pouch, placing an unlined index card on the back side of the document and directly behind the location where the slit will be cut.

12. Laminate.

13. Using an X-Acto knife and a straight edge, carefully cut an appropriately sized slit directly over the index card. Be sure to cut through the front side of the laminate, and up to the index card, without cutting through the index card.

Directions for Response Objects

14. Open a new drawing document in a graphics program such as *AppleWorks®, FreeHand®,* or *Illustrator®.*

15. Turn on Grid and Rulers. (Refer to the previous section on *Grid and Rulers* in *Graphic Skills*.)

16. Copy an appropriately sized image to the clipboard that relates to the image on the page. (Or, be prepared to resize a smaller or larger image once it has been pasted. Refer to the previous section on *Scale* in *Graphic Skills*.)

17. Paste the image from the clipboard into the document. Using the Select Tool, select and move the image on the page to allow room for pasting other images.

18. Continue copying and pasting images for all pages.

19. Print one copy.

20. Laminate.

21. Cut the images out by cutting along the outside edge of each image. (See *Cutting Tip* for **Creating a Tab**.)

Illustration 12

You might find tigers in a cage at the zoo.

(See Illustration 12.)

INTERACTIVE BOOK TYPE EIGHT

Book Type Eight uses a window that is cut in the printed page to create see-through "cages," "windows," and the like. The window is cut out of the page right before it is laminated. Once laminated, you can see right through the window. A pocket is then created by laminating an additional "patch" onto the back of the page. This is done by covering an unlined index card with a single thickness of another laminating pouch and then laminating the document again. A slit is then cut on the front side of the page to access the pocket of the see-through window.

DIRECTIONS FOR INTERACTIVE BOOK TYPE EIGHT—
Interactive Book with See-Through Window

1. Open a new drawing document in a graphics program such as *AppleWorks®, FreeHand®,* or *Illustrator®*.

2. Turn on Grid and Rulers. (Refer to the previous section on **Grid and Rulers** in **Graphic Skills**.)

3. Using the Line Tool, split the page in half by drawing a horizontal reference line the width of the page located 5½ inches from the top edge of the page.

4. Set the text size to 48 points.

5. Using the Text Tool, type a simple sentence.

6. Using the Select Tool, select and move the text to approximately 1 inch below the horizontal reference line and centered on the page. *(See Illustration 12.)*

7. Using the Rectangle Tool, draw a rectangle 4 x 5 inches.

8. Fill the rectangle with black from the Color Palette.

9. Using the Rectangle Tool, draw a rectangle 3¾ x ¾ inches.

10. Fill the rectangle with white from the Color Palette.

11. Duplicate the smaller rectangle 3 times.

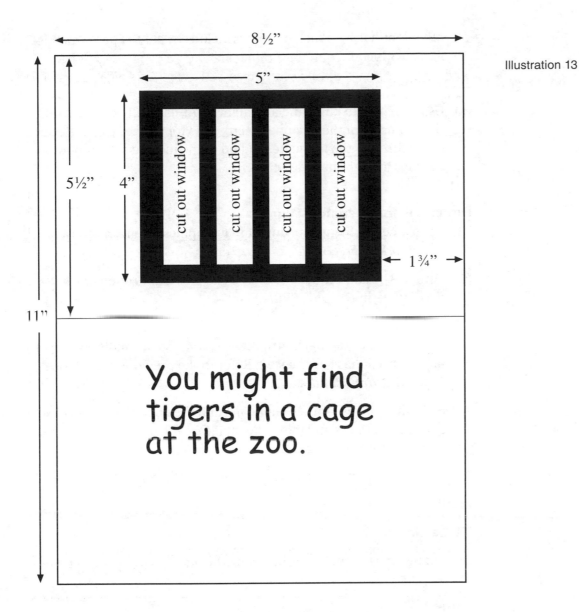

Illustration 13

12. Using the Select Tool, select and move the four smaller rectangles, placing them equidistant within the larger rectangle (½ inch from the left and right side and approximately ³⁄₈ inches a part).

13. Using the Select Tool, select and move all five rectangles together 1¾ inches from the right side of the page and approximately ¾ inches above the horizontal reference line. *(See Illustration 13.)*

14. Delete the horizontal reference line that splits the page.

15. Print one copy.

16. Using an X-Acto knife and scissors, cut out the windows. *(See Illustration 13.)*

17. Laminate.

18. Place a 4 x 6 inch unlined index card on the back side of the document. Cover the index card with a "patch" cut from one side of an-

other laminating pouch (a single thickness), cut to approximately 4½ x 5½ inches.

19. Laminate again.

20. Using an X-Acto knife and a straight edge, carefully cut a slit on the front side of the document across the top of the "cage." Be sure to cut through the laminate, and up to the index card, without cutting through the index card.

Directions for Response Objects

21. Open a new drawing document in a graphics program such as *AppleWorks®, FreeHand®,* or *Illustrator®*.

22. Turn on Grid and Rulers. (Refer to the previous section on **Grid and Rulers** in **Graphic Skills**.)

23. Copy an appropriately sized image to the clipboard that relates to the text on the page. (Or, be prepared to resize a smaller or larger image once it has been pasted. Refer to the previous section on **Scale** in **Graphic Skills**.)

24. Paste the image from the clipboard into the document. Using the Select Tool, select and move the image on the page to allow room for pasting other images.

25. Continue copying and pasting images for all pages.

26. Print one copy.

27. Laminate.

28. Cut the images out by cutting along the outside edge of each image.

DESIGN VARIATION

You can create other types of windows, but the trick is that the dimension of the window can be no greater than the size of the "patch" laminated onto the back of the page. So if you are using a 4 x 6 inch un-lined index card to create the patch, the window cannot be larger than 4 x 6 inches. *(See Illustrations 14 and 15.)*

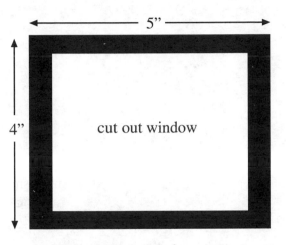

Illustration 14

Use this window for creating an aquarium for fish or a stage for actors.

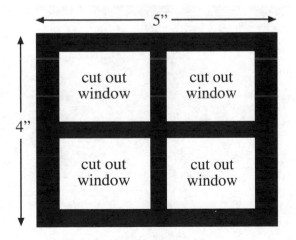

Illustration 15

Use this window for creating a peek into a little house.

SENTENCE BUILDING PARTS OF SPEECH

What You'll Need

Materials
- White printer paper or printable card stock, 8½" x 11" and 8½" x 14"
- Laminating pouches, 8¾" x 11¼" and 8¾" x 14¼"
- Clear business card pockets, 3¾" x 2⅜", top loading
- Self-adhesive VELCRO® coin fasteners
- Plastic binding comb

Tools
- Scissors
- Heat laminator
- Comb binder

Art
- Scanned images, computer graphics, or clip art

Software
- Graphics program

Hardware
- Color printer

Level of Difficulty
- Moderate

After a great deal of hard work and a bit of creative design, Ashley overcame significant challenges to acquire some rather impressive reading skills. The previous pages are a testament to her hard work. Naturally, I began to wonder if I could teach Ashley one more skill: to construct her own sentences from a bank of individual words.

To help her along, I created a set of materials that color-coded the parts of a sentence. I designed:
- a color-coded pocket strip comprised of different pockets for the different parts of speech
- a bank of color-coded sentence strips
- a bank of color-coded word cards, and
- a color-coded book to store all the words in the word bank

Ashley began by matching: placing the appropriate word cards directly on top of the sentence strip by matching color and text. Then she used the sentence strip as a model, selecting the appropriate words and then placing each in the correct pocket of the pocket strip to create an identical sentence. Lastly, Ashley created sentences of her own, selecting words from each color category of the color-coded work bank and then filling each pocket of the pocket strip by matching the color of the word to the color of the pocket. I then read her sentences aloud and together we replaced nouns, verbs, or articles with others if the sentences she created were not quite right (for example, "I eat the apple." rather than "I drink the apple.").

For Ashley, this was a wonderful method for her to bring individual words together to create thoughts of her own. You can use this "low tech" activity with your child as a bridge to other "high tech" communication and language strategies.

Skills to Teach

Visual perception
Math
● Language
● Communication
● Reading
Handwriting
Self-help

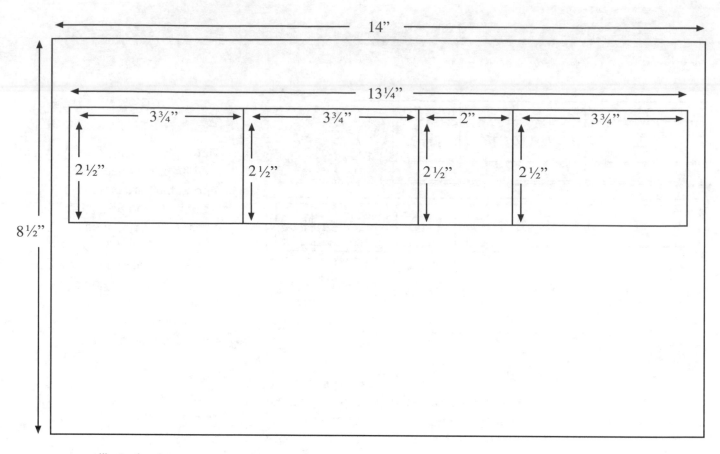

Illustration 1

DIRECTIONS FOR POCKET STRIP

1. Open a new drawing document in a graphics program such as *AppleWorks®, FreeHand®,* or *Illustrator®.*

2. In the File Menu, select Page Setup. Change paper Orientation to Landscape. (Refer to the previous section on *Document Settings* in *Graphic Skills*.)

3. Change the document size to Legal.

4. Turn on Grid and Rulers. (Refer to the previous section on *Grid and Rulers* in *Graphic Skills*.)

5. Using the Rectangle Tool, draw a rectangle 2½ x 3¾ inches.

6. Duplicate the rectangle 2 times so that you have three rectangles.

7. Using the Rectangle Tool, draw a rectangle 2½ x 2 inches.

8. Using the Select Tool, select and move one of the larger rectangles approximately ⅜ inch from the left side of the page and within the top half of the page. Select and move the other rectangles so that they are aligned horizontally, touching, and placed in the order in which they appear in *Illustration 1*.

9. Fill each rectangle with its own distinct color from the Color Palette. (See *Design Tip* for **Choosing Colors for the Parts of Speech**.)

QUICK TIPS

DESIGN TIP
■ **Using the "Duplicate" Command**
Duplicate makes an exact copy of a selected image with one simple command without the use of the Clipboard. The images can then be selected and moved to their permanent locations. Duplicate cannot be used between documents, but is great for creating multiple copies of the same image within the same document.

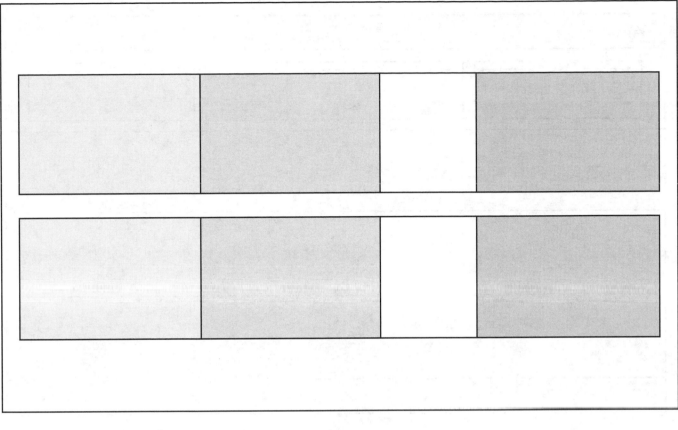

Illustration 2

10. Using the Select Tool, simultaneously select all four rectangles by dragging the pointer over all four shapes. (See *Making An Exact Copy: Using the Group Command* in *Graphic Skills*.)

11. Copy to the clipboard and paste (or use Duplicate).

12. While selected, move the new set of rectangles together below the first set of rectangles. *(See Illustration 2.)*

13. Print one copy on legal sized paper (8½ x 14 inches).

14. Laminate.

15. Cut out each pocket strip.

16. Because the plastic around the clear top-loading business card pockets makes them slightly larger than the large rectangles, trim the excess plastic around the edges of the three pockets.

17. Remove the paper backing and adhere the three clear pockets over the three largest rectangles of one pocket strip.

18. Cut one business card pocket to fit the smallest rectangle (the top and one side will now be open). Remove the paper backing and adhere the last pocket.

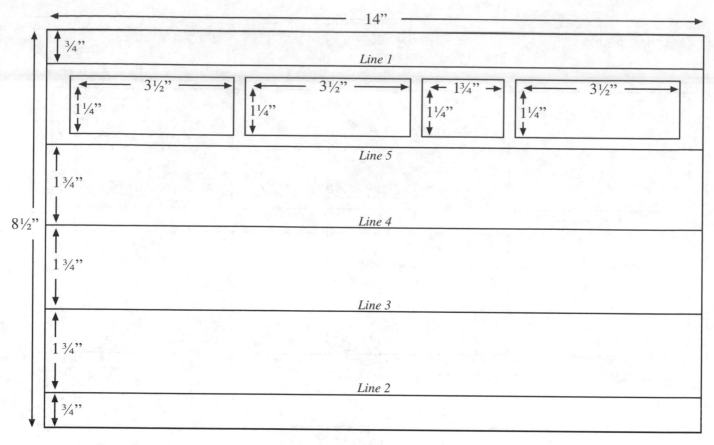

Illustration 3

DIRECTIONS FOR SENTENCE STRIPS AND WORD CARDS

19. Open a new drawing document in a graphics program such as *AppleWorks®, FreeHand®,* or *Illustrator®.*

20. In the File Menu, select Page Setup. Change paper Orientation to Landscape. (Refer to the previous section on **Document Settings** in **Graphic Skills**.)

21. Change the document size to Legal.

22. Turn on Grid and Rulers. (Refer to the previous section on Grid and Rulers in Graphic Skills.)

23. Using the Line Tool, draw the following lines:
    - **Line 1:** a horizontal line the width of the page located ¾ inch below the top edge of the page
    - **Line 2:** a horizontal line the width of the page located ¾ inch above the bottom edge of the page
    - **Line 3:** a horizontal line the width of the page located 1¾ inches above Line 2
    - **Line 4:** a horizontal line the width of the page located 1¾ inches above Line 3
    - **Line 5:** a horizontal line the width of the page located 1¾ inches above Line 4 *(See Illustration 3.)*

24. Using the Rectangle Tool, draw a rectangle 1¼ x 3½ inches.

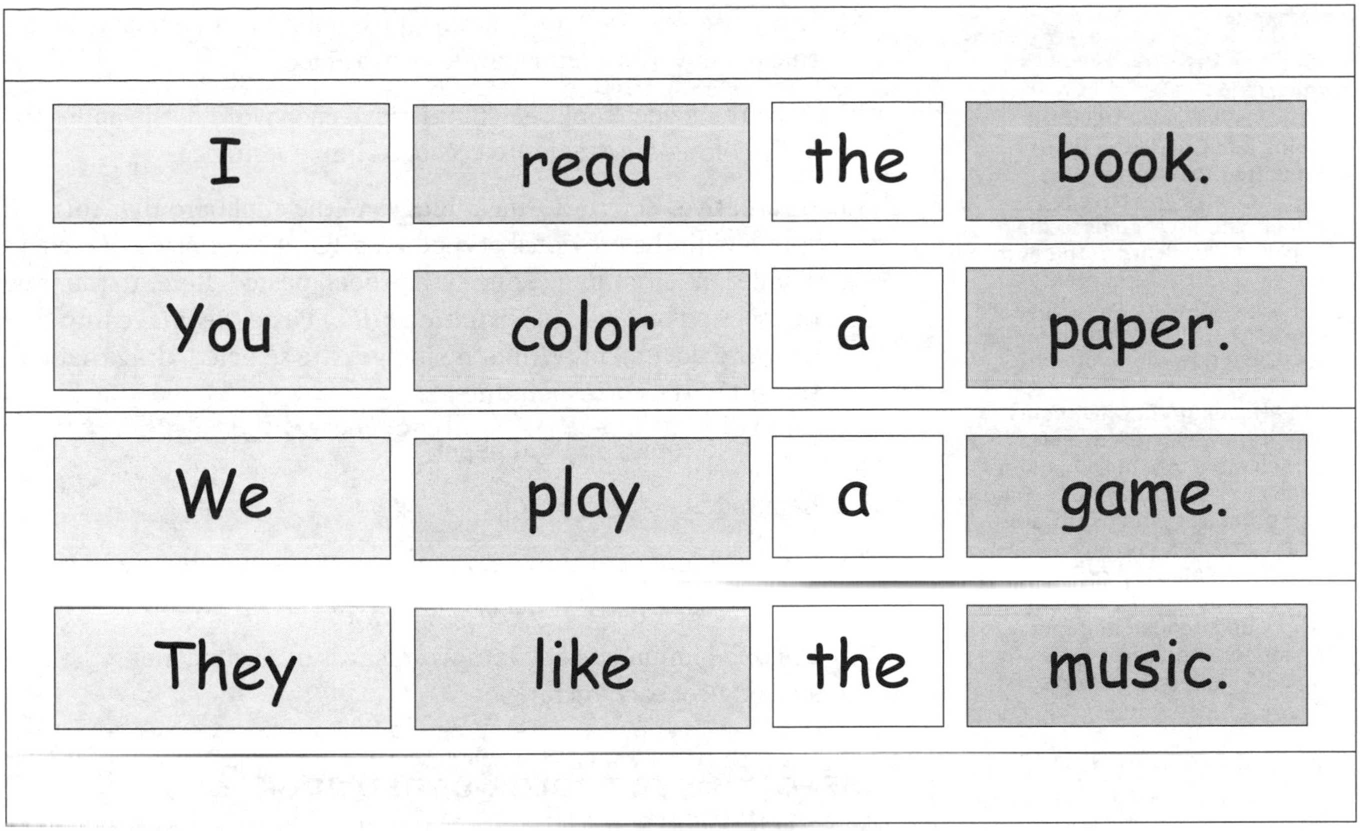

I	read	the	book.
You	color	a	paper.
We	play	a	game.
They	like	the	music.

Illustration 4

25. Duplicate the rectangle 2 times so that you have 3 rectangles.

26. Using the Rectangle Tool, draw a rectangle 1¼ x 1¾ inches.

27. Using the Select Tool, select and move one of the larger rectangles ½ inch from the left side of the page and between the top two horizontal lines. Select and move the other rectangles so that they are aligned horizontally, ¼ inch apart, and placed in the order in which they appear in *Illustration 3*.

28. Fill each rectangle with its own distinct color from the Color Palette that corresponds to the colors on the previously created pocket strip.

29. Using the Select Tool, simultaneously select all four rectangles by dragging the pointer over all four shapes. (See **Making An Exact Copy: Using the Group Command** in **Graphic Skills**.)

30. Copy to the clipboard and paste (or use Duplicate).

31. While selected, move the new set of rectangles together between the next set of horizontal lines. *(See Illustration 4.)*

32. Repeat steps 29-31 twice more.

33. Set the text size to 48 points.

34. Using the Text Tool, type nouns, pronouns, verbs, and articles so that each word is in a separate text frame.

35. Using the Select Tool, select and move each word to the appropriately colored rectangles to create a simple sentence.

36. Alternative: Copy 1 x 1 inch images to the clipboard that correspond with the previously typed text. (Or, be prepared to resize a smaller or larger image once it has been pasted. Refer to the previous section on *Scale* in *Graphic Skills*.) Paste the image into the drawing document. While the images are selected, drag them to the left of the corresponding text.

37. Print two copies on legal paper.

38. Laminate.

39. Cut one laminated copy into sentence strips by cutting along the five horizontal lines.

40. Cut one laminated copy into word cards by cutting along the outside edge of each rectangle.

DIRECTIONS FOR COLOR-CODED BOOK FOR THE WORD BANK

41. Open a new drawing document in a graphics program such as *AppleWorks®, FreeHand®,* or *Illustrator®.*

42. Turn on Grid and Rulers. (Refer to the previous section on *Grid and Rulers* in *Graphic Skills*.)

43. Using the Rectangle Tool, draw a 10 x 7½ inch rectangle centered on the page.

44. Fill the rectangle with its own distinct color from the Color Palette using the same colors as the ones to create the pocket strip, word cards, and sentence strips.

45. Save the document with a unique name, such as "Word Bank Page 1."

46. Fill the rectangle with another color from the previously created materials and save the document with a unique name, such as "Word Bank Page 2."

47. Fill the rectangle with another color from the previously created materials and save the document with a unique name, such as "Word Bank Page 3."

48. Open a new drawing document in a graphics program such as *AppleWorks®, FreeHand®,* or *Illustrator®.*

49. Turn on Grid and Rulers. (Refer to the previous section on *Grid and Rulers* in *Graphic Skills*.)

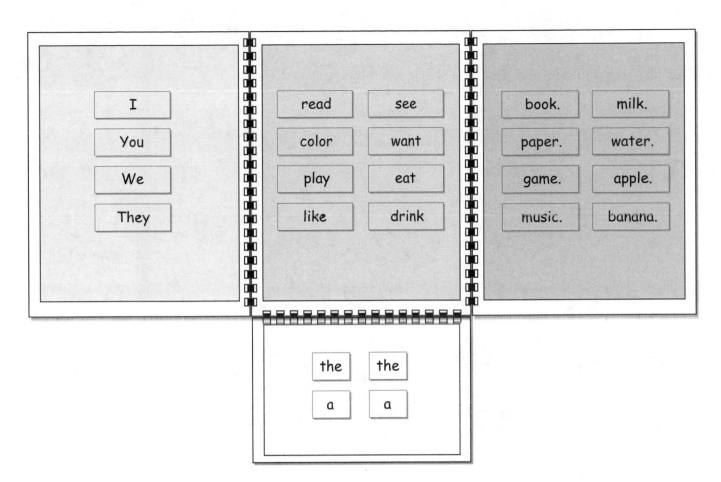

Illustration 5

50. Using the Rectangle Tool, draw a 5 x 7½ inch rectangle centered on the page.

51. Fill the rectangle with the last color from the previously created materials and save the document with a unique name, such as "Word Bank Page 4."

52. Print all four pages.

53. Laminate all four pages.

54. Cut off the excess page for the smallest rectangle.

55. Comb bind all four pages together *(see Illustration 5)*, trimming the excess binding comb off the shortest side.

56. Attach VELCRO® coins to the back of each word card and then attach the word cards to the corresponding page of the Word Bank Book according to their color.

QUICK TIPS

USAGE TIP
▪ **A Bridge to "High Tech"**
There are many "high tech" strategies for creating sentences that can speak! Progams like *IntelliTalk*® (a "talking word processor and flexible authoring tool") from IntelliTools® (www.intellitools.com) and *Speaking Dynamically™ Pro* (a "dynamic screen communication software") from Mayer-Johnson, Inc. (www.mayer-johnson.com) are both examples of programs that can be used to author talking sentence building.

The "low tech" strategy in this activity can be used as a bridge to "high tech," or as a parallel activity.

JOURNAL WRITING

What You'll Need

Materials
- White printer paper, 8½" x 11"
- Photos
- Glue stick

Tools
- None

Art
- None

Software
- Graphics program
- *School Fonts for Beginning Writing* or *Transitional Fonts for Emerging Writers*

Hardware
- Color printer

Level of Difficulty
- Simple

Journaling is a common classroom activity Ashley has encountered in many grades. But Ashley cannot participate in the traditional sense. Unable to handwrite independently and unable to speak, it has been challenging for her to freely express herself. In addition, her keyboarding skills were not developed enough for independent writing. I knew Ashley had something to say; the challenge was to find a way for her to say it. The computer to the rescue again!

In the months-long quest to find a method for Ashley to learn to write, or at least to experience the motor movement of handwriting, I created a series of fonts called *School Fonts for Beginning Writing* and *Transitional Fonts for Emerging Writers*. Each letter in these fonts consists of a series of dashed lines to trace over. Using photographs of Ashley and our family, I designed a number of pages, each with a box large enough for Ashley to attach a 4 x 6 inch photo. Using either *School Fonts* or *Transitional Fonts*, I created simple sentences to correspond with the photos. Given the photos and page of text, Ashley could attach the photos and then trace over the dashed text.

By using *School Fonts* or *Transitional Fonts*, nearly all children can participate in creating a journal. Even those who have a difficult time communicating their own thoughts through writing can participate if they can learn to trace over dashed text. More proficient readers can read the text and place the appropriate photo on the corresponding page; less proficient readers can be shown where the photo goes. Or, your child can be encouraged to dictate his or her own story while you keyboard it in dashed text to be traced over later.

Approaching journal writing in this way enables all students to experience success, ownership, and pride in producing a meaningful document.

Skills to Teach

Visual perception
Math
- Language
- Communication
- Reading
- Handwriting
Self-help

Illustration 1

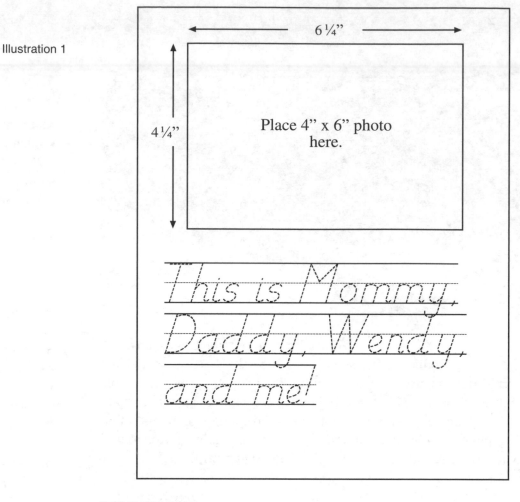

DIRECTIONS

1. Open a new drawing document in a graphics program such as *AppleWorks®, FreeHand®,* or *Illustrator®.*

2. Turn on Grid and Rulers. (Refer to the previous section on **Grid and Rulers** in **Graphic Skills**.)

3. Using the Rectangle Tool, draw a 4¼ x 6¼ inch rectangle. (Making the rectangle slightly larger than the photo makes it easier for your child to paste the photo in it.) While the rectangle is selected, move it to the center of the page and place it approximately 1 inch from the top of the page. *(See Illustration 1.)*

4. Set the text size to 48 pts. or greater.

5. Choose one of the dashed fonts from *School Fonts for Beginning Writing* or *Transitional Fonts for Emerging Writers.*

6. Using the Text Tool, create a sentence that corresponds with the photo that will be attached to the page.

7. Using the Select Tool, select and move the text below the rectangle that will hold the photo.

8. Print.

QUICK TIPS

DESIGN TIP

■ **Using Digital Photos**

Rather than using traditional photographs, consider using digital photos. Many photographic processing centers will provide a CD-ROM of your photo images in a digitized format. Crop, copy, and paste the digitized images. Digitized photos have great value since they can be used over and over again.

HANDWRITING TRANSPARENCY

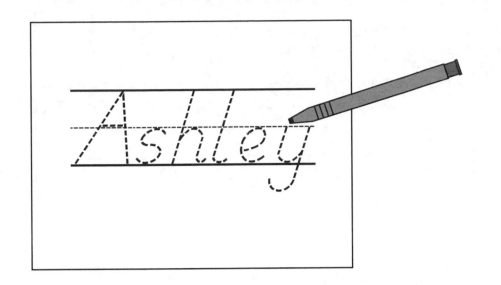

Like all kids, Ashley needs to practice certain skills over and over, like writing her name, address, and telephone number, to name a few. Rather than creating a document and printing on paper that would be thrown away, I began thinking of a way I could create something that she could use again and again. I realized that if I printed something on an inkjet transparency with words in dashed text, Ashley could trace over the dashed text with a write-on/wipe-off pen (such as a Vis-a-Vis®). The transparency could be wiped clean and then she could repeat the process. This not only saved on paper, but the wiping and repeating held Ashley's interest.

Transparencies can be used for many children at home or at school. A teacher could create a personalized pad for practicing handwriting for writing certain personal information. Each student could also have his or her own transparency that could be used over and over again. Plus, because they are smooth plastic, the surface provides a different type of feedback to the hand (less drag).

Transparencies are very versatile. They can be used directly on a tabletop or desk. I have also used them with a light box. Using drafting tape, tape the transparency down to the light box and then tape a blank piece of white paper on top of it. When you use the transparency with a blank sheet of paper on a light box, your child can trace over the dashed text onto the paper, remove the paper, and walk away with a slick product with no remnants of dashed text under the handwriting. His work looks like everyone else's!

Read on and let's get writing!

Illustration 1

Ashley Voss
555-5555

11"

8½"

DIRECTIONS

1. Open a new drawing document in a graphics program such as *AppleWorks®, FreeHand®,* or *Illustrator®.*

2. In the File Menu, select Page Setup. Change paper Orientation to Landscape. (Refer to the previous section on ***Document Settings*** in ***Graphic Skills.***)

3. Turn on Grid and Rulers. (Refer to the previous section on ***Grid and Rulers*** in ***Graphic Skills.***)

4. Set the text size to 72 pts. or greater.

5. Choose one of the dashed fonts from *School Fonts for Beginning Writing* or *Transitional Fonts for Emerging Writers.*

6. Using the Text Tool, create one or more lines of dashed text. *(See Illustration 1.)*

7. Using the Select Tool, select and move the text if it is not properly placed.

8. Print on the rough side of the inkjet transparency.

9. Allow the transparency to completely dry before using.

10. Write on and wipe off the slick side of the inkjet transparency.

QUICK TIPS

MATERIALS TIP

■ **Using Drafting Tape**

Drafting tape is designed to hold things in place temporarily and then peels off easily from vellum, transparencies, and paper without damaging the media.

If you don't have drafting tape, you can remove some of the stickiness from a small piece of masking tape by repetitively sticking and then removing it from your fingers.

PRINTING TIP

■ **"My Ink Won't Dry!"**

In all likelihood, if your ink will not dry after printing your inkjet transparency, you have printed on the wrong side of the transparency. Sorry!

DESIGN VARIATION

An inkjet transparency is ideal for creating a method to practice filling out a check. Scan the image of a check (or find or create a graphic image; one is included on the CD-ROM), erase old personal information, and then add personal information pertaining to your child (name, address, etc.). Have your child fill in the rest. *(See Illustration 2.)*

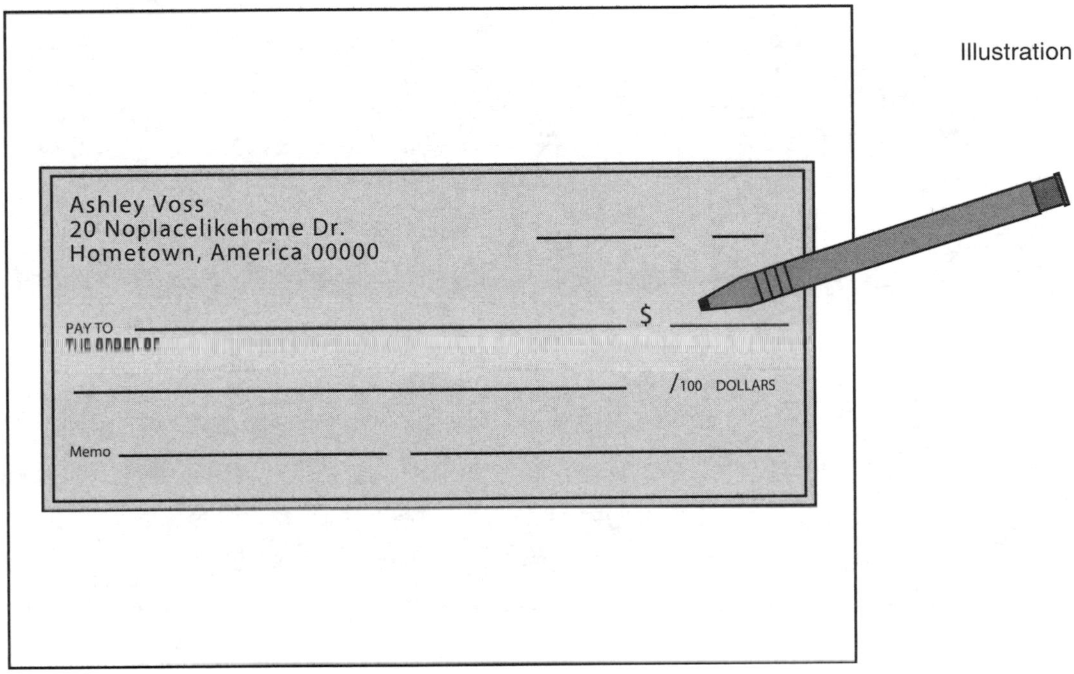

Illustration 2

You can also use dashed text in the appropriate places if your child cannot write or fill in the blanks independently. Have her trace over the dashed text. *(See Illustration 3.)*

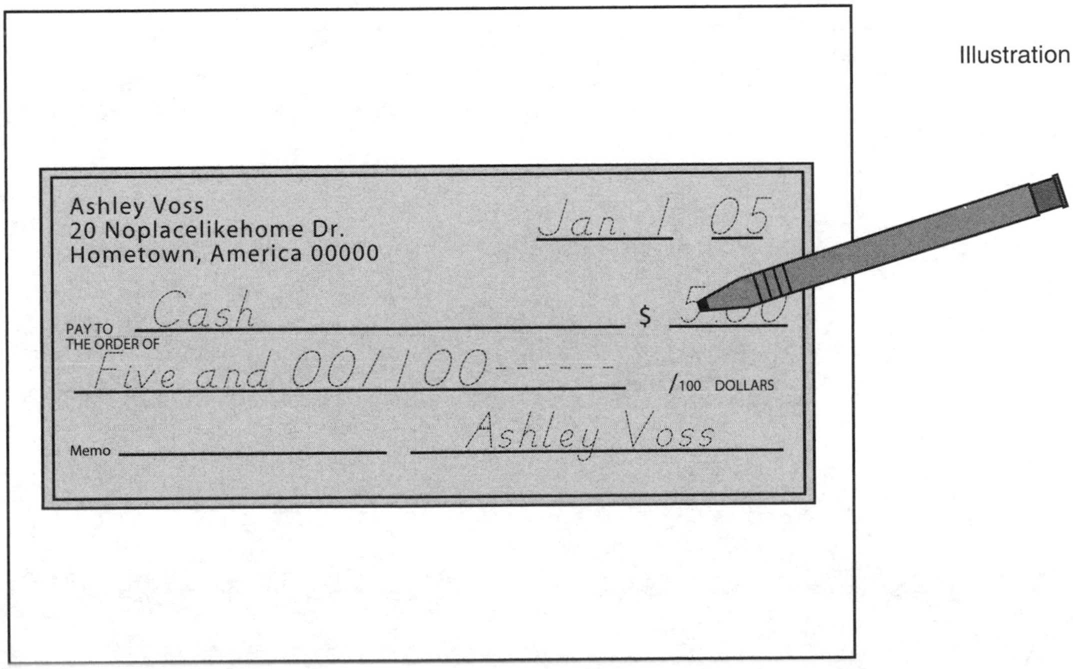

Illustration 3

NAME LABELS

There are times when Ashley needs to write her name or the name of a classmate, but her challenges with handwriting get in the way. Who would think that inkjet labels could address the problem? But they can! They have allowed Ashley to participate in activities she would have otherwise been left out of. Inkjet labels have allowed Ashley to put her name on school papers, address Valentine cards to friends, or "sign" friends' yearbooks. Created using a dashed font, Ashley places them on the top of a school paper, on the outside of an envelope, or in a yearbook. She can then trace over the text with a pen or marker and feel a sense of accomplishment as if she were writing independently.

Formatting a document to create a page of labels is not difficult when you use a template. A template document serves as the foundation for creating various sets of labels. It is used to determine where to place the text (and/or images) on each label. There are essentially 4 ways to do so:

- create your own template in a graphics program
- download a specific template from the label manufacturer (such as www.avery.com) to be used in programs like Microsoft® *Word* or *WordPerfect*®
- use something like *AppleWorks*® *Assistant* or Microsoft® *Wizard* to walk you through the necessary steps to create a format for a particular label product, or
- use a software application specifically designed for formatting labels, such as Avery® *DesignPro*® (Windows® only) available for free download at www.avery.com

Read on to find out how to design your own label template and the many ways you can use inkjet labels. And don't forget: both permanent and repositionable inkjet labels are commercially available!

Illustration 1

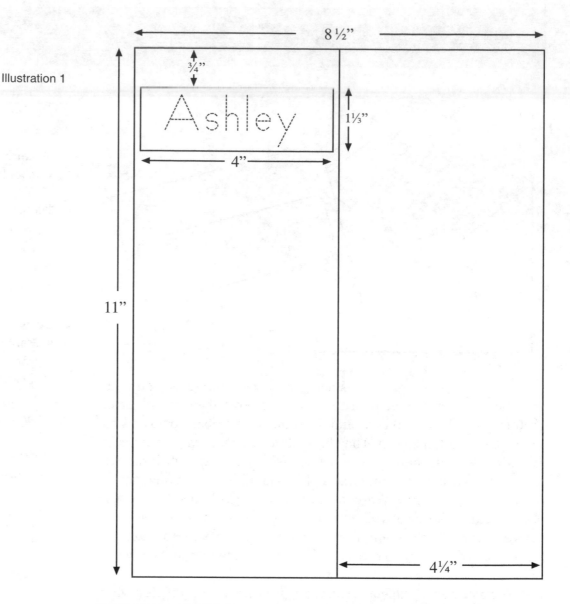

DIRECTIONS FOR USING A GRAPHICS PROGRAM TO CREATE A TEMPLATE FOR 1⅓" X 4" LABELS (AVERY 8162™)

1. Open a new drawing document in a graphics program such as *AppleWorks®, FreeHand®,* or *Illustrator®.*

2. Turn on Grid and Rulers. (Refer to the previous section on **Grid and Rulers** in **Graphic Skills**.)

3. Using the Line Tool, split the page in half by drawing a vertical line the length of the page located 4¼ inches from the right edge of the page.

4. Using the Rectangle Tool, draw a 1⅓ x 4 inch rectangle.

5. Select and move the rectangle ¾ inch below the top edge of the page and ⅛ inch from the left side of the page. *(See Illustration 1.)*

6. Set the text size to 48 pts. or greater.

7. Choose one of the dashed fonts from *School Fonts for Beginning Writing* or *Transitional Fonts for Emerging Writers.*

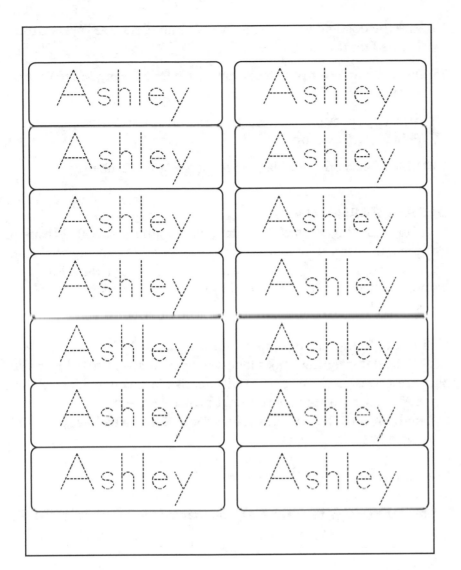

Illustration 2

8. Using the Text Tool, type your child's name.

9. Using the Select Tool, select, move, and center the text inside the rectangle.

10. Using the Select Tool, simultaneously select both the rectangle and the text inside it by dragging the pointer over both images.
   (See *Making An Exact Copy: Using the Group Command* in *Graphic Skills*.)

11. Copy to the clipboard and paste (or use the Duplicate command).

12. While selected, move the text and rectangle together directly below the first rectangle.

13. Continue this process 5 more times, lining the rectangles up vertically in the left column.

14. Repeat the same process to create the 7 labels for the right column.
   (See Illustration 2.)

QUICK TIPS

DESIGN TIPS
■ **Using the "Duplicate" Command**
"Duplicate" is used to make a copy of a selected item within the same document.

■ **Creating a Dashed Print Name Rubber Stamp**
Check with your local office supply store about creatng a custom rubber stamp of your child's name in dashed text. A child, parent, or teacher can use the stamp on top of school papers, inside greeting cards, and more, and the child just traces over the text. Self-inking stamps make it really neat with no messy ink pads!

QUICK TIPS

PRINTING TIP
- **Printing a Test Copy**
  When using specialty papers, it is always best to run a test copy on standard printer paper first. Place the test copy on top of the specialty paper, hold both up to the light, and determine whether all images and text are properly aligned. This is a good habit when printing such things as labels, decals, and pre-perforated papers. Specialty papers are significantly more expensive than standard printer paper, therefore, it is worth the effort to take the time to run a test before printing your final copy.

15. Save the document with a distinct file name, such as "Avery 8162" (named for this label type).

16. Delete all lines (or read the *Drawing Tip* for **Making Lines Disappear Without Deleting Them**) leaving only the text.

17. Print a test copy on standard printer paper (See *Printing Tip* for **Printing a Test Copy**.)

18. Print a final copy on a blank sheet of Avery 8162 labels.

DESIGN VARIATION

Downloading a template from a label manufacturer's website or using a built-in assistant in a word processing program may be simpler than creating your own template in a graphics program. But, either way, it's not hard! So consider these other ideas for using inkjet labels to address your child's needs:

"Fill In the Blank" With Inkjet Labels

Consider creating inkjet labels for the answers to a fill-in-the-blank test. Design the test sheet with blanks large enough to hold the label. And use repositionable labels to provide more than one chance to respond correctly. It's a great strategy for children who have a difficult time writing their answers!

Create Name Labels With Standard Text

Nothing says you have to create name labels with dashed text for your child to trace. You can also create name labels with standard text if handwriting is not your goal.

Label Lists

Create a page of labels for your child to select from to create a list, removing selections to put on a blank page. Use this for creating grocery lists, a list of favorite things, a list of items to pack in a suitcase, etc.

Mailing Labels

Create a page of address labels: return labels for your child and address labels for family and friends. Add a photo next to the name and address of your child, family, or friend so that your child knows exactly whose label it is.

COLOR WITHIN THE LINES

What You'll Need

Materials
- White inkjet embossing paper or inkjet vellum, 8½" x 11"
- Embossing powder

Tools
- Embossing heat tool
- Small paintbrush

Art
- Scanned image, computer graphic, or clip art

Software
- Graphics program

Hardware
- Color printer

Level of Difficulty
- Simple

Learning to color within the lines was no snap for Ashley. With her visual impairments, as well as her handwriting deficits, it was not an easy assignment for her to learn or for me to teach.

At one point, we tried using Wikki Stix®, a wax covered yarn that can be shaped, twisted, and stuck to just about anything. They were used to physically mark the outside edge of an image Ashley was to color. This gave her "physical boundaries" that her crayon or marker could bump up against to keep her in the lines. Wikki Stix® are great for a lot of things, but using them for this purpose is terribly time consuming and next to impossible with anything other than the simplest images. Plus, the presence of Wikki Stix® made Ashley's coloring activity look different than everyone else's.

I've also seen "puff paint"—a dimensional paint that is squeezed out of a tube—used to create an outside boundary to color within. But this is also very labor intensive, carefully applying puff paint to all the lines of an image.

In time, I have found a quicker method that creates a product that appears different only upon closest inspection. Using a special inkjet embossing paper, an image is printed. Embossing powder is then quickly applied while the ink is still wet. A heat tool is used to warm up the powder until it melts, creating a raised ("embossed") effect. This method is quick and easy. It gives children a boundary they can "feel" with their fingers, hands, or writing instrument. And it allows for embossing more complex images that your child can then color, using the raised edge to keep them in the lines.

What could be simpler? Create your own coloring pages using images from the Internet. Then quickly provide tactile input to help your child color within the lines. And, you can do it in a way that doesn't make your child look or feel different.

Consider using this method for creating other materials where it would be helpful for a child to feel, and not just see, the lines.

Skills to Teach

Visual perception
Math
Language
Communication
Reading
● Handwriting
● Self-help

DESIGN TIP
■ **Finding Coloring Images to Print**
The Internet is full of images to create your own coloring book pages. Search the Internet for "print coloring page" and the sites go on and on. Look for your child's favorite cartoon character, or images of holiday or seasonal interest. Some images are printed directly from the Internet.

Check out these sites:
www.coloring-page.net
www.coloringbookfun.com
www.crayola.com
www.janbrett.com
www.sesameworkshop.org/
   sesamestreet/coloringpages/

MATERIALS TIP
■ **Selecting a Paper for Embossing**
The trick to embossing is keeping the ink wet long enough to apply the embossing powder. Embossing works for images printed from your inkjet printer because the ink takes a bit longer to dry on special papers used for embossing, giving you time to apply embossing powder to the wet ink.

But some papers dry faster than others. Multipurpose paper and card stock will not work since the paper is porous and the ink dries too quickly. But some papers, such as inkjet vellum, inkjet transparencies, and inkjet paper made especially for embossing, are good candidates since they do not dry as quickly as other papers.

EMBOSSING TIP
■ **Choosing an Embossing Powder**
There are different levels of coarseness for embossing powder. "Fine" or "Extra Fine" works best for embossing fine lines. "Medium" or "Coarse" works better for broader lines.

Embossing powder also comes in an array of colors. Black (opaque) powder can visually enhance the black lines of your image. Transparent embossing powder gives definition to lines without changing their color.

DIRECTIONS

1. Open a new drawing document in a graphics program such as *AppleWorks®*, *FreeHand®*, or *Illustrator®*.

2. Turn on Grid and Rulers. (Refer to the previous section on **Grid and Rulers** in **Graphic Skills**.)

3. Copy an image to color to the clipboard. (Or, be prepared to resize a smaller or larger image once it has been pasted. Refer to the previous section on **Scale** in **Graphic Skills**.) (See *Design Tip* for **Finding Coloring Images to Print**.)

4. Paste the image into the document. Using the Select Tool, select and move the image on the page to your desired location.

5. Change your printer settings to apply the most ink. (See *Printing Tip* for **Applying the Most Ink for Embossing**.)

6. Print on inkjet embossing paper. (See *Materials Tip* for **Selecting A Paper for Embossing**.)

7. Quickly apply embossing powder over the areas where ink has been applied by the printer. (See *Embossing Tip* for **Choosing An Embossing Powder**.)

8. Shake and tap off the excess embossing powder into a clean, dry container. (This powder can be saved and used again.)

9. Use a small, clean paintbrush to lightly remove the excess embossing powder from around the image.

10. Using the embossing heat tool, slowly warm up the embossing powder. Continue applying heat to the powder until it begins to melt and raise.

11. Allow the embossed areas to completely cool before using.

DESIGN VARIATION

There are a number of creative ways to use embossed inkjet printer images. Here are just a few:

■ Emboss letters of the alphabet for tactile input, including your child's name.
■ Create stained glass coloring pages by embossing images of plants, animals, and insects on inkjet vellum. Have your child color the images with crayons or markers. Then hold them up to the light.
■ Make a "rubbing" of an embossed image by covering it with a blank piece of paper and then coloring over it with a crayon or pencil. The image will appear on the top piece of paper. This is another method to provide tactile input and increase your child's awareness of texture.

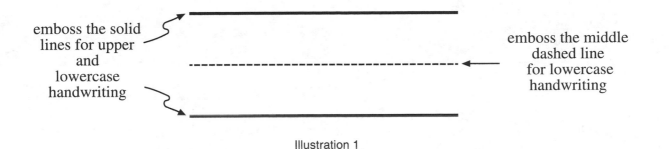

emboss the solid lines for upper and lowercase handwriting

emboss the middle dashed line for lowercase handwriting

Illustration 1

- Locate a "Braille font" on the Internet and download the appropriate version for your computer. Print letters and words using the Braille font and then emboss them to provide awareness for students with and without disabilities regarding the use of Braille.
- Use a dashed font (*School Fonts for Beginning Writing* or *Transitional Fonts for Emerging Writers*) to create a blank handwriting line to practice writing the letters of the alphabet. Emboss the top and bottom solid lines, and middle dashed line to practice writing lowercase letters; emboss only the top and bottom solid line to practice writing uppercase letters. *(See Illustration 1.)*

GAME SPINNER

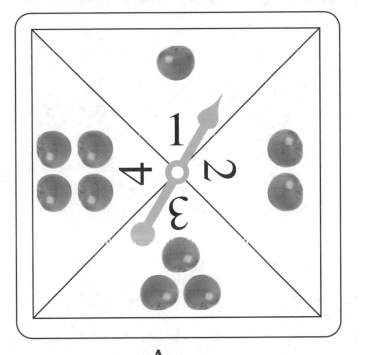

Although it might be true that "work is work," learning doesn't always have to feel like it. Ashley, like most children, lights up when educational opportunities are tied to social interaction. Presenting "lessons" as "games" is a wonderful way to accomplish this because games are usually played with two or more people. There is interaction and conversation. And there is always the opportunity to practice "turn taking."

Many common board games come with their own spinners. However, these generic spinners often pose educational problems for some children and can't be modified. For example, the numbers on a spinner may be too small to be read easily. The numbers on the spinner may need to be represented as words. Or, it may be preferable to represent the numbers on a spinner by the comparable number of objects (such as "4" represented by four apples). Without the ability to modify the spinner, the entire game may be inaccessible to your child.

Custom-made spinners can also be created to turn just about any activity into a game: Who sweeps the floor and who empties the dishwasher; what restaurant to go to for a special outing; what word to spell with a set of plastic letters; what coin configuration to pay for an item costing 25 cents.

Entire board games and corresponding spinners can be created using almost any household item as game pieces: beads, coins, hard candy, buttons, or pasta shapes. Put your imagination to work. The opportunities are limitless, and creating game spinners, as you will see, is easy.

Illustration 1

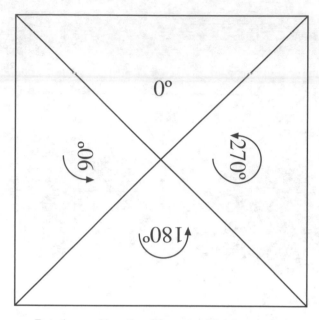

Rotation and location for each of the four images.

DIRECTIONS

1. Open a new drawing document in a graphics program such as *AppleWorks®, FreeHand®,* or *Illustrator®.*

2. Turn on Grid and Rulers. (Refer to the previous section on **Grid and Rulers** in **Graphic Skills**.)

3. Using the Rectangle Tool, draw a 4 x 4 inch square.

4. Using the Line Tool, divide the square into 4 equal parts by drawing a diagonal line from the upper right corner to the lower left corner and a diagonal line from the upper left corner to the lower right corner.

5. Individually copy to the clipboard and then paste 4 1 x 1 inch images into the drawing document. (Or, be prepared to resize a smaller or larger image once it has been pasted. Refer to the previous section on **Scale** in **Graphic Skills**.)

6. Using the Select Tool, select each image, rotate it and then move it to its location according to *Illustration 1.* (Refer to **Rotate** in **Graphic Skills**.)

7. Print.

8. Cut out the 4 x 4 inch square by carefully cutting along the outside edge.

9. Cut along one interior line from the outside edge of the square to the point where the 2 lines intersect. *(See Illustration 2.)*

10. Using a single hole punch, punch a hole at the point where the 2 lines intersect. *(See Illustration 3.)*

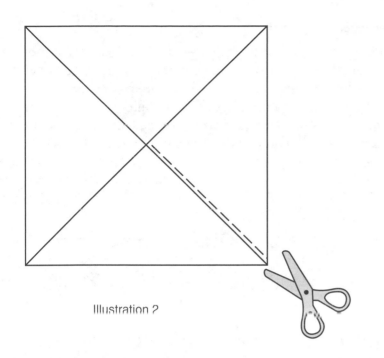

Illustration 2

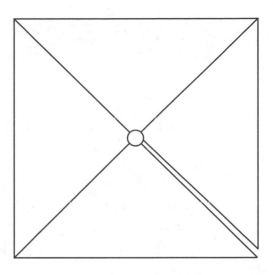

Illustration 3

11. Spray on a light coat of spray adhesive on the back side of the printed square. Adhere the square to the blank game spinner, carefully adjusting the square around the spinner arrow until it is properly placed.

Pre-made blank game spinners can be purchased in two formats: transparent and opaque. Each are 4½ inches x 4½ inches in size and come with washable faces and incorporated metal spinners. They can typically be found at teacher supply stores or from Learning Resources (www.learningresources.com). The face of the game spinner can be quickly and easily created by following the previous directions. It can then be printed from a color printer, cut out, and pasted to the blank spinner.

Additionally, a game spinner can be created using an individual metal spinner arrow, a brass plated fastener, and a piece of cardboard. These metal spinner arrows are also typically found at teacher supply stores or from Frank Schaeffer Publications (www.teacherspecialty. com). By using this method, you are not bound by the dimensions of ready-made spinners. A larger or smaller face of the game spinner can also be easily created using a computer and color printer, limited only by the size of the printer paper.

QUICK TIPS

DRAWING TIPS
- **Drawing Squares**
  To simplify drawing squares, hold down the Shift key while dragging the Rectangle Tool.

- **Drawing Lines**
  To simplify drawing lines horizontally, vertically, or at constrained angles, hold down the Shift key while dragging the Line Tool.

- **Determining Pen Width**
  Setting the Pen Width or Line Width to Hairline will draw guide lines for cutting which will be imperceptible once they have been cut.

DESIGN VARIATIONS

Use the designs below *(see Illustration 4)* to make a wide variety of game spinners from the simple to the more complex. By drawing circles and lines, the game spinner can be divided into as many divisions, or as few, as necessary. But keep in mind that using too many divisions may make the spinner more difficult and confusing to read. Strike a balance between complexity, which challenges your child, and clutter, which could confuse her.

Illustration 4

Game spinner to select fast food restaurant.

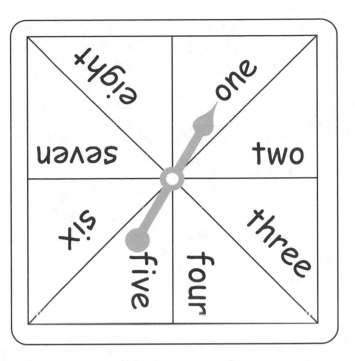

Game spinner with words to represent numbers.

Game spinner with enlarged numbers.

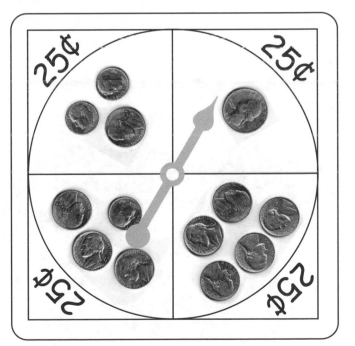

Game spinner with various coin configurations to
pay for a 25 cent item.

CARD GAMES

I came from a family of game players. Whether it was Chess, Scrabble, or Bridge, it was not uncommon for us to clear the table after a weekend meal and pull out a board game or a deck of cards. A little healthy competition, good conversation, and a few laughs were hard to beat.

But, unfortunately, it hasn't been the same for our family and Ashley. As she has grown up, I have become keenly aware of how limited the choices are for family leisure activities in which Ashley can truly be included.

Most of us pick up a deck of cards and think nothing of its appearance. But it must be incredibly confusing for Ashley with numbers and unfamiliar symbols with funny names like "spades" and "clubs." It is challenging both visually and cognitively.

But, with the assistance of a computer, an inkjet printer, and specialty paper, I can create a deck of cards that Ashley can relate to and understand. It is yet one more way for Ashley to interact with text and images...and people! And it can be for your child, too. It's social and it's fun!

A game of "Go Fish" can be more meaningful when the a deck of cards has images of fruits or vegetables, or family faces, or even fish! The following instructions show how to create your own customized deck of cards and includes a bunch of neat ideas for their use.

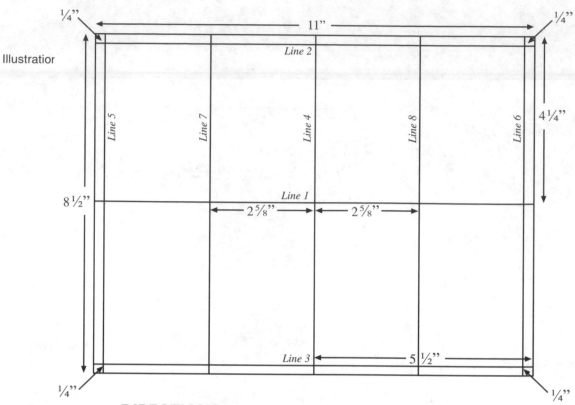

Illustration

DIRECTIONS

1. Open a new drawing document in a graphics program such as *AppleWorks®, FreeHand®,* or *Illustrator®.*

2. In the File Menu, select Page Setup. Change paper Orientation to Landscape. (Refer to the previous section on ***Document Settings*** in ***Graphic Skills***.)

3. Turn on Grid and Rulers. (Refer to the previous section on ***Grid and Rulers*** in ***Graphic Skills***.)

4. Using the Line Tool, draw the following lines:
   - **Line 1:** a horizontal line the width of the page located 4¼ inches below the top edge of the page
   - **Line 2:** a horizontal line the width of the page located ¼ inch below the top edge of the page
   - **Line 3:** a horizontal line the width of the page located ¼ inch above the bottom edge of the page
   - **Line 4:** a vertical line the length of the page located 5½ inches from the right edge of the page
   - **Line 5:** a vertical line the length of the page located ¼ inch from the left edge of the page
   - **Line 6:** a vertical line the length of the page located ¼ inch from the right edge of the page
   - **Line 7:** a vertical line the length of the page located 2⅝ inches to the left of the center vertical line
   - **Line 8:** a vertical line the length of the page located 2⅝ inches to the right of the center vertical line *(See Illustration 1.)*

strawberry	strawberry	strawberry	strawberry

Illustration 2

5. Copy a 2 x 2 inch image to the clipboard. (Or, be prepared to re-size a smaller or larger image once it has been pasted. Refer to the previous section on **Scale** in **Graphic Skills**.)

6. Paste the image into the drawing document. While the image is selected, drag and center it within one of the 8 large rectangles.

7. Continue this same process of copying, pasting, and centering 7 additional 2 x 2 inch images into the last 7 empty rectangles. *(See Illustration 2.)*

8. Set the text size to 24 pts.

9. Using the Text Tool, type the name that corresponds with each of the 8 images.

10. Using the Select Tool, select, move, and center the text inside each of the 8 rectangles. *(See Illustration 2.)*

11. Delete all lines leaving the text and images.

12. Print a test copy on standard printer paper. (See *Printing Tip* for **Printing a Test Copy**.)

13. Print a final copy on the blank playing card paper.

14. Fold the paper back and forth along the perforations and remove the cards.

DESIGN VARIATION

If you look at a standard deck of playing cards, you will notice that the card number appears in the upper left and lower right hand corner. That is because when the cards are fanned out in the hand, only the upper left hand corner shows while the rest of the card is hidden.

Take this into consideration when designing a deck of playing cards. If the cards are going to be held in your child's hand and fanned out, consider placing a scaled down image of what appears in the middle of the card in both the upper left and lower right corner, rotating the image in the lower right hand corner 180 degrees. *(See Illustration 3.)* And if your child is a "lefty," watch out because it may all be reversed!

If the cards are to be used for games like War/Battle or Concentration, the entire face of the card will show and it is unnecessary to add these additional images in the corners. *(See Illustration 4.)*

Illustration 3

Illustration 4

CARD HOLDERS

It is not always just the appearance of a deck of cards that can make playing card games a challenge. Little hands or limited hand function can make holding a handful of playing cards difficult to manage.

But there are products that help. Card holders that sit on the tabletop make playing a game of cards "hands free." And there are card holders that consist of two discs and a piece of foam pad in between. The cards are inserted into the disc and the disc is then held rather than the individual cards, making it easy to remove cards without others falling.

Check out www.maxiaids.com and www.lssproducts.com.

Play Go Fish
with Simple Shapes

Play Old Maid
with Animals

Play Go Fish
"Do you have words that
begin with /br/?"

Play Go Fish
"Do you have Megan?"

Play Go Fish
with a Deck of Antonyms/Opposites

Play War/Battle with a Deck
of Math Facts

Play Concentration Finding Pairs of
Antonyms/Opposites

Play Concentration with a Deck
of Math Facts

CUSTOM GAME PIECE

When we play board games at our house, the first and seemingly most important decision is who gets what game piece. We all know that Ashley's sister Wendy with red hair has "dibs" on a game piece of a red headed girl, or a simple red game piece. Her sister Megan is always the brunette, or the game piece in her favorite color, blue.

Once we begin, it is easy for everyone to remember which piece is theirs; everyone, that is, except Ashley. This task is not so simple for Ashley. The colors may or may not have any significance to her. Once she is assigned a game piece, it is difficult for her to identify that piece as "Ashley." When it is her turn and she spins a five, the concept of "Ashley, you move five" makes no sense. She must be thinking "Move what five?" I decided to fix this. Rather than trying to get Ashley to connect to a game piece that is supposed to represent her, I made Ashley into a game piece!

Using a full length digital photo of her, I printed the image on a shrink art media, a color inkjet compatible plastic media that shrinks when baked in a conventional oven. I cut out the image, placed it on a cookie sheet, and baked it, shrinking it to about one-third its original size, and much thicker and stiffer than the original media.

I placed the image in a game piece stand. Voila! I've created a customized board game piece for Ashley! Now her piece is easy for her to identify. And when she spins a five and is asked to move, it makes sense.

Follow these simple instructions and you can create a customized game piece for your child, too!

Illustration 1

DIRECTIONS

1. Take a "head to toe" photograph of the subject. *(See Illustration 1.)*

2. Take the picture using a digital camera, or render the image in a digitized format by either scanning the photograph or processing the film in a digitized format.

3. Open the photo image in an image editing program such as Adobe *Photoshop*®, or a graphics program such as *FreeHand*® or *Illustrator*®.

4. Crop and resize the image to approximately 8 x 3 inches. (Or, be prepared to resize the image once it has been pasted. Refer to the previous section on *Scale* in *Graphic Skills*.)

5. Open a new 8½ x 11 inch document in an image editing program such as Adobe *Photoshop*®, or a graphics program such as *Free-Hand*® or *Illustrator*®.

6. In the File Menu, select Page Setup. Change paper Orientation to Landscape. (Refer to the previous section on *Document Settings* in *Graphic Skills*.)

7. Turn on Grid and Rulers. (Refer to the previous section on *Grid and Rulers* in *Graphic Skills*.)

QUICK TIPS

PRINTING TIP
■ **Printing a Test Copy**
When using specialty papers, it is always best to run a test copy on standard printer paper first. Place the test copy on top of the specialty paper, hold both up to the light to determine whether all images and text are properly aligned. This is a good habit when printing such things as labels, decals, and pre-perforated papers. Specialty papers are significantly more expensive than standard printer paper, therefore, it is worth the effort to take the time to run a test before printing your final copy.

← 11" →

↕ 8½"

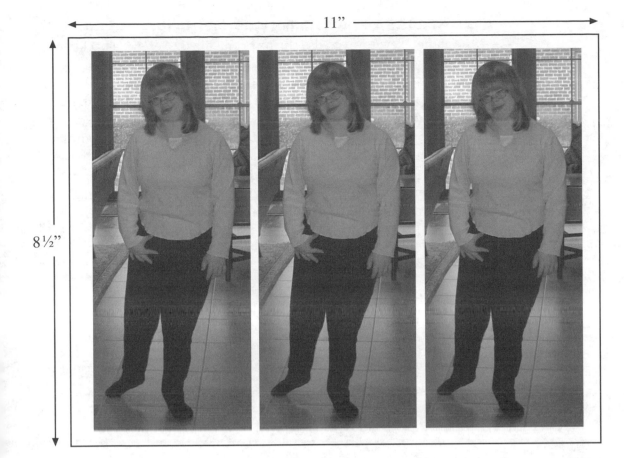

Illustration 2

8. Using the Select Tool, select the cropped image. Copy it to the clipboard.

9. Paste the image from the clipboard three times into the new document. As each image is pasted, use the Select Tool to select and move it around on the page, allowing for some printer clipping around the outside edges. *(See Illustration 2.)*

10. Print a test copy on standard printer paper. (See *Printing Tip* for **Printing a Test Copy**.)

11. Print the document on the shrink art media.

12. Carefully cut out each "head to toe" image from the shrink art media, squaring off the bottom of the image so that it can be placed in a plastic stand-up base.

13. Follow the baking directions on the shrink art media packaging.

14. Spray the printed image side with a clear acrylic spray to protect the ink.

QUICK TIPS

SHRINKING TIP
▪ **Baking Shrink Art Media**
Baking and shrinking shrink art media is not difficult but will go more smoothly by following a few tips:

- Be sure to preheat your oven.
- Shrink your first image by itself as a "dry run."
- Use a cookie sheet without a layer of air between the top and bottom of the sheet; they are not recommended.
- Watch the process. It is expected that the shrink art media will curl while shrinking. But it will typically "uncurl" itself and flatten out. But occasionally it can stick to itself while curling so carefully remove it from the oven and help it flatten out.
- If holes are desired in your shrink art, hole punch images before shrinking.

ANOTHER IDEA FOR SHRINK ART MEDIA

Another clever way to use shrink art media is to create a backpack tag similar to a luggage tag. Take a picture of your child or student, copy and paste the image into a basic shape (star, circle, square), add their name, print it on shrink art media, and cut it out to bake. Be sure to hole punch it before you bake it. And remember to make the hole big because the hole shrinks too! Use goldtone bead key chains (www.shrinkydinks.com) to attach it to your child's backpack.

The same can be made with paper, laminated, and hole punched. But it is not as thick, not transparent, and not nearly as cool!

QUICK TIPS

DRAWING TIP
■ **Removing the Background around an Image**
Probably the "lowest tech" method to remove the background around an image is by using scissors; once the image has been printed, the background is cut away.

But the background can also be removed by more "high tech" methods on the computer before it is printed.

One method is by simply using the Eraser Tool in a drawing application program. This works just fine but is rather tedious and time consuming.

A better method is by using the Magnetic Lasso, available in Adobe® *Photoshop*®. The Magnetic Lasso selects objects by detecting color differences and snaps to the edge of the object. The Magnetic Lasso is best used on objects that have a distinct edge. Therefore, if you intend to use the Magnetic Lasso to remove the background around a subject, take the photograph against a background with high color contrast. *(See Illustration 3.)*

Illustration 3

CARDS FOR AUDIO CARD READER

cat

What You'll Need

Materials
- White printer paper, 8½" x 11"

Tools
- Scissors
- Blank audio cards
- Rubber cement

Art
- Scanned image, computer graphic, or clip art

Software
- Graphics program

Hardware
- Color printer

Level of Difficulty
- Simple

An audio card reader plays recorded sound from a card that is fed through the machine. Each card has a strip of magnetic tape. Sound can be recorded onto the magnetic strip using the audio card reader, much like a cassette tape. When the card is run back through the audio card reader, the message is played.

Audio card readers are most often used with kids with speech and language disorders (but probably not as severe as Ashley's). Although considered by some to be "old technology," I have had great success using an audio card reader with Ashley to enhance her speech and language. She listens attentively to a familiar voice on the card. She sees the target word and the associated icon as the card passes through the machine. And, she is prompted to speak by the presence of a hand held microphone to record the message. Ashley has learned to run the audio cards through the reader independently, involving her motor skills. And she can listen to them as many times as she would like.

You would not believe the speech we get from her when we use this. And when she makes a close approximation of a word, I re-record the word with her speaking. She needs every reminder I can come up with that she is a speaking individual. We have to celebrate speech every day...every word.

Pre-recorded cards can be hard to come by and, frankly, I prefer to create my own. By doing so, I can be consistent with the images I select and the text I use. I can produce them in color. And, most importantly, I can target the vocabulary of my choosing, whether individual sounds, words, or phrases.

Blank magnetic strip cards can be purchased to make your own audio cards. The following instructions give you the proper page layout for creating your own cards using your inkjet printer and graphics program.

Skills to Teach

Visual perception
Math
● Language
● Communication
● Reading
Handwriting
Self-help

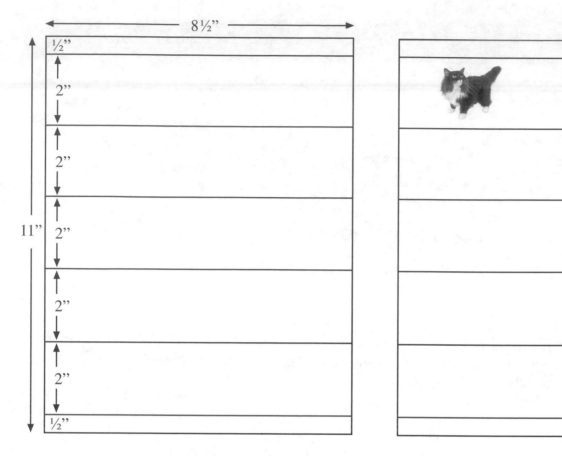

Illustration 1   Illustration 2

DIRECTIONS

1. Open a new drawing document in a graphics program such as *AppleWorks*®, *FreeHand*®, or *Illustrator*®.

2. Turn on Grid and Rulers. (Refer to the previous section on **Grid and Rulers** in **Graphic Skills**.)

3. Using the Line Tool, draw 6 horizontal lines at 2 inch intervals, beginning ½ inch below the top edge of the page. *(See Illustration 1.)*

4. Copy a 1½ x 1½ inch image to the clipboard for a target word. (Or, be prepared to resize a smaller or larger image once it has been pasted. Refer to the previous section on **Scale** in **Graphic Skills**.)

5. Paste the image into the drawing document. Using the Select Tool, select and move the image between the top two horizontal lines and along the left side of the page. *(See Illustration 2.)*

6. Copy and paste 4 additional 1½ x 1½ inch images for the rest of the target words. Using the Select Tool, select and move each image between two horizontal lines, lining them up with the initial image.

7. Set the text size to 72 points.

Illustration 3: Individual Words

Illustration 4: Simple Phrases

8. Using the Text Tool, type the text that corresponds with each image (individual words and simple phrases). Using the Select Tool, select and move the text to the right of each image. *(See Illustrations 3 and 4.)*

9. Print one copy of the document.

10. Cut the document apart into 5 individual strips.

11. Using rubber cement, paste each strip onto a blank audio card.

12. Record and use.

QUICK TIPS

DRAWING TIP

▪ **Determining Pen Width**
Setting the Pen Width or Line Width to "Hairline" will draw guide lines for cutting which will be imperceptible once they have been cut.

ADHESIVE TIP

▪ **Using Rubber Cement on Audio Cards**
There are real advantages to using rubber cement for creating audio cards. Rubber cement does not wrinkle paper and, most importantly, it can be easily removed from most surfaces by rubbing your finger across the glue once it has dried. Unlike other adhesives, rubber cement can be removed if any gets on the magnetic strip of the audio card. Additionally, using rubber cement allows audio cards to be recycled: the glue and anything glued to the audio card can be removed, and a new message can be recorded on the magnetic strip.

SOURCE TIP

▪ **Finding Audio Card Readers**
The name Language Master might be familiar, a trade name for the old audio card readers manufactured by Bell and Howell. These "dinosaurs" can often be found in school libraries, or in the closet of a speech language pathologist. I have purchased a couple of them on eBay. Although new machines are still manufactured and are commercially available, they are an often forgotten piece of useful technology.

RESOURCES

COMPUTER RELATED

GRAPHICS PROGRAMS: VECTOR

CorelDraw® (Win)
Corel Corporation
1600 Carling Avenue
Ottawa, Ontario
Canada
K1Z 8R7

Phone: 800-772-6735
www.corel.com

FreeHand® (Mac/Win)
Macromedia, Inc.
600 Townsend Street
San Francisco, CA 94103
Phone: 415-252-2000
FAX: 415-626-0554
www.macromedia.com

Illustrator® (Mac/Win)
Adobe Systems Incorporated
345 Park Avenue
San Jose, CA 95110-2704
Phone: 408-536-6000
FAX: 408-537-6000
www.adobe.com

PowerPoint® (Mac/Win)
Microsoft Corporation
One Microsoft Way
Redmond, WA 98052-6399
Phone: 425-882-8080
FAX: 425-936-7329
www.microsoft.com

Publisher® (Win)
Microsoft Corporation
One Microsoft Way
Redmond, WA 98052-6399
Phone: 425-882-8080
FAX: 425-936-7329
www.microsoft.com

GRAPHICS PROGRAMS: BITMAP

AppleWorks® (Mac)
Apple
1 Infinite Loop
Cupertino, CA 95014
Phone: 408-996-1010
www.apple.com

PaintShop® Pro (Win)
Corel Corporation
1600 Carling Avenue
Ottawa, Ontario
Canada
K1Z 8R7
Phone: 800-772-6735
www.corel.com

SCREEN CAPTURE PROGRAMS

SnagIt® (Win)
TechSmith Corporation
2405 Woodlake Drive
Okemos, MI 48864-5910
Phone: 517-381-2300
FAX: 517-913-6121
www.techsmith.com

SnapzPro® (Mac)
Ambrosia Software, Inc.
P.O. Box 23140
Rochester, NY 14692
Phone: 585-325-1910
800-231-1816
FAX: 585-325-3665
www.ambrosiasw.com

Available at on-line store

Available at office supply stores

Available at teacher supply stores

Available at craft stores

FONTS

School Fonts for Beginning Writing (Mac/Win)

This is a set of thirteen fonts designed by Kim Voss to make educational materials for students. They are provided in both TrueType and PostScript. Twelve of the fonts feature the Palmer manuscript style of handwriting, similar to simple printing.

Each set of fonts includes 12 dashed fonts, in 6 different design variations, either with or without a dashed line. The thirteenth font is the "Hands-On" font that matches the Lakeshore plastic letters.

Mayer-Johnson, Inc.
P.O. Box 1579
Solana Beach, CA 92075-7579
Phone: 800-588-4548
FAX: 858-550-0449
www.mayer-johnson.com

Transitional Fonts for Emerging Writers (Mac/Win)

This is a set of twelve fonts designed by Kim Voss to make educational materials for students. They are provided in both TrueType and PostScript. This set features the slanted D'Nealian style of handwriting, utilizing only three letter heights, making it easy for students to learn. All modern manuscript letters except f, i, j, t, and x are formed with a single continuous stroke. This requires few pencil lifts and creates a smooth writing flow and reduces letter reversals.

Each set of fonts includes 12 dashed fonts, in 6 different design variations, either with or without a dashed line.

Mayer-Johnson, Inc.
P.O. Box 1579
Solana Beach, CA 92075-7579
Phone: 800-588-4548
FAX: 858-550-0449
www.mayer-johnson.com

GRAPHIC IMAGES

Commercially Available

Boardmaker™ (Mac/Win)

Boardmaker™ is a searchable graphic database of over 3,500 bitmapped and vector drawn Picture Communication Symbols (PCS). These icons are provided in a set of color symbols, as well as in black and white. Each symbol is labeled with at least one identifiable name used to search the database. The images within the database are listed in multiple languages from English and Spanish to Italian and Dutch.

Initially comprised of the most frequently used words, there are now over 6,000 additional symbols, including a collection of sign language symbols, that can be added to the Boardmaker™ database. These symbols cover a wide spectrum of categories from cooking and grooming to leisure and school activities. Boardmaker™ can be used to create an array of educational and communication materials.

Mayer-Johnson, Inc.
P.O. Box 1579
Solana Beach, CA 92075-7579
Phone: 800-588-4548
FAX: 858-550-0449
www.mayer-johnson.com

News-2-You® (Mac/Win)

News-2-You® is a weekly subscription newspaper that is "designed for individuals who need concise, visual concepts." The newspaper is downloaded from the Internet as a pdf. The unique News-2-You® images are available weekly with a newspaper subscription or can be purchased from a year's worth of newspapers available annually on a CD-ROM. The images come in black & white and color. They are provided in Boardmaker™ formats so that they can be added to Boardmaker's™ searchable database.

News-2-You®
P.O. Box 550
Huron, OH 44839
Phone: 800-697-6575
419-433-9800
FAX: 419-433-9810
www.news-2-you.com

Lots O'Logos (Mac/Win)

This is a collection of over 14,000 black & white and full color digital corporate logos and trademarks in vector (eps) format.

Images are copyright protected, but are available for personal use.

Typesetting, Ink
1144 S. Robertson Boulevard
Los Angeles, CA 90035-1404
Phone: 301-273-3330
FAX: 301- 273-0733
www.lots-o-logos.com

Photo-Objects® (Mac/Win)
The Big Box of Art™ (Mac/Win)

Hemera sells digital images in a number of ways: CD, DVD, or downloaded from the Internet, individually or through subscription. Hemera sells stock photos, clip art, illustrations, Photo Clip Art, and their signature image type, the Hemera Photo-Objects® image.

Images are provided in 72 ppi (on-screen display), 150 dpi (good quality), 200 dpi (high quality), and 300 dpi (professional quality) against a transparent background.

Images are royalty-free.

Hemera Technologies, Inc.
490 St-Joseph Boulevard
Hull, Quebec
Canada
J8Y 3Y7
Phone: 819-772-8200
FAX: 819-778-6252

www.hemera.com

Picture This (Mac/Win)

Picture This (Standard and *Pro)* is a collection of child-friendly photographs (2,700 for *Standard* and over 5,000 for Pro). Additional photo collections for *Places You Go, Things You Do, Functional Living Skills and Behavioral Rules,* and *School Routine and Rules* are also available.

Images are 240 dpi, taken against a non-transparent "plain background." A library of the digitized photos is available for *Boardmaker™* so that they may be accessed in *Boardmaker's™* searchable database.

Images are copyright protected.

Silver Lining Multimedia, Inc.
P.O. Box 2201
Poughkeepsie, NY 12601
Phone: 888-777-0876
FAX: 888-777-0875
International Phone: 845-462-8714
International FAX: 845-463-0437

www.silverliningmm.com

Subscription-Based On-line Images
clipart.com™ (Mac/Win)

This is an on-line service of downloadable images. It includes over 5 million clipart images, photos, fonts, and sounds. Subscriptions are from weekly to yearly (1 week, 3 months, 6 months, 1 year)

Images are royalty-free.

JupiterImages
5232 E. Pima Street
Suite 200C
Tucson, AZ 85712
Phone: 877-CLIPART (877-254-7278)
Phone: 800-482-4567
FAX: 520-881-1841
www.clipart.com

Stock Image Source
Publishing Perfection
21155 Watertown Road
Waukesha, WI 53186-1898
Phone: 800-782-5974
International: 262-717-0600
www.pubperfect.com

Online Photo Services

Kodak Easy Share Gallery
www.kodakgallery.com

Mpix™
www.mpix.com

PhotoWorks®
www.photoworks.com

Snapfish
www.snapfish.com

Free Stock Photos and Clipart

The Internet is a wonderful source of web sites with royalty free and public domain photographs that can be used for personal, educational, and noncommercial use.

Photos

bigfoto.com
www.bigfoto.com
Categories include America, Asia, Europe, Africa, and others.

FreeFoto.com
www.freefoto.com
FreeFoto.com claims to be "the largest collection of free photographs for private non-commercial use on the Internet." A large stock photo library from Britain.

FreeImages.co.uk
www.freeimages.co.uk
Stock photography from Britain. Free for personal or commercial use.

FreeStockPhotos.com
www.freestockphotos.com
Free for personal and commercial use.

Holy Land Photos
www.holylandphotos.org
Free, high resolution images of the Holy Land.

Images of the World
www.imagesoftheworld.org
Photos from around the world and the U.S. for personal and educational use only.

Portrait Gallery
www.lib.utexas.edu/photodraw/portraits/
These images are in the public domain.

stock.xchng®
www.sxc.hu
Over 100,000 free stock photos.

The Coin Page
www.coinpage.com
Free images of coins.

United States Government Public Domain Photography Web Sites

The following is an enormous source of amazing images related to various departments and agencies of the federal government.

United States Government Graphics and Photos
www.firstgov.gov/Topics/Graphics.shtml
The portal to numerous government sites of images.

Library of Congress—LOC
www.loc.gov
Just about everything under the sun–historical, political, and educational.

National Aeronautics and Space Administration—NASA
www.nasa.gov/multimedia/imagegallery/index.html

Hubble Space Telescope—NASA
http://hubblesite.org/newscenter/

Johnson Space Center Earth From Space—NASA
http://earth.jsc.nasa.gov/

National Oceanic and Atmospheric Administration—NOAA
Photo Library
www.photolib.noaa.gov

National Park Service—NPS
Digital Image Archive
www.nps.gov/pub_aff/imagebase.html
Beautiful photos of national parks, monuments, battlefields, and historic sites.

Smithsonian Photographic Services
http://photo2.si.edu/
Online Smithsonian photography free for personal use; a charge for commercial use.

Smithsonian Images
www.smithsonianimages.com
Free download for personal and educational use; a charge for commercial use. E-cards available.

United States Department of Agriculture—Agricultural Research Service
www.ars.usda.gov/is/graphics/photos

United States Department of Agriculture—USDA
www.usda.gov/oc/photo/opclibra.htm
Useful photos depicting general agriculture, health, economics, resource conservation, forestry, etc.

United States Department of Defense—USDoD
www.defenselink.mil/multimedia/

United States Department of Health and Human Services-Public Health Image Library (PHIL)
http://phil.cdc.gov/Phil/home.asp
This library includes subject matter that might be unsuitable for children.

United States Fish and Wildlife Service—USFWS
http://images.fws.gov/
Photos of widlife, plants, and National Wildlife Refuges.

United States Geological Survey—USGS
www.usgs.gov/picturingscience/collections.html
Photos related to biology, ecosystems, geology, geography, hydrology, and national parks.

United States Mint
www.usmint.gov/pressroom/
Images of various coins, contemporary and historical.

Clipart

Microsoft Office Clipart and Media Home Page
http://office.microsoft.com/clipart/
Over 45 categories of clipart and media.

Royalty-free Clip Art Collection for Foreign/Second Language Instruction
www.sla.purdue.edu/fll/JapanProj/FLClipart/
Categories include verbs, adjectives, buildings, food and drinks, people and animals, sports, things and events, time, vehicles and medical.

World Flag Database
www.flags.ndirect.co.uk
A complete collection of the world's flags. For personal use.

Classroom and Coloring Book Clipart

Author Jan Brett's Home Page: A Great Place for Ideas
www.janbrett.com
Wonderful images from children's book author/illustrator Jan Brett.

Classroom Clipart
www.classroomclipart.com
A large collection of free images for the classroom.

ColoringBookFun.com
www.coloringbookfun.com
Numerous image categories to choose from, including familiar cartoon characters.

Coloring-Page.net
www.coloring-page.net
Mazes, dot-to-dots, as well as coloring pages of cartoon characters.

Crayola Creativity Central
www.crayola.com
Cool site. Over 900 arts & crafts ideas, over 1,000 coloring & activity pages, and more. Requires registration.

DLTK's Crafts for Kids
www.dltk-kids.com
Many craft projects and coloring pages.

Enchanted Learning®
www.enchantedlearning.com
> A wide variety of educational projects, including science-related activities and printable books.

Sesame Street Workshop—Coloring Pages
www.sesameworkshop.org/sesamestreet/coloringpages/
> Numerous coloring pages with favorite Sesame Street characters.

CRAFT MATERIALS AND OFFICE SUPPLIES

INKJET MEDIA

Multipurpose Paper, Inkjet, Card Stock, Colored Paper, Vellum, Photo, Transparency, Labels & Stickers

Epson Paper

Phone: 800-873-7766
www.epson.com
> Multipurpose, card stock, inkjet, photo, transparency, labels/stickers, and other specialty media.

Great White Paper
www.greatwhitepaper.com
> Multipurpose, inkjet, photo, and transparency.

Hammermill Paper
www.hammermill.com
Phone: 800-242-2148
> Multipurpose, card stock, inkjet, colored, and photo.

Hewlett Packard
www.hp.com
Phone: 800-888-0262
> Card stock, inkjet, photo, transparency, labels/stickers, and other specialty media.

Kodak
Eastman Kodak Company
343 State Street
Rochester, NY 14650
www.kodak.com
> Multipurpose, inkjet, photo, and transparency.

Strathmore
www.strathmoreartist.com
> Vellum, photo, labels/stickers, and other specialty media.

Wausau Paper
100 Paper Place
Mosinee, WI 54455-9099
Phone: 715-693-4470
FAX: 715-693-2082
www.wausaupapers.com
> Multipurpose, card stock, inkjet, and colored.

Xerox®
800 Long Ridge Road
Stamford, CT 06904
Phone: 800-ASK-XEROX
800-275-9376
www.xerox.com
> Multipurpose, card stock, inkjet, colored, transparency, labels/stickers, magnet sheets, and other specialty media.

National Office Supply Stores

Office Depot®
www.officedepot.com

Office Max®
www.officemax.com

Staples®
www.staples.com

Playing Cards

PlainCards
Freshwater Bay Co.
2308 Freshwater Bay Road
Port Angeles, WA 98363
www.plaincards.com

Puzzles

Compoz-A-Puzzle, Inc.
2 Secatoag Avenue
Port Washington, NY 11050
Phone: 800-343-5887
FAX: 516-883-2314
www.compozapuzzle.com

Flip Puzzle™
Micro Format, Inc.
830-3 Seton Court
Wheeling, IL 60090
Phone: 847-520-4699
800-333-0549
FAX: 847-520-0197

www.imaginationgallery.net

Joslin Photo Puzzle Co.
302 Bel Air Road
Southampton, PA 18966-3322
Phone: 215-357-8346
FAX: 215-357-0307

www.jigsawpuzzle.com

Clear Decals

Avery®
Consumer Service Center
50 Pointe Drive
Brea, CA 92821
Phone: 800-GO-AVERY, 800-462-8379
FAX: 800-831-2496

www.avery.com

DecalPaper.com
10913 N.W. 30th Street, Suite 103
Miami, FL 33172
Phone: 305-406-9507
FAX: 305-593-1011

www.decalpaper.com

The Crafty PC™
1075 Easton Avenue, #308
Somerset, NJ 08873
Phone: 732-873-8055
FAX: 732-873-3424

www.thecraftypc.com

Printable Index Cards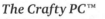

Avery®
Consumer Service Center
50 Pointe Drive
Brea, CA 92821
Phone: 800-GO-AVERY, 800-462-8379
FAX: 800-831-2496
www.avery.com

Oxford Custom Printable Index Cards
Esselte®
44 Commerce Road
Stamford, CT 06902-4561
Phone: 800-645-6051
www.esselte.com

Printable Magnet Sheets

Avery®
Consumer Service Center
50 Pointe Drive
Brea, CA 92821
Phone: 800-GO-AVERY, 800-462-8379
FAX: 800-831-2496
www.avery.com

DecalPaper.com
10913 N.W. 30th Street, Suite 103
Miami, FL 33172
Phone: 305-406-9507
FAX: 305-593-1011
www.decalpaper.com

Dick Blick Art Materials
P.O. Box 1267
Galesburg, IL 61402-1267
Phone: 800-828-4548
FAX: 800-621-8293
www.dickblick.com

McGonigal Paper
P.O. Box 134
Spinnerstown, PA 18968
Phone/FAX: 215-679-8163
www.mcgpaper.com

The Crafty PC™
1075 Easton Avenue, #308
Somerset, NJ 08873
Phone: 732-873-8055
FAX: 732-873-3424
www.thecraftypc.com

Xerox®
800 Long Ridge Road
Stamford, CT 06904
Phone: 800-ASK-XEROX
800-275-9376
www.xerox.com

Fuzzy Paper

McGonigal Paper
P.O. Box 134
Spinnerstown, PA 18968

Phone/FAX: 215-679-8163
www.mcgpaper.com

The Crafty PC™
1075 Easton Avenue, #308
Somerset, NJ 08873
Phone: 732-873-8055
FAX: 732-873-3424
www.thecraftypc.com

Rotary Cards

Avery®
Consumer Service Center
50 Pointe Drive
Brea, CA 92821
Phone: 800-GO-AVERY, 800-462-8379

FAX: 800-831-2496
www.avery.com

Rolodex® Necessities
Phone: 800-323-0749
www.eldonoffice.com

Temporary Tattoo Paper

DecalPaper.com
10913 N.W. 30th Street, Suite 103
Miami, FL 33172
Phone: 305-406-9507
FAX: 305-593-1011
www.decalpaper.com

McGonigal Paper
P.O. Box 134
Spinnerstown, PA 18968
Phone/FAX: 215-679-8163
www.mcgpaper.com

Fabric Paper

Dick Blick Art Materials
P.O. Box 1267
Galesburg, IL 61402-1267
Phone: 800-828-4548

FAX: 800-621-8293
www.dickblick.com

June Tailor®

P.O. Box 208
2861 Highway 175
Richfield, WI 53076
Phone: 262-644-5288 or 800-844-5400
FAX: 262-644-5061 or 800-246-1573
www.junetailor.com

Print & Shrink

McGonigal Paper
P.O. Box 134
Spinnerstown, PA 18968
Phone/FAX: 215-679-8163
www.mcgpaper.com

Shrinky Dinks
K & B Innovations, Inc.
P.O. Box 223
N78 W31401 Kilbourne Road
North Lake, WI 53064-0223
Phone: 262-966-0305
FAX: 262-966-0306
www.shrinkydinks.com

Embossing Paper

McGonigal Paper
P.O. Box 134
Spinnerstown, PA 18968
Phone/FAX: 215-679-8163
www.mcgpaper.com

Waterslide Decal Paper

DecalPaper.com
10913 N.W. 30th Street, Suite 103
Miami, FL 33172
Phone: 305-406-9507
FAX: 305-593-1011
www.decalpaper.com

Lazertran LLC
5535A N.W. 35th Avenue
Fort Lauderdale, FL 33309
Phone: 800-245-7547
FAX: 954-578-7300
www.lazertran.com

Iron-On Transfer Paper

Epson Paper
Phone: 800-873-7766

www.epson.com

June Tailor®
P.O. Box 208
2861 Highway 175
Richfield, WI 53076
Phone: 262-644-5288 or 800-844-5400
FAX: 262-644-5061 or 800-246-1573
www.junetailor.com

McGonigal Paper
P.O. Box 134
Spinnerstown, PA 18968
Phone/FAX: 215-679-8163
www.mcgpaper.com

OFFICE SUPPLIES

 Office Depot®
www.officedepot.com

 Office Max®
www.officemax.com

 Staples®
www.staples.com

Brads/Fasteners
Creative Xpress!!
295 West Center Street
Provo, UT 84601
Phone: 800-563-8679
www.creativexpress.com
        gold and silver: circles, stars, and trees

Loose-Leaf Rings

Heat Laminator
ibico®
www.ibico.com

Laminating Pouches
GBC Office Products Group
5700 Old Orchard Road
Skokie, IL 60077
Phone: 847-965-0600
800-541-0094
FAX: 847-965-0912
www.gbcoffice.com

ibico®
www.ibico.com

Self-Adhesive Diskette Pocket
Cardinal Brands
HoldIt® Pockets
108 Summer Court
Georgetown, KY 40324
Phone: 800-282-7261
FAX: 800-282-7329
800-750-7530
www.cardinalbrands.com

Rotary Card File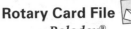
Rolodex®
Phone: 800-323-0749
www.eldonoffice.com

Top-Loading Sheet Protectors
Acco Wilson Jones®
300 Tower Parkway
Lincolnshire, IL 60069
Phone: 800-989-4923
FAX: 800-247-1317
www.wilsonjones.com

Avery®
Consumer Service Center
50 Pointe Drive
Brea, CA 92821
Phone: 800-GO-AVERY, 800-462-8379
FAX: 800-831-2496
www.avery.com

Comb Binder & Plastic Binding Combs
ibico®
www.ibico.com

3-Ring Easel Binder
Avery®
Consumer Service Center
50 Pointe Drive
Brea, CA 92821
Phone: 800-GO-AVERY, 800-462-8379
FAX: 800-831-2496
www.avery.com

CRAFTING SUPPLIES

VELCRO® Coins

Mayer-Johnson, Inc.
P.O. Box 1579
Solana Beach, CA 92075-7579
Phone: 800-588-4548
FAX: 858-550-0449
www.mayer-johnson.com

Laminator, Sticker Maker, Magnet Maker

XYRON®
7400 E. Tierra Buena Lane
Scottsdale, AZ 85260
Phone: 480-443-9419
800-793-3523
FAX: 480-443-0118
www.xyron.com

MISCELLANEOUS MATERIALS

Spinner Arrows

Frank Schaeffer Publications
P.O. Box 141487
Grand Rapids, MI 49514-1487
Phone: 800-417-3261
FAX: 888-203-9361
www.teacherspecialty.com

Game Spinners

The Learning Resources
380 N. Fairway Drive
Vernon Hills, IL 60061
Phone: 847-573-8400
www.learningresources.com

Magnetic Write-On/Wipe-Off Lapboards and Stands

Teaching Resource Center
TRC
P.O. Box 82777
San Diego, CA 92138-2777
Phone: 800-833-3389
FAX: 800-972-7722
www.trcabc.com

Plastic Letters

Mayer-Johnson, Inc.
P.O. Box 1579
Solana Beach, CA 92075 7579
Phone: 800-588-4548
FAX: 858-550-0449
www.mayer-johnson.com

Playing Card Holders

Disability Products
5447 East Elmwood Street
Mesa, AZ 85205
Phone: 800-688-6794
www.disabilityproducts.com

LS&S
P.O. Box 673
Northbrook, IL 60065
Phone: 800-468-4789
FAX: 847-498-1482
www.lssproducts.com

Maxi-Aids, Inc.
42 Executive Boulevard
Farmingdale, NY 11735
Phone: 800-522-6294
FAX: 631-752-0689
www.maxiaids.com

Audio Card Reader & Blank Audio Cards

Lakeshore® Learning Materials
2695 E. Dominguez Street
Carson, CA 90810
Phone: 800-421-5354
310-537-8600
www.lakeshorelearning.com

Super Duper® Publications
P.O. Box 24997
Greenville, SC 29616
Phone: 800-277-8737
864-288-3536
FAX: 800-978-7379
864-288-3380
www.superduperinc.com

Molded Plastic Stand-up Bases

Shrinky Dinks
K & B Innovations, Inc.
P.O. Box 223
N78 W31401 Kilbourne Road
North Lake, WI 53064-0223
Phone: 262-966-0305
FAX: 262-966-0306

www.shrinkydinks.com

Goldtone Bead Key Chains

Shrinky Dinks
K & B Innovations, Inc.
P.O. Box 223
N78 W31401 Kilbourne Road
North Lake, WI 53064-0223
Phone: 262-966-0305
FAX: 262-966-0306
www.shrinkydinks.com

Communication/Porta Books

Crestwood Communication Aids, Inc.
6625 N. Sidney Place, Dept. 21F
Milwaukee, WI 53209-3259
Phone: 414-352-5678
FAX: 414-352-5679
www.communicationaids.com

Mayer-Johnson, Inc.
P.O. Box 1579
Solana Beach, CA 92075-7579
Phone: 800-588-4548
FAX: 858-550-0449
www.mayer-johnson.com

Color Coded Measuring Cups and Spoons

LS&S
P.O. Box 673
Northbrook, IL 60065
Phone: 800-468-4789
FAX: 847-498-1482

www.lssproducts.com

OXO
GOOD GRIPS®
1200 South Antrim Way
Greencastle, PA 17225
Phone: 800-545-4411
FAX: 800-685-3950

www.oxo.com

Photo Sleeves

Exposures®
1 Memory Lane
P.O. Box 3615
Oshkosh, WI 54903-3615
Phone: 800-222-4947
www.exposuresonline.com

Bear Counters

Didax Educational Resources
395 Main Street
Rowley, MA 01969
Phone: 800-458-0024
FAX: 800-350-2345
www.didax.com

Gestalts

Rotary Cards

Card Games

Interactive Spelling Cards

Sight Words

Color Within the Lines

Spelling Your Name

Custom Game Piece

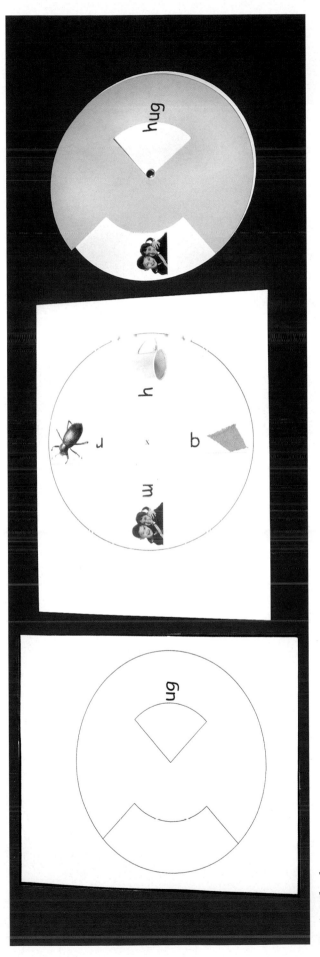

Basic Wheel

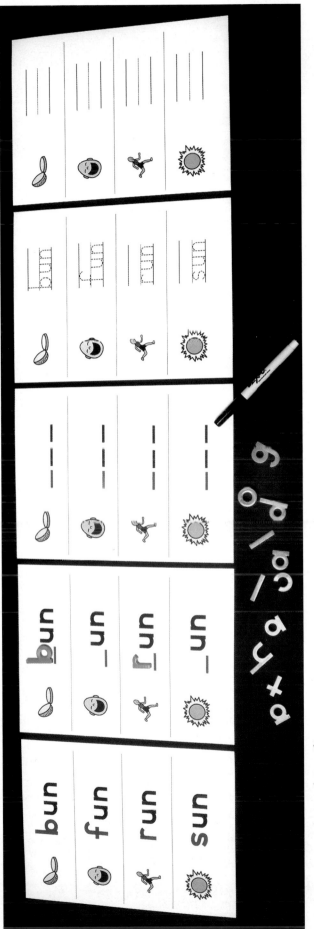

Decoding Text with Word Families

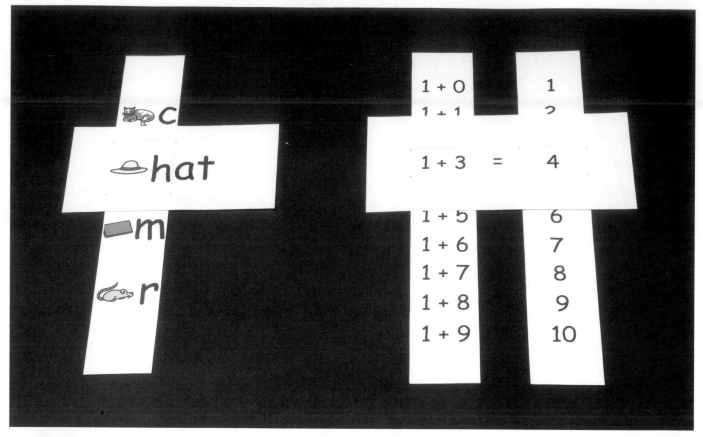

Simple Slider and Double Slider

c		
hat		
m		
r		

1 + 0		1
1 + 1		2
1 + 3	=	4
1 + 5		6
1 + 6		7
1 + 7		8
1 + 8		9
1 + 9		10

bus
it
nut
just
bag
wig

eggs
milk
butter
yogurt
bread
bananas
apples
grapes
broccoli

1+0=1
2+0=2
3+0=3
4+0=4
5+0=5
6+0=6
7+0=7
8+0=8
9+0=9

Pocket Slider

Symmetry Game

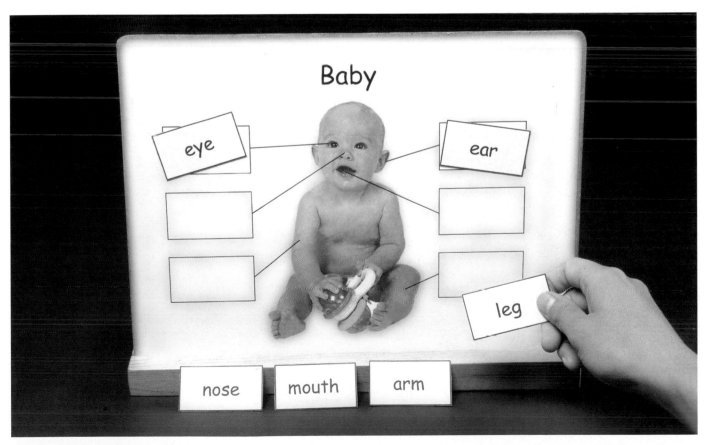

Fill in the Blank: Word Magnets & Decal

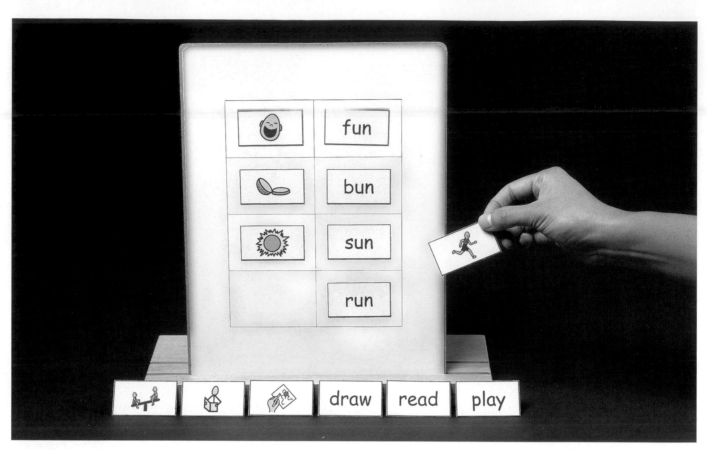

Reading Inventory: Word Magnets & Decal

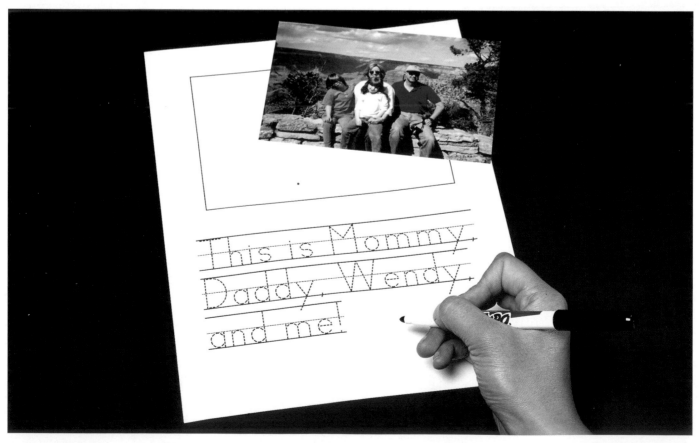

Journal Writing

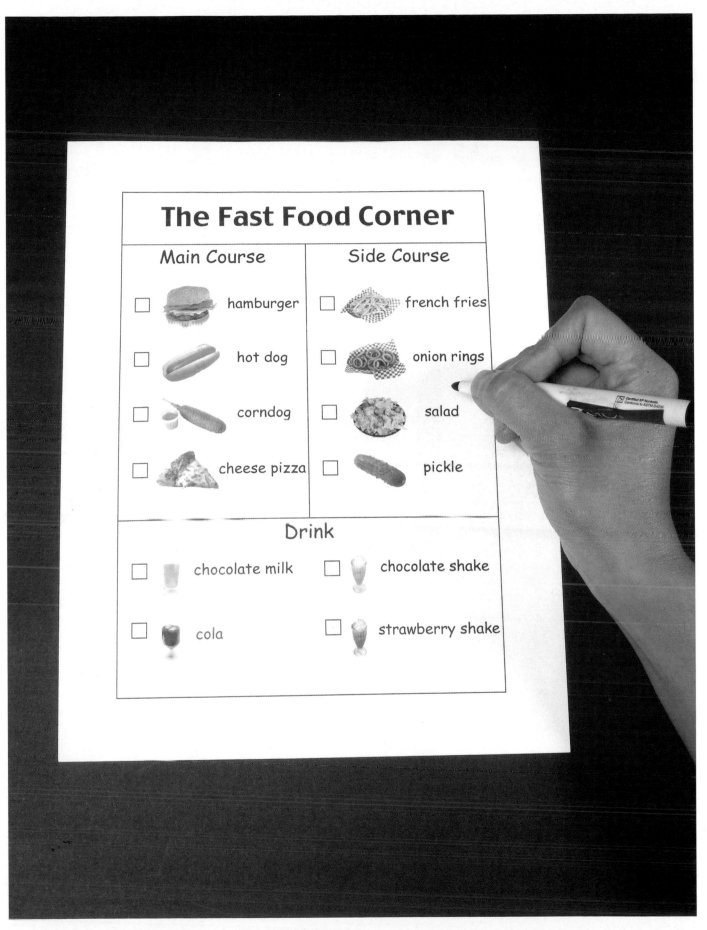

INDEX

ABOUT THE AUTHOR

Kimberly S. Voss is the creator of *School Fonts for Beginning Writing* and *Transitional Fonts for Emerging Writers*, published by Mayer-Johnson, and used for creating customized educational materials. She has nearly two decades of experience modifying and creating materials to teach her daughter to read, write, spell, and communicate. She speaks nationally on the use of computer technology in special education and rehabilitation. She lives with her husband and three daughters in Tulsa, Oklahoma.